Women in the Judiciary

Does gender matter in judging? And if so, in what way? Why were there so few women judges only two or three decades ago, and why are there so many now in most countries of the Western world? How do women judges experience their work in a previously male-dominated environment? What are their professional careers? How do they organise and live their lives? And, finally and most notably: do women judge differently from men (or even better)?

These are the questions dealt with in this collection of contributions by seven authors from six countries (UK, Australia, USA, Canada, Syria and Argentina), contrasting views from common law and civil law countries. In spite of differences in the two legal systems, as well as greater gender diversity on the bench and the overall higher income and prestige enjoyed by judges in common law countries, women judges in all these countries – Syria included – share many problems. Diverse and intriguing facets are added to a debate that started thirty years ago but continues to leave ample space for further discussion.

This book was originally published as a special issue of *International Journal of the Legal Profession.*

Ulrike Schultz, a qualified lawyer, is a senior academic in the Law Faculty of the Fern University in Hagen, Germany, specialised in media work, didactics, and communications trainings for lawyers and judges, while her teaching and research is concentrating on Gender and Law and the Sociology of the Legal Professions.

Gisela Shaw, Emeritus Professor in German, chaired the national Women in German Studies Association, and was awarded a personal chair at the University of the West of England, where she held the post of Director of Research for Modern Languages and European Studies until her retirement in 2002.

Women in the Judiciary

Edited by
Ulrike Schultz and Gisela Shaw

Routledge
Taylor & Francis Group
LONDON AND NEW YORK

First published 2012
by Routledge
4 Park Square, Milton Park, Abingdon, Oxon OX14 4RN
605 Third Avenue, New York, NY 10017

Routledge is an imprint of the Taylor & Francis Group, an informa business

This book is a reproduction of the *International Journal of the Legal Profession*, vol. 15, issue 1-2. The Publisher requests to those authors who may be citing this book to state, also, the bibliographical details of the special issue on which the book was based.

British Library Cataloguing in Publication Data
A catalogue record for this book is available from the British Library

ISBN13: 978-0-415-50861-2 (hbk)

Typeset in Times New Roman
By Taylor & Francis Books

Publisher's Note
The publisher would like to make readers aware that the chapters in this book may be referred to as articles as they are identical to the articles published in the special issue. The publisher accepts responsibility for any inconsistencies that may have arisen in the course of preparing this volume for print.

Contents

INTRODUCTION

Gender and Judging

Does gender matter in judging? And if so, in what way? Who are the women judges? How did they get into office? How do they organise and live their lives? What are their professional careers? What constitutes a good judge? And finally: do women judge differently from men (or even better)?[1] These are the questions which a Collaborative Research Network (CRN) of the Law and Society Association (LSA) on 'Gender and Judging' has put on its agenda.

Work started in 2006 at the LSA Conference in Baltimore, and has since been continued vigorously at a number of major subsequent events: a conference for women lawyers in Latin America organised by Beatriz Kohen in Buenos Aires in April 2007; the international socio-legal conference in Berlin in July in 2008 organised jointly by the LSA, the Research Committee on Sociology of Law (RCSL) and national socio-legal organisations (where five panels presented a total of 18 papers); the LSA conference in Montreal in May 2008; the meeting of the Working Group for the Comparative Study of Legal Professions in Berder, France, in June 2008; the RCSL Conference in Milano in July 2008, a special workshop on gender and judging at the International Institute for the Sociology of Law in Oñati, Spain, in June 2009[2], the meeting of the Legal Profession Group in Paris in 2010 and several panels at the LSA conferences in Denver 2009, Chicago 2010 and San Francisco 2011. In short, 'Gender and Judging' has emerged as an issue of considerable and lasting interest to socio-legal scholars.

The 'Gender and Judging' project, a truly international venture with contributors from around the world, builds on work of the Women and Gender in the Legal Profession Group (a sub-group of the RCSL Working Group on Legal Professions). This Group was established in 1994 and can, by now, point to a range of publications, most prominently the collection *Women in the World Legal Professions*[3] and a special issue of this journal[4]. In addition, many articles in books and journals have been inspired by the work of the group.

The CRN on 'Gender and Judging' focuses on the following areas:

- gender aspects of judicial education and training
- gender aspects of selection and careers
- women judges at work (job satisfaction, stress, coping strategies)

- gendered construction of judges in the media
- gendered judging
- judging in family courts
- gendered communication in the courtroom
- female judicial leaders (eminent women judges, first women judges, the pioneers)

In keeping with its international character, the project adopts a comparative perspective (including a historical dimension) with the aim of identifying any differences between the way in which women and men approach and conduct their judicial work, as well as between the impact of their gender and work on the judicial system. In this book, which is the first collection of articles on 'Gender and Judging', all the issues listed above are addressed in some form, be it merely in passing or in greater depth. Common to all contributions is the central question: do women judges judge differently from men judges? Do women judges add a different voice? This was a question first raised in the 1990s under the influence of 'difference feminism'[5] and today remaining as topical as ever.

Four contributions deal with women judges in common law countries (UK, Australia, USA), two with women judges in a civil law system (Argentina and Syria), and another with women judges and dissenting opinions in a mixed jurisdiction (Canada), although dissenting opinions are rather more a feature of common law than civil law systems.

In comparing developments regarding women judges in different countries, it is important to keep in mind a number of relevant fundamental differences between civil law and common law systems. In civil law countries, a judicial career is one of a number of separate career paths open to law graduates, which means that judges start their careers at the age of between twenty-five and thirty-five. As they are public servants, entry later in life is, as a rule, not possible, and formal qualifications are crucial to access to the judiciary. By contrast, in common law countries, judges are chosen from among experienced legal practitioners, the key criterion being professional achievement.

In the two legal systems, the very process of judicial decision-making is governed by contrasting ideologies. In civil law countries, judges pass judgments in the name of the state or the people as anonymous interpreters of the law and representatives of state power. Judges in common law countries have more discretion in the process of finding the law by 'distinguishing' the case from precedents. They 'make the law'. The judgment is therefore more closely connected to their personality, and the reasoning in the decision will be more often scrutinized and criticized with a view to their personal character and background, i.e. financial status, political affiliation, life experience as a man or woman, religious belief, sexual orientation, ethnicity and personal qualities.

In common law countries, the judiciary commands a higher social status as well as higher incomes, than in the civil law world. Both factors may work as hidden mechanisms to keep women out or hinder them from getting in. In civil law countries it is easier for women to enter the judiciary, as key access criteria for judicial office, such as formal qualification and examination results, are more rational and transparent and therefore more easily met by women than those in the common law world, where professional visibility, favourable evaluations of professional achievement, and access to – traditionally male – networks are of crucial weight. The increase in the number of women in the judiciary in civil law countries therefore happened about two decades earlier than in common law countries, and more of them have by now reached career positions. On the other hand, the question remains whether an increase in the proportion of women in the judiciary may not actually contribute to a lowering of judicial prestige and income, as women traditionally have not been associated with perceptions of personal importance and the role of breadwinner of the family. Possible developments will have to be watched closely.

All of these differences explain why problems of women's access to judicial careers have been more frequently analyzed and discussed in the common law than in the civil law world. One important further reason is that the civil law ideology of judicial objectivity, of the neutral judge applying the law in strict compliance with formalised rules, makes it almost a taboo to discuss influences of gender on judging in civil law countries. Yet, the subject is equally important, and there are, of course, shared problems.

Common law countries represented in this collection are more familiar with issues of diversity. The colonial past, multi-cultural societies and migration have created diversity on the bench earlier and more visibly than in most civil law countries. This adds to the differences in perception of the issue at stake. The intersection of gender with another of the above mentioned qualities or with biographical features (religion, sexual orientation, age, ethnicity) may have led to a more intense experience of discrimination on the part of judges in the common law world as well as of their clients. So-called intersectional discrimination in the European Union is an important issue for anti-discrimination policies.

What makes a judge a feminist judge? Do feminist judges make a difference? What can women expect from feminist judges? These are the fundamental questions addressed by Rosemary Hunter. Do feminist judges (which may well include men) by definition practise feminist judging, i.e. introduce women´s perspectives and experiences, a conscious pro-care agenda; or are they more likely to adapt to the system or to be transformed by it? Rosemary Hunter identifies four major aspects of judging where feminist judges may differ from others:

- court process
- case outcome
- reasons given for a decision
- 'extra-curricular' activities.

She concludes 'that while it is unrealistic to make generalisations or to impose demands upon women judges as a whole, feminist judges both can and ought to make a difference'.

Baroness Hale, the first female Law Lord in the UK, describing herself as 'just a bit different', is convinced that difference on the bench 'subtly changes and ultimately improves the judicial product'. Erika Rackley uses the House of Lords' decision in *Secretary of State for the Home Department v K(FC); Fornah (FC) v Secretary of State for the Home Department* [2006] as 'a lens through which to explore the "difference" of the woman judge and, in particular, the developing jurisprudence of Baroness Hale'. The case, involving a claim for asylum based on danger of female mutilation in the home country, demonstrates that Baroness Hale brings to bear a better understanding of life realities and legal problems encountered by women on account of their sexuality than her male colleagues. Erika Rackley concludes however that the mere suggestion of difference in the context of adjudication remains contentious, and she rejects the 'different voice' as a dangerous myth. Acknowledging that women on the bench are an irritant disrupting established patterns of masculinity, she considers diversity on the bench as important because it attracts the best, facilitates a better chance of understanding problems facing people, and thereby creates greater public confidence in the judiciary.

Reg Graycar, drawing on her experience as a barrister, takes a deep and critical look at the consequences of diversity on the bench and at how otherness may colour a judgment. She warns that we need to pay careful attention to what judges know about the world, how the things they know translate into activities as judges. Giving examples of cases from various common law countries, she analyses how the concepts of bias, partiality and perspective are connected via notions of 'otherness' to outsider judges and 'other' legal decision makers.

An important source of differing opinions between women and men are dissenting and concurring votes in judicial judgments. This provides the focus for the contribution of Marie-Claire Belleau and Rebecca Johnson, with special reference to the Supreme Court of Canada. Belleau and Johnson have kept careful track of female dissenters over the years, concluding that dissenting and even concurring votes (i. e. dissenting opinions but final consent) were much more frequent among women than among men. However, in recent years the number of such votes has declined, giving rise to speculation and discussion as to whether key issues in the context of women's rights have now been settled. Is there less need now to break with traditions? Have women adapted more to a general norm? Do they, in times of unrest, feel more strongly in need of unanimity among judges of both sexes?

Interesting insights on this question may derive from research by Bryna Bogoch from Israel[6] who has analysed judgments published in legal databases. She not only found that decisions by women are underrepresented in the databases but also that women´s decisions are significantly longer. Is it because they differ in their arguments? Or do they want to explain their reasoning in more detail to the parties?

Sally Kenney analyses the literature on women judges by political scientists over the past decades in the US, arguing that 'carefully examining the body of work of three pioneering scholars, Beverly Blair Cook, Elaine Martin, and Sue Davis, yields insights beyond the particular subject matter and helps us to understand sex and gender more generally'. One suggestion is that we should understand gender as producing tendencies among generational cohorts rather than trying to identify essential sex differences. Differences in entry and career can be related to sex, but sex differences will not necessarily lead to different judgments giving gendered views, and judges in general influence others but not in a gendered and predictable way.

Finally, Monique Cardinal and Beatriz Kohen deal with questions of gender in the judiciary of civil law countries. Both show that, although in these countries there is awareness that they cannot waste the competence of their well-educated women; the problems faced by women keen on a judicial career are comparable to those of their sisters in the Western world.

Monique Cardinal, on the basis of comprehensive empirical research on women and the judiciary in Syria (where the first female judge was appointed in 1975), describes the appointment process, training and judicial career path, making a valuable contribution to our limited knowledge of the role and place of women lawyers in a Muslim Arab country.

Beatriz Kohen sets out to find answers to the question whether the participation of women changes the judiciary. She does so by empirical research on gender differences in the values and attitudes of family judges in the City of Buenos Aires using Gilligan´s ethic of care approach. She explores how men and women judges perceive their office, how they imagine the 'ideal' judge, what their motivation is to become a judge, and how they assess the special contribution of women judges to the judiciary. Judges of both sexes do identify differences. She herself finds that women tend to apply a more interdisciplinary approach to reaching a decision, not only relying on their professional techniques but integrating to a greater extent social workers and other family experts in their work. However, she, too, concludes (concurring with her fellow authors) that, overall, there is no evidence of clear-cut gender-based differences.

These articles add diverse and fascinating contributions to a debate that started thirty years ago but leaves ample space for further discussion.

Ulrike Schultz & Gisela Shaw
September 2008

Notes

1 Cf. Ulrike Schultz, Richten Richterinnen richtiger? In *Frauenbilder*. Ed. by Ulrike Schultz for the Northrhine-Westfalian Ministery of Health, Social Matters, Women and Family, Düsseldorf, 2005, 117 – 126
2 Organisers: Sally Kenney (USA), Ulrike Schultz (Germany), Gisela Shaw (UK) ed. by Ulrike Schultz and Gisela Shaw, Oxford: Hart, 2003
3 *Women in the Legal Profession*, in *IJLP* vol. 10, no. 2, July 2003
4 About the notion of different voice: Gilligan, Carol, 1982. *In a Different Voice.* Cambridge, Mass: Harvard University Press
5 Still unpublished work, presented at the LSA Conference in Montreal in May 2008

Can *feminist* judges make a difference?

Rosemary Hunter
Kent Law School, University of Kent, Canterbury, UK

Abstract *Many of the expectations and aspirations about the 'difference' that women judges would make have proved unrealistic, given the inevitable diversity and often conservatism of women appointed as judges. On the other hand, we might reasonably expect feminist judges to 'make a difference'. This essay focuses on feminist judges, and seeks to identify what it is that we might reasonably expect of them. This in turn requires consideration of who counts as a feminist judge, what might be included in a feminist approach to judging, and what institutional norms inherent within the judicial role might constrain the adoption of a feminist approach. The essay concludes that feminist judges both can and ought to make a difference across a wide range of judicial activities.*

> The idea of women on the bench may have gained acceptance ... but the proper role for female jurists once they get there is still a work in progress. (L'Heureux-Dubé, 2001, p. 30)

Introduction

This paper is the first product of what is intended to be a larger project on feminism and power. One of the objectives of liberal feminism has been to get women into positions of power, but it has not developed any theory of what women should do when they get there. At least part of the reason for this has been the assumption that women would make a difference simply by *being* there. According to this view, if the problem was women's (illegitimate) exclusion from public institutions, then they had merely to be included in order to transform those institutions. Once women visibly occupied powerful positions for which they were equipped and qualified, they would demonstrate by their very presence that the previous exclusion of women was indeed illegitimate, and would also ensure that women's perspectives and experiences were brought into the decision-making processes undertaken by those institutions.[1]

These assumptions about the difference that women in power would make, however, now appear at best naïve and at worst essentialist. Why did we think that women would transform institutions without simultaneously—or alternatively—being transformed by them (see Menkel-Meadow, 1986)? Why did we believe that women appointed to positions of power would be 'representative' of women as a group, rather than being those who most resemble the traditional incumbents and are thus considered least likely to disturb the status quo?[2] Why did we assume that women appointed to these positions would have the capacity to represent the whole, diverse range of women's perspectives and experiences? And why did we imagine that individual women would want potentially to risk their newly-acquired status by taking a stand on behalf of other women, when it would be much safer for them to keep their heads down and attempt to gain some legitimacy amongst their sceptical peers and jealous subordinates? After all, women have not exactly been welcomed into the halls of power with open arms, and invited to rearrange the furniture.

Consequently, it seems more useful at this juncture to ask about *feminism* and power, rather than *women* and power. Feminists do have a political agenda (leaving aside, for the moment, exactly what that might be). Feminism might be seen as a kind of voluntary community of belief, like religious congregations and political parties (Cotterrell, 2006, p. 72). Such communities are based on shared beliefs or values and stress solidarity and interdependence; participation is "conscious and considered" (Cotterrell, 2006, pp. 69, 72). To identify as a feminist necessarily involves assuming a commitment to other women. It might legitimately be expected, therefore, that feminists in positions of power will exercise their power in a feminist way. But *is* that a legitimate expectation in all institutional contexts? Is it easier, for example, to follow a consciously pro-woman political agenda as a politician or union official than as a judge? And if it is a legitimate expectation, what precisely might a feminist deployment of power look like? This essay seeks to provide the beginnings of an answer to these questions.

Who is a feminist judge?

It is not my intention in this essay to engage in a purely descriptive discussion of feminist judging. To the extent that the essay does describe a feminist approach to judging, it is an approach that may (and I hope will) be adopted by any judge. My concern, however, is also to make a normative claim about what might reasonably be *expected* of a feminist judge. Consequently, it is necessary to identify the judges who may be the subject of these expectations. In other words, while any judge *may* engage in feminist judging, it would only be reasonable for feminists to *expect* feminist judging of feminist judges. So it is necessary to identify which judges fall within this category.

Two issues arise in this context. First: is it necessary for a feminist judge to be a woman, and secondly: is it necessary for a feminist judge to identify as a feminist? My tentative answer to the first question is yes (I take the experience of being gendered female to be a crucial element of feminism), but I am also aware that there is much scope for disagreement on this point, and insufficient space in this essay to argue it fully. For now, therefore, I will not offer a conclusive answer, but will move to the second and more important question about identification.

I do maintain that a feminist judge must identify her- (or him-) self as a feminist. Some women judges specifically and emphatically insist that they are not feminists, often by reference to the social construction or caricature of feminism as something negative, wrongheaded and/or dangerous.[3] I would argue that one cannot be a feminist while accepting and perpetuating this negative characterisation of feminism. Feminists, if we can agree on little else, do tend to value feminism.

What, then, of judges who refuse to declare a position or remain equivocal, but whose judgments and actions evince feminist sympathies? Some women judges in particular have been identified as feminists by (some) other feminists, without themselves embracing the label. There seem to be two issues here. First, referring back to the understanding of feminism as a voluntary community of belief which gives rise to legitimate expectations about how its members will behave, it seems that if we are going to hold *expectations* about the judicial behaviour of feminist judges, then the element of voluntariness must be respected. If participation in the feminist community includes the assumption of certain commitments, then such participation must indeed be "conscious and considered".

Secondly, however, there is the issue of judges who do not identify as feminists, but to whom we may wish to refer as exemplars of 'feminist judging'. Perhaps the most obvious example in this category is Justice Bertha Wilson of the Supreme Court of Canada, who "demonstrate[d] an understanding and engagement with feminism" (McGlynn, 2003, p. 308) in speeches such as the famous "Will Women Judges Really Make a Difference?" (Wilson, 1990), in judgments such as *Lavallee*[4] and *Morgentaler*,[5] and in the report of the Canadian Bar Association Task Force on Gender Equality in the Legal Profession (1993), which she chaired; but who, according to her biographer, rejected the label of 'feminist' (Anderson, 2001, pp. xiv, 135–6, 197; see also McGlynn, 2003, p. 308; Rackley, 2007, p. 80). As noted above, however, feminist judging is not necessarily the exclusive province of feminist judges. While we may only *expect* a consistently feminist approach of feminist judges, this does not mean that other judges may not also make decisions, give speeches or engage in projects that are recognisably feminist at least some of the time. Referring to someone as an exemplar is not the same as imposing expectations upon them. So there is no necessary contradiction between excluding someone from the category of 'feminist judge' for normative purposes, yet referring to one or more of their judgments or speeches as examples of feminist judicial practice for descriptive purposes.

Further, in the specific case of Justice Wilson, her rejection of feminism must be understood in the particular legal and social context of her time. She came from a generation before the women's movement, having entered law school in 1954 and begun work as a lawyer in 1959. This may have affected her subsequent attitude towards feminism, both substantively and strategically. According to Backhouse, women lawyers of this generation typically denied their experiences of discrimination (see also Hunter, 2002) and "cautiously adopted strategies of responding to male exclusion and hostility with politeness and persistence" (Backhouse, 2007, p. 10). By contrast, Backhouse notes that the substantial increase in women entering law schools in Canada from 1970 "brought a certain 'safety in numbers' and many of the women who became lawyers after 1970 recognized that they had the luxury of identifying with feminism because they were able to offer each other protection and support" (Backhouse, 2007, p. 4). Thus, we should remain aware of the fact that the rejection of feminism has had different generational meanings. Although the generation of women judges still on the bench who pre-dated the women's movement is now shrinking, we should also be sensitive to other contexts in which it may be difficult for a judge to identify as a feminist, while nevertheless (at least sometimes) behaving as one. My definition of who counts as a feminist judge for normative purposes is thus, necessarily, temporally and culturally specific.

It follows from the identification requirement that there are likely to be relatively few feminist judges (and also that those judges are quite likely to be women[6]). Nevertheless, the category of feminist judges is not an empty one, even at the highest levels of the judiciary. Once again, however, I wish to stress that it is not my contention that feminist judging is the exclusive province of feminist judges as defined here. Empirically, it can also be done by men and by women who do not identify as feminists. Indeed, another Canadian Supreme Court judge, Justice Claire L'Heureux-Dubé, has argued that 'making a difference' should not only be seen as the responsibility of women judges (L'Heureux-Dubé, 1997a, p. 7). Rather, everyone in a position of power should take responsibility for understanding different perspectives and reflecting them in law, and all judges should "develop an increased sensitivity ... to the diverse human experiences which are presented to courts on a daily basis" (L'Heureux-Dubé, 1997a, p. 9). Normatively, however, I would argue that we can only *expect* feminist judges to engage in feminist judging. Before turning to the question of whether this is a reasonable expectation in all aspects of the judicial role, I deal with a further definitional issue: what constitutes feminist judging?

What should a feminist judge do?

The question of what constitutes feminist judging has received considerable attention in previous literature, and that literature yields an array of suggestions as to how a feminist judge may or ought to approach her role. Many of these suggestions are procedural—that is, they set out ways to go about judging as a feminist, rather than dictating any specific substantive results. But feminism does have substantive goals, in particular the achievement of equality and justice for women, in the legal system and in society. These substantive goals may also translate into expectations of feminist judges.

Asking the woman question

In a well-known article, US feminist legal theorist Katharine T. Bartlett identified one of the key feminist legal methods as 'asking the woman question', that is, examining and highlighting "the gender implications of rules and practices which might otherwise appear to be neutral or objective" (Bartlett, 1990, p. 837). Judith Resnik, for example, notes a consistent finding of US court gender bias task forces, that while most male judges reported that gender had little or no effect on the process or outcome of most cases, "significantly higher percentages of women judges (whether at trial or appellate level, in administrative tribunals or in courts) report occasions in which they deem gender to be relevant" (Resnik, 1996, p. 963). Bartlett also argues that 'asking the woman question' can (and should) lead to asking questions about other forms of exclusion (on the basis of race, religion, sexuality, etc.) that may be operating in the particular case (Bartlett, 1990, p. 848).

Including women

Having identified the relevance of gender, the feminist judge should then judge inclusively. This has two aspects. First, as Christine Boyle has argued, she should not make decisions that protect male interests masquerading as human interests, but should try to take into account women's as well as men's interests (Boyle, 1985, pp. 101–2). In doing so, she demonstrates that the male perspective is not a neutral norm against which other narratives can be evaluated, but represents only a partial view of reality (L'Heureux-Dubé, 1997a, p. 3; C. Young, 2004, p. 235).

Secondly, Justice L'Heureux-Dubé has identified the hope that women judges will be "more willing and able to hear and understand the stories of women litigants" (L'Heureux-Dubé, 1997a, p. 3). While this will not be true of all women judges, it does suggest that a feminist judge should listen carefully and respectfully to stories of women's lives, and should also tell those stories in her decisions (Graycar, 1995, p. 281), thereby putting gendered (and racialised, and other previously excluded) experience into legal discourse (see, e.g. Rush, 1993, p. 609; Kobayashi, 1998, p. 203; Rackley, 2006, p. 176). While she sat on the Canadian Supreme Court, for example, Justice L'Heureux-Dubé explained that "I recognize that women's diverse experiences have been sadly lacking in many areas of law and I have continually emphasized the necessity of incorporating them in our judicial decisions" (1997a, p. 6).

The feminist judge's ability to hear and understand the stories told by women litigants may be based partly on her own gendered experience, which enables her to respond sympathetically when other women speak of similar experiences. However, a judge's personal experience alone cannot possibly encompass the diversity of experiences that women litigants bring to court. Consequently, Christine Boyle has argued that the feminist judge "would need to continue to talk with other women to learn how they experience the world", and also to refer to research on women's experience, in order to gain a broader understanding (Boyle, 1985, pp. 102–3). For instance, Elizabeth Sheehy notes that Justice L'Heureux-Dubé "consistently attempted to enrich her knowledge of the experience of the 'other' by reading and integrating material" from sources such as women's organisations and reports of government bodies, "in order to craft sounder legal doctrine" (Sheehy, 2004b, p. 12).

Challenging gender bias

A third major element of feminist judging identified in the literature is the process of intervening to challenge hegemonic discourses of sexism, racism and heteronormativity. This may involve questioning the current legal construction of 'woman', rejecting 'stock stories' about women's reactions and behaviour, not relying on stereotypical or gender-biased assumptions about sexual difference or behaviour,[7] challenging myths and stereotypes about women, and critiquing previous judgments or the decisions of 'brother' judges that adopt such myths and stereotypes (L'Heureux-Dubé, 1997a, pp. 5–6; Boivin, 2003, pp. 88–94; Backhouse, 2003, p. 192). In addition to attempting to identify and overcome gender bias in legal principles and doctrines (L'Heureux-Dubé, 1997a, p. 3), this process extends to confronting sexism and gender bias in the legal profession.

Contextualisation, particularity and attention

Fourthly, a feminist judge may engage in what Bartlett describes as "feminist practical reasoning", that is, reasoning from context, focusing on the reality of women's lived experience in each situation, and producing a decision that is individualised rather than abstract (Bartlett, 1990, pp. 849–50). Other feminist legal scholars have also emphasised the importance of contextualisation (Sherry, 1986, pp. 604–9; Gilbert, 2003, p. 2; Boivin, 2003, pp. 75–6), avoiding abstraction (Boyle, 1985, pp. 103–4), and focusing on the realities of people's lives rather than on narrow doctrinal issues (Westergren, 2004, p. 691; Rush, 1993, p. 623). Contextualisation may include considering the specific situation of the parties, the circumstances in which particular legislation was enacted, and/or the broader social context within and upon which the legal rules in question operate. In order to understand this social context, it may be necessary to refer to social science research literature and policy reports—so-called 'social framework evidence' (see, e.g. Boyd, 2004, pp. 169–70, 175–6, 178; C. Young, 2004, pp. 234–5; Sheehy & Boyle, 2004, p. 249; Sullivan, 2004, pp. 63–7; Sparks, 2004, p. 381).

In relation to individualised decision making, Helen O'Sullivan has produced what she refers to as a 'particularity model' of judging, which involves the judge taking into account (in a criminal trial) the particular circumstances of the accused, the accuser and the case, "*really looking*" at the parties before her, treating both the accused and the accuser as people with reason, emotion and vulnerabilities, and as worthy of equal respect and dignity, and avoiding categorisation and the rigid application of universal rules, but rather rendering a 'fresh judgment' in every case (O'Sullivan, 2007, ch. 6, pp. 9–35; see also Murdoch, 1970, p. 91; Derrida, 1990, p. 961). Similarly, Patricia Cain has offered the following feminist recasting of Judge Learned Hand's advice to judges:

> When you listen as a judge, you must transcend your sense of self, so that you can really listen. Listen to the story that is being told. Do not prejudge it. Do not say this is not part of my experience. But listen in such a way as to make it part of your experience. Find some small part of your own self that is like the Other's story. Identify with the Other. Do not contrast. Only when you have really listened, and only then, should you judge. (Cain, 1988, p. 1955)

The 'particularity model' has resonances with Carol Gilligan's (1982) 'ethic of care'—the notion that women speak in a different moral voice, specifically one that is relational, connected, caring, nurturing, responsible and just, rather than abstract, distanced, calculating, disengaged and legalistic (see, e.g. Sherry, 1986, p. 580;

Resnik, 1988). The 'ethic of care' has proved problematic, however, as both a hypothesis and an aspiration. Clearly, not all women judges do speak in such a 'different' moral voice (nor do all male judges conform to its masculine opposite). Neither is it clear that we should want all feminist judges to speak in this 'different' voice. Not only does the 'ethic of care' represent a somewhat stereotypical view of femininity that we might wish to contest (see, e.g. DuBois *et al.*, 1985, pp. 73–5), but alternative feminist visions have argued for the virtues of detached attention rather than care and connection. As explained by Helen O'Sullivan:

> [Simone] Weil describes 'attention' in this way:
>
> > Attention consists of suspending our thought, leaving it detached, empty, and ready to be penetrated by the object; it means holding in our minds, within reach of this thought, but on a lower level and not in contact with it, the diverse knowledge we have acquired which we are forced to make use of. (Weil, 1977, p. 49)
>
> Weil regards "paying attention" as a widening of focus resulting from detachment, which involves "[s]tepping back from the immediate objects of concern which tend to cause a distortion of moral perception" (Van Marle, 2004). Detachment leads to a reliable perception of the individual. (O'Sullivan, 2007, ch. 6, p. 16)[8]

Although elements of the 'ethic of care' remain valuable (such as taking responsibility for one's decisions, and the ability to think relationally), a combination of feminist practical reasoning, the particularity model and detached attention in Weil's sense appear to represent a preferable feminist approach to judging.

Remedying injustices, improving women's lives, promoting substantive equality

Much of the US empirical research on women judges has sought to determine whether women judges adopt a 'representative role'; that is, to what extent do they adopt a 'woman's viewpoint' on 'women's issues' (matters directly impacting on women as a group) (Allen & Wall, 1993, p. 158)? Allen and Wall's survey, for example, found that women judges who identified as feminist were twice as likely as all other respondents to advance 'pro-woman' positions in response to hypothetical cases involving women's issues (Allen & Wall, 1993, p. 158; see also Martin, 1989, pp. 78–81). But they also found in a study of actual voting patterns that the majority of women judges adopted a representative role across a range of cases involving women's issues—sex discrimination, sexual abuse, medical malpractice, property settlements, and child–parent relations (Allen & Wall, 1993, p. 161). Similarly, Martin and Pyle found that judicial gender had the greatest impact on pro-wife decisions in divorce cases (Martin & Pyle, 2000, p. 1231; see also Davis *et al.*, 1993; Martin, 1993; Westergren, 2004).

Arguably, feminist judges should attempt to identify and remedy injustices of any kind, attempt to achieve concrete improvements in women's lives, and provide a vision of a better world in which justice for women would prevail (Backhouse, 2003, p. 192;

Boivin, 2003, pp. 75–6, 97; Lakeman, 2004, p. 48). Arguably, too, feminist judges should promote a substantive view of equality—one which seeks to accommodate women's differences, to take account of historic and systemic disadvantages, and to revise norms and standards to incorporate women's positions and experiences (Gaudron, 1997; Gilbert, 2003, p. 2).

It would be too simplistic, however, to expect that feminist judges should always adopt a 'representative role' or take a 'pro-woman' stance. In some cases, what constitutes a 'pro-woman' decision or a feminist outcome may be considerably less than obvious. Is it 'pro-woman', for example, to protect a vulnerable young woman from potential harm, or to allow her the autonomy to make her own (possibly harmful) decisions? What 'representative role' should a feminist judge adopt in a case concerning the validity of a rule banning the wearing of headscarves by women in employment or education? What would be the 'pro-woman' position in a case in which a mother and grandmother were contesting custody of a child? Is it 'pro-woman' to increase the wages paid to child care workers, when this will benefit some women (child care workers) at the expense of others (women who may now be unable to afford child care and thus have their employment options curtailed)?

Making feminist choices

In cases where there may be no clear or single feminist answer, we are compelled to revert once again to procedural guidance. One element of such guidance might be to be wary of judging other women simply because they have made different choices from the ones the feminist judge might have made in their position.[9] Another would be for the feminist judge to think carefully about the consequences of her or his judicial choices. As Sonia Lawrence has observed, exercising power "is a complicated task that risks implicating feminists in various forms of oppression and subordination" (Lawrence, 2004, p. 588). A decision may not only exclude some women, but contribute to a worsening of their situation or cause them material harm (Lawrence, 2004, p. 594). Whatever choices are made, therefore, the feminist judge must be open about the priorities she sets and the tradeoffs she makes, and be prepared to justify her choices and to be accountable for the balance she strikes in each case (Lawrence, 2004, p. 597). A third element of procedural guidance would be to remain up-to-date with feminist legal literature, and to draw upon discussions of difficult issues in that literature and the resolutions proposed therein.

Full-time feminism

Is it reasonable to expect feminist judges *always* to deliver feminist judgments? On the Australian High Court, for example, Justice Mary Gaudron tended to be feminist on civil law issues, but pro-defendant on criminal law issues, including those that might adversely affect women and children. I would argue, however, that a judge who identifies as a feminist cannot be selectively feminist. Neither can her feminism be confined to cases involving 'women's issues', since there is no clear dividing line between cases involving 'women's issues' and those that do not. Justice Wendy Baker has observed that equality issues present themselves in court every day in all manner of proceedings: tort, contract, tax, administrative law, labour law, crime, evidence, civil procedure and family law (Baker, 1996, p. 208). Moreover, feminist legal theory has developed analyses of just about every area of law, including contracts, commercial law, corporate law, constitutional law, evidence and civil procedure, as well as the more obvious areas of tort, criminal law, family law, medical law, labour law, equity and trusts, and human rights. This is another reason for feminist judges to maintain familiarity with feminist legal literature. Arguably, they have a responsibility to do so, and to make use of it to consider whether and if so how a feminist analysis may be undertaken in every case coming before them. Sheila McIntyre has noted, for example, that Justice L'Heureux-Dubé considered judging to be a scholarly activity—an intellectual challenge and a learning process requiring her to read widely and to constantly expand and update her jurisprudential resources (McIntyre, 2004, p. 314).

Supporting other women

A final aspect of feminist judging is the provision of support and encouragement to other women lawyers and judges. As suggested above, this does not mean always agreeing with each other, but it does mean adopting a general stance of solidarity and mutual assistance, and thinking carefully about where and how disagreements, when they arise, are expressed.

Is feminist judging permissible?

Turning now to the key question for this paper, the judicial oath sworn by English judges is "to do right to all manner of people, according to the laws and usages of the realm, without fear or favour, affection or ill will" (Hale, 2005, p. 286). This expresses the judicial norms of fairness, decision-making according to law, independence and impartiality—which incorporates both impartiality as between litigants and impartiality as between arguments (Wilson, 1990; Hale, 2001, p. 498).

In reflecting on the second element of this formulation (decision-making according to law), Lord Bingham of Cornhill has suggested that judicial decisions must be "legally motivated" (Bingham, 2005, p. 70). Decisions are precluded which are motivated

> not by legal but by extraneous considerations, as by the prejudice or predilection of the judge, or worse, by any personal agenda of the judge, whether conservative, liberal, feminist, libertarian or whatever. (Bingham, 2005, p. 70)

On this view, a decision motivated by feminist considerations would be impermissible. But what of the case of mixed motives? As Brenda Hale has argued:

> [T]he business of judging, especially in the hard cases, often involves a choice between different conclusions, any of which it may be possible to reach by respectable legal reasoning. The choice made is likely to be motivated at a far deeper level by the judge's own approach to the law, to the problem under discussion and to ideas of what makes a just result. (Hale, 2007, pp. 2–3)

Hale also goes on to point out that "an important project of feminist jurisprudence has been to explode the myth of the disinterested, disengaged, and distant judge" (Hale, 2007, p. 3). Fairness, decision-making according to law, independence and impartiality do not—indeed cannot—require the judge to become a blank slate upon which the evidence and arguments in each case are written afresh. At a recent discussion in London on feminism and judging, one of the participants observed that suggesting that one's gender is likely to affect one's experience and hence one's judgments is seen as highly divisive and somehow 'letting the side down'.[10] But such a view is only tenable within a system which takes (privileged, white) male perspectives to be universal and neutral.

A more pluralist and realist perspective might accept that a judge's religious and political beliefs, including feminism, are likely to inflect his or her decision-making, but should not intrude to the extent that the judge allows him- or herself to prejudge the issue or to be biased against particular parties or particular arguments. This is consistent with Justice Wendy Baker's argument that "Feminism in a judge is not [*automatically*] evidence of judicial partiality, nor a threat to judicial independence" (Baker, 1996, p. 199). But it also accepts that feminism in a judge will (or at least ought to) be trumped by the need for fairness, decision-making according to law, impartiality and independence should a conflict arise. In other words, a feminist approach or a feminist agenda must always be subordinated to judicial norms. But this allows considerably more scope for feminism than one might expect, especially when one recalls that judging is not just about making decisions.

When I discussed this project with a feminist trial judge, who spends her working life presiding over a fairly unalloyed diet of rape, sexual assault and child sexual abuse cases, she observed that feminist judging makes her "bloody tired". This reminded me that her practice as a feminist judge includes at least the following:

(a) listening to endless stories of the physical and emotional abuse visited upon other women and children;
(b) attempting to provide a trial process that minimises the trauma for the victims, against the constant efforts of defence counsel to push the boundaries of aggressive defence;
(c) feeling responsible for the outcomes of these cases and attempting to deliver some kind of justice to the victims of abuse in a legal system heavily weighted against them;
(d) reaching and delivering sentencing decisions;
(e) constantly having to defend her legitimacy as a feminist judge in the face of challenges, official complaints, sniping and disrespect from non-feminist colleagues (both male and female) and other detractors inside and outside the legal profession; and
(f) the extensive extra-curricular activities she undertakes (in her case, working for legal and procedural reforms relating to the reception of children's evidence).

While I have undoubtedly missed some other things that make her tired, it is notable that this list does not include decision-making (in the sense of determining the outcome of the case) at all.

I would argue, indeed, that previous analyses of the potential 'difference' that women judges might make have been either too optimistic (ascribing to women judges an unfettered capacity to change the law and the legal system), too pessimistic (asserting that law and the legal system are completely impervious to women's voices), or otherwise too dogmatic (contending that feminism is incompatible with being a judge), because they have adopted too generalised an understanding of judging. In order to arrive at a more nuanced and defensible assessment of the relationship between judging and feminism, it is necessary to develop a more detailed description of the practice of judging, and then to determine at each point whether a feminist approach would be consistent with judicial norms of fairness, decision-making according to law, impartiality and independence.

There appear to be four major aspects of judging which I will consider separately below—the court process, the outcome of the case, the reasons given for a decision, and extra-curricular activities. I acknowledge at the outset that this is a description of the practice of judging in common law systems, and that judging may involve different activities, or the same activities may be done differently, in civil law systems.

The court process

As noted above, part of the role of a feminist trial judge is to listen to stories of abuse visited upon other women and children, and to attempt to provide a trial process that minimises trauma for the victims of abuse, against the constant efforts of defence counsel to push the boundaries of aggressive defence. Managing the first instance trial or hearing process is a little-explored aspect of (feminist) judging (see Martin, 1989, p. 75; Hale, 2007, p. 22).

In terms of contextualisation and particularity, I have argued elsewhere that judges should not, in civil cases involving violent relationships, simply accept any terms of settlement between the parties that are handed up, but should scrutinise the terms of proposed settlements to ensure that the agreement protects the safety of the survivor of violence and any children involved (Hunter, 2007, p. 169). This approach involves paying attention to the context of the proceedings and the realities of the situation, rather than succumbing to abstraction and universal rules (the notion that settlement is automatically preferable to adjudication, and that if the parties have agreed, the court should remain neutral as to the terms of settlement).

Further, the precepts of particularity and attention would require the feminist judge to treat all parties, including victims/complainants/vulnerable witnesses, with equal dignity and respect. This would include offering litigants compassion and concern, engaging with the lives and the pain of the people appearing before her (Resnik, 1988, pp. 1922–3), and taking active steps to minimise their trauma in the courtroom. It would include the close supervision of cross-examination (Schultz, 2001, p. 64), making decisions about the admission or exclusion of evidence, and implementing available protections for vulnerable witnesses, in order to ensure that witnesses are not humiliated, patronised or bullied, and are given a fair opportunity to give their best evidence (Hale, 2007, p. 24). I once saw a very good example of this in a family law case in which the unrepresented father, who was alleged to have subjected the mother to serious violence, was set to cross-examine her directly. The mother was clearly terrified of the father, but the (feminist) judge arranged things so that she (the judge) acted as a physical intermediary between the two parties, enabling the father to ask his questions without confronting the mother, and the mother to answer without collapsing in fear. (All this while the mother's own barrister appeared to have no clue as to the point of the judge's efforts.) A feminist judge concerned to accord equal dignity and respect to all litigants would also make certain that they understood what was happening in court.

The imperatives to challenge gender bias and improve women's lives would mean that a feminist judge would not minimise the gravity or the effects of domestic violence. It has also been argued that judges in domestic violence restraining order proceedings ought to express their support and sympathy for the victims of domestic violence, while impressing upon perpetrators the unacceptability of violence, and the seriousness of breaching the orders being made (Ptacek, 1999, pp. 106–9). This, too, could fall within the feminist approach of promoting substantive equality.

The 'right' approach to take in such cases, however, may not always be clear. In the context of domestic violence, some feminist lawyers and sympathetic judges have taken the position that victims of abuse should, as far as possible, be spared the stress and trauma of speaking in open court about their experiences. Yet other research suggests that while some women welcome the opportunity to remain silent, others are very keen to tell their stories and to have them publicly heard and affirmed (Hunter, 2005; see also Schultz, 2001, p. 63). Should a feminist judge therefore minimise speaking requirements/opportunities, or ascertain in each case whether a survivor of violence wishes to speak or would prefer not to do so? The elements of feminist judging outlined above might suggest that an approach that gives women the opportunity to tell their stories and have them heard and understood, to be represented in legal discourse, to be considered as unique individuals, and to receive a 'fresh judgment' in each case—i.e. one that recognises women's diversity—would be preferable to one that generalised about victims of violence as a group, or exhibited paternalism. This would also be consistent with the feminist literature and research evidence rather than relying only on limited personal experience. In any event, the feminist judge would need to reflect on the possible consequences of her choice, and be able to justify it as a feminist position.

Do any of these suggestions constitute unreasonable expectations of a feminist judge? Scrutinising proposed settlements to ensure that violence is not perpetuated involves no partiality or unfairness to either party, and does not raise any issues in relation to legal decision-making or judicial independence.

It is also difficult to see how impartiality and fairness would be compromised if all litigants are treated with equal dignity and respect. Taking steps to minimise complainants' trauma, attempting to make them feel comfortable, and protecting vulnerable witnesses do not limit the defendant's ability to put his case, and can only be conducive to the effective administration of justice. This may not be how impartiality has traditionally been interpreted (Resnik, 1988, pp. 1922–3), but impartiality simply means lack of partiality for one side or another; it does not have to mean indifference or disengagement. Likewise, no issue of judicial independence is raised. In relation to the judge's decisions whether to exclude certain evidence, the judge must apply the rules of evidence, but those rules often confer a discretion, or the weighing of factors such as 'probative value' and 'prejudicial effect', which may in turn be exercised, or interpreted, in a way that challenges gender bias and takes into account the context of the case and the particularity of each party. In sum the feminist approach of contextualisation, particularity and attention appears to offer an entirely acceptable, and considerably more attractive model of judging, albeit a much more demanding one for the judge. As Brenda Hale has argued:

> In criminal trials, properly protecting the prosecution witnesses while allowing the defence properly to deploy its case is a hugely demanding task. It is so much easier to sit back and let defence counsel rip. It is also much safer: appellate courts do not usually have the opportunity to criticise trial judges for failing to protect vulnerable witnesses properly; but they have plenty of opportunities to criticise trial judges for 'descending into the arena' and intervening too much. Enabling all the witnesses, on either side, to give their best evidence is a much more radical idea than you might think. ... But the process of enabling witnesses to give their best evidence, of listening carefully to the stories being told even if alien to one's own experience, can only enhance the fairness of the trial. A feminist trial should be a fairer trial. (Hale, 2007, p. 24)

Similarly, challenging gender bias in attitudes towards domestic violence is inherently an approach that enhances fairness and impartiality rather than undermining them. But the concern to improve women's lives and promote substantive equality in the court process is not so clear-cut. At first blush, this may appear to be the opposite of impartiality. In fact, however, it is simply the opposite of *neutrality*, in a situation in which neutrality is not called for. Parliament has enacted laws designed to protect victims of domestic violence and to reduce its incidence. Once a decision has been made, on the basis of admissible evidence, that violence has occurred, or that there is a legally significant risk of its occurrence, then emphasising the gravity of that finding, expressing concern and support towards the victim, and reinforcing the unacceptability of violence to the perpetrator, is entirely in line with legislative policy. It is premised on decision-making according to law, and does not compromise fairness, impartiality, or judicial independence.

Finally, the example given makes it clear that there is nothing inherent in the process of making feminist choices about how the trial or hearing should be run that would take that process outside the bounds of permissible judicial action. Thus, it appears that feminist judges can adopt the full range of feminist approaches towards the court process without contravening judicial propriety. Consequently, it would be reasonable to expect feminist judges to act consistently *as* feminists at this level.

The result of the case

A feminist judge may make decisions that challenge gender- and other forms of entrenched bias. One such example might be Canadian Judge Corinne Sparks's decision in *RDS*,[11] in which she acquitted a Black defendant charged with obstructing police—a different decision from the one that might ordinarily have been made, and one that refused to perpetuate "the spiral of racialized injustice" (Kobayashi, 1998, p. 208). Another might be Australian magistrate Pat O'Shane's decision to dismiss charges of malicious damage against a group of women who had defaced a billboard which depicted a man sawing a semi-clad woman in half. In doing so, she stated that "The crime in this situation is the erection of those billboards depicting violence towards women". This decision provoked conservative outrage about O'Shane's cavalier disregard for property interests, but it also generated a great deal of public and private support, and a sense that she had empowered people to stand up against violence towards women (O'Shane, 1994, pp. 4–6).

The precepts of contextualisation, particularity and attention would result in sentencing decisions in criminal cases that reflected the interests of the community, the defendant and the victim, rather than accepting formulaic submissions.

A feminist judge would also be concerned to make decisions that remedied injustices, improved women's lives, and promoted substantive equality. As well as dealing with the substantive issues in dispute, this would include ensuring that the level of damages awarded appropriately reflected the nature of the harm suffered—a particular issue for women in sex discrimination, sexual harassment and abuse, medical negligence, and criminal compensation cases.

An interesting case study in this regard is provided by Eliane Junqueira, who has observed that Brazilian women judges are generally seen and see themselves as being tougher than their male colleagues on women seeking maintenance in divorce cases. They see this tough approach as helping women to break free from economic dependency on their husbands and to "better develop and fulfil their potential as human beings". They also see this stance as being most in tune with the constitutional principle of the equality of men and women, which does not permit any presupposition that women are less self-sufficient than men. They may be sympathetic to the actual labour market position of some women (for example those who are older or have few qualifications), and so might grant temporary maintenance until they are able to find their own feet. But they also express antipathy towards women who appear not to want to work and to remain dependent on their husbands (Junqueira, 2003, p. 448).

Yet while women's economic independence from men is a key feminist aspiration, this approach involves a fairly rigid insistence upon formal equality, with only limited regard for context, and a somewhat punitive, 'maternalistic' exercise of power to discipline divorced women and force them to behave in an approved feminist fashion. Insisting that divorced women acquire economic self-sufficiency may be an example of false gender neutrality that in fact serves men's interests (i.e. they are not required to pay maintenance to wives who may have sacrificed much of their income-earning potential to the marriage). It is also an example of adversely judging women who make different choices, rather than respecting the diversity of women's experience. By contrast, a more inclusive, contextualised and particularised approach would be more likely to achieve substantive equality between women and men in the post-divorce context. Clearly, one of the perils of a substantive equality analysis is that in taking into account the undesirable social realities of women's lives, there is a risk of reinforcing them (Mossman, 2004, p. 309). But from the position of a judge dealing with individual cases (as opposed to a policy-maker), the consequences of refusing to take account of social realities and insisting upon formal equality are likely to be more disadvantageous for women litigants than the consequences of pursuing a substantive equality approach.

How far are these kinds of feminist results possible within the boundaries of the judicial role, in particular the need for decision-making according to law? The answer depends on the situation. If the case directly raises issues of equality and discrimination—as many cases do in countries that have adopted constitutional or legislative human rights instruments—then a decision that promotes substantive equality is likely to be "consistent with the fundamental principles of the law" (Hale, 2007, pp. 26–7), and as such, is hardly objectionable (Hale, 2005, p. 286).

Secondly, if the feminist judge is exercising a discretion—as in the cases of the award of maintenance to a divorced wife, the dismissal of charges, the amount of damages to be awarded for non-economic loss, or sentencing in a criminal case—there is likely to be some scope for feminist decision-making. Discretion is not, of course, entirely unconstrained. It must be exercised within the bounds of any statutory or common law criteria to be taken into account, and more generally within the bounds of fairness, impartiality and judicial independence. It must also be exercised by reference to the arguments and evidence presented by the parties. As Justice Wendy Baker has observed:

> judicial sensitivity and training cannot compensate for a failure by counsel to properly analyse, plead or prove matters concerning gender or racial equality or cultural diversity arising in a lawsuit. Judges cannot substitute 'judicial notice' for evidence or compensate, to any significant extent, for a failure by counsel to identify the issues and present the appropriate facts and law. (Baker, 1996, p. 206–7)

Nevertheless, discretionary decision-making is an area in which a feminist philosophy may come into play. In this respect, the feminist judge is in no different position from the judge who exercises discretion in accordance with his or her predisposition towards liberalism, conservatism, the Christian faith, defendants, the state, institutions, or individuals. The same may be said for the interpretation of ambiguous statutory language and divergent precedents, and other instances of legal indeterminacy.

In relation to shaping legal doctrine in a way that is informed by a feminist analysis, judges who are members of the highest court in the relevant court hierarchy clearly have more room to manoeuvre than those at lower levels.[12] But it must be acknowledged that a lower or intermediate level judge faced with clear legislative provisions and/or clear precedent may have very little opportunity for feminist decision-making (unless, of course, the relevant precedent is itself the product of feminist decision-making by a higher court). Likewise, a trial judge may actively supervise the court proceedings, make evidential rulings, and emphasise certain issues in her summing up, but the decision is ultimately made by the jury. This is another reason why the feminist trial judge referred to earlier finds her job tiring:

while she feels responsible for the outcomes of her cases—for trying to deliver some kind of justice to victims of abuse—ultimately she cannot make up for deficiencies in the prosecution case, change the law, or prevent the jury from acquitting defendants she believes to be guilty. The best she can do is to make her conduct of the proceedings and her directions to the jury as appeal-proof as possible.

Reasons for decision

The fact that judges, particularly in lower level courts, are bound to follow existing rules and precedents, which may leave little scope for creativity or difference in their decisions, has led some authors to question whether women judges simply become assimilated into the masculine legal culture (Davis, 1993, p. 171; Graycar, 1995, pp. 268–9). But even if the outcome of a case is constrained, this does not mean that the feminist judge is compelled, in Berns's terms, to "become one with the law she speaks" (Berns, 1999, p. 53). Arguably, in cases other than those where the decision is made by a jury, there always remains scope for a judge to deploy a feminist analysis in her reasons for decision. Even if the law is clear and compels a decision one way or another, the reasons given for arriving at that decision may still evince a feminist approach.

Reasons for decision may be both implicit (referred to consciously or otherwise in the process of fact-finding) and explicit (the contents of the published judgment). On appellate courts, there is also the issue of the influence (or lack thereof) of the feminist judge on the reasoning of her judicial colleagues. Each of these points is considered in turn.

(i) Fact finding and assessments of credibility. A great deal of what judges do at lower levels of the court hierarchy is fact-finding. There has been very little discussion of this topic in the literature to date (see, e.g. Hale, 2001, p. 500, 2007, pp. 22–3), however it was raised at the conversation about feminism and judging referred to earlier. At that event, one of the participants noted that in chairing tribunals dealing with cases of equal pay and sex discrimination, her own experiences of discrimination and inequitable pay arrangements tend to make her more open-minded to the evidence of complainants, and she also encourages her fellow tribunal members to be similarly open-minded (see also Omatsu, 2005, p. 75). Likewise, another participant observed that judges do rely on their own experiences in the fact-finding process, which in the case of a woman judge includes understanding what it is like to be the only woman working in a male-dominated environment—something of which male judges have no experience. As a result, in her view, the under-representation of women on a tribunal that deals with discrimination and harassment cases limits the quality of its decisions. A third participant said that when hearing evidence, she understands where women are coming from, thereby providing access to justice for those women where it was not previously available. These are all examples of judging inclusively.

Similarly the Chief Justice of New Zealand, Dame Sian Elias, observed at a recent conference that her life experience as a woman has made her sensitive to humiliation and conscious of the importance of human dignity.[13] And Maryka Omatsu notes that:

> To the extent that gender, class, race or ethnicity affect one's behaviour on the stand, direct experience will also help judges to interpret a witness's demeanour, for instance to assess credibility. (Omatsu, 2005, pp. 75–6)

While experience as a woman is something that women judges as a whole rather than specifically feminist judges may bring to the bench, as noted earlier, a feminist judge would understand women's experience to be socially constructed, hence her willingness both to acknowledge her own experiences of discrimination and gender bias, and to connect those experiences to those of other women (compare Hunter, 2002). As suggested earlier, too, in order to judge inclusively, a feminist judge would not simply rely on her own experience in fact-finding and assessing the plausibility of litigants' stories, but would also refer to research and to interactions with other women in order to understand the diversity of women's experiences—for example the range of sometimes contradictory reactions experienced by victims of sexual assault and domestic violence.

Fact finding and assessing witness credibility may also involve challenging gender bias—for example consciously rejecting 'stock stories' about women's reactions and behaviour. At the feminism and judging event, for instance, two of the participants suggested that a feminist approach to fact-finding would include trying not to rely on stereotypical or gender-biased assumptions about sexual difference or behaviour.

Reg Graycar has argued that:

> we need to pay careful attention to what judges know about the world, how they know the things they do, and how the things they know translate into their activity as judges. (Graycar, 1995, p. 267)

If judicial knowledge is singular, derived from homogeneous (masculine) sources, and rarely reflected upon, then it will be difficult to achieve fairness towards all litigants. It is notable that all three judges at the conversation on feminism and judging characterised the process of judging from (gendered) experience as one of *providing justice* to women litigants. That is, their ability to comprehend what women were talking about produced overall fairness rather than partiality for one side. By contrast, a system in which all or most judges were men was implied to be *unfair* because it denied women the possibility of an empathetic hearing. Similarly, an approach to fact-finding that eschewed sexist (or other kinds of) assumptions and stereotyping arguably would perfect rather than violate judicial norms of fairness and impartiality.

(ii) Written judgments. There is, by now, quite a catalogue of exemplary feminist judgments available, and a developing literature analysing them—especially those penned by appellate judges at the highest level. These judgments 'ask the woman question', incorporate women's lives (and social science research evidence and feminist legal scholarship) into legal discourse, and challenge gender bias, myths and stereotypes. Examples include Justice Claire L'Heureux-Dubé's decisions on tax deductibility of childcare;[14] spousal support following divorce;[15] the admissibility of sexual history evidence[16] and counselling records,[17] and the issue of consent,[18] in

rape cases; and judicial bias[19] (see also L'Heureux-Dubé, 1997a, pp. 5–6; Sheehy, 2004a). In the latter case, she and Justice Beverley McLachlin held that the reasonable person in Canada is an informed and thinking member of society who subscribes to the principles of the Charter, including equality, and is aware of historical discrimination against minorities. Significantly, in French, this person was rendered as "la personne raisonnable".[20]

The judgments of Brenda Hale in the UK's High Court (Family Division), Court of Appeal and House of Lords, have been similarly wide-ranging, including decisions on child contact and the impact of family violence in family law,[21] evidence in sexual assault cases,[22] and medical negligence affecting women's reproductive choices. In the wrongful conception case of *Parkinson v. St James and Seacroft University Hospital NHS Trust*,[23] the Court of Appeal, composed of Hale and two male judges, reached a unanimous decision on the outcome, but in their judgments told the story of the case in quite different ways. In Rackley's words, Hale gave an "extraordinarily vivid account of pregnancy, childbirth and parenthood" (2006, p. 175) which shed new light on 'wrongful pregnancy' cases, and she also put forward an understanding of the invasion of the woman's autonomy in such cases as not merely something physical (which would therefore end at the child's birth), but as involving the imposition of an unwanted caring relationship (which thus continued throughout the child's dependency) (Rackley, 2006, p. 176).

Feminist judges such as Claire L'Heureux-Dubé and Mary Gaudron have also developed a significant jurisprudence of equality.[24] Both understood equality in substantive rather than formal terms. For Gaudron, equality involved "the recognition of genuine difference and, where it exists, differential treatment adapted to that difference" (Gaudron, 1997). Similarly, L'Heureux-Dubé's equality framework involved "a contextualized approach ... that emphasized the social history and vulnerability of disadvantaged groups", with a greater focus on the effects of discriminatory practices than on the black-letter search for a ground of discrimination recognised in existing Charter jurisprudence (Gilbert, 2003, p. 2; see also M. Young, 2004, p. 289).

The question then arises as to whether feminist judging in this sense violates judicial norms of fairness, impartiality, or decision-making according to law. The observation of fairness and impartiality requires that the arguments of both sides in the adversarial contest are given equally careful attention. If, in the course of a feminist judgment, the arguments with which the judge disagreed were ignored or summarily dismissed, this could create an appearance of partiality. But so long as a feminist judgment acknowledged and gave plausible reasons for rejecting opposing arguments, then no problem of unfairness or partiality would arise. Indeed, to the extent that such a judgment paid careful attention to arguments on behalf of women that were dealt with cursorily in other judgments, it would represent a fairer approach. In relation to decision-making according to law, whatever other sources the feminist judge may rely upon or refer to, ultimately, a judgment must be crafted from admissible evidence, social facts that might be the subject of judicial notice, and legal doctrine. The exemplary judgments discussed above certainly conform to these strictures.

(iii) Influence. Contrary to what I have just argued, Sandra Berns contends that a feminist judgment is an oxymoron. In her view, the conventions governing judicial

texts require the eradication of judicial difference (Berns, 1999, p. 204), and thus judgments will be most successful when judicial particularity is completely expunged. Judgments must be written as if it is "the law that has spoken" rather than the individual judge (Berns, 1999, p. 205). To the extent that judicial particularity remains, the authority of the judgment is diminished. Thus, for a judge to self-consciously speak with a different voice constitutes an abrogation of responsibility, a failure to justify the decision and to persuade the interpretive community in the most compelling way possible (Berns, 1999, p. 205): "whatever justification is proffered is incomplete, a failed attempt" (Berns, 1999, p. 206).

> To the extent that she speaks with a 'different voice', universality collapses into particularity. Judgment ceases to be a plausible continuation of an authoritative legal narrative and becomes a break with tradition. As rhetoric it may serve to challenge long standing traditions and in that way have persuasive force, but within law, as the continuation of an ongoing legal story, it is likely to be a failure. (Berns, 1999, p. 206)

I think that this argument is overstated, and that law is not nearly as monolithic and closed as Berns makes out. But even if one were to accept the argument as it stands, it does not negate the *possibility* of feminist judgment. Rather, it goes to the persuasiveness or influence of feminist judgments, which is a different matter.

Some of the exemplary feminist judgments identified above—and many others—have been dissenting opinions. At appellate level, a feminist judge who takes a different view of the case from other members of the court can always dissent. Claire L'Heureux-Dubé, for example, has been described as one of the Canadian Supreme Court's "great dissenters" (Gilbert, 2003, p. 27), and she herself argued for the value of dissenting opinions (L'Heureux-Dubé, 2000a). While a dissenting judgment does not change the law, it does put previously excluded experiences into legal discourse, educate students, lawyers and judicial colleagues about those experiences, demonstrate a different way of thinking about the issues in the case, provide an opportunity for judges to debate and analyse the merits of alternative approaches to those issues, and potentially lay the groundwork for future legal development (see also L'Heureux-Dubé, 2000a, pp. 496, 508, 511–2; Sparks, 2004, p. 382; Hale, 2007, pp. 21–2). Further, a dissenting judgment can not only preserve the judge's personal integrity, but also strengthen judicial independence (L'Heureux-Dubé, 2000a, p. 513).

L'Heureux-Dubé saw the authority of a dissenting opinion as being conferred by the quality of its reasoning (2000a, p. 514), while in Rackley's words, "the persuasive success of a dissenting narrative lies in its ability to challenge the majority's story and weaken its hold on our collective imagination" (Rackley, 2006, p. 181). In two cases decided by the US Supreme Court in 2007, in which majorities of the court upheld limitations on women's hard-won rights to abortion[25] and pay equity,[26] Justice Ruth Bader Ginsburg underlined the strength and power of her feminist objections by reading her dissenting judgments from the bench. As one journalist noted: "To read a dissent aloud is an act of theatre that justices use to convey their view that the majority is not only mistaken, but profoundly wrong" (Greenhouse, 2007).

In other cases, feminist appellate judges may be able to persuade their judicial colleagues to their point of view, and to join them in their reasons for decision and/or in the ultimate result of the appeal. For example, Justice Bertha Wilson managed to persuade other members of the Canadian Supreme Court to join her in the *Lavallee* decision, upholding the admissibility of expert evidence to explain the thought-processes and dispel myths about battered women who kill their abusers.[27] In the Rwandan genocide case, *Prosecutor v. Akayesu,* Justice Pillay wrote for the International Criminal Tribunal for Rwanda in finding that rape and sexual violence can be forms of genocide.[28] According to Rackley, Pillay's empathetic connection with the victims who gave evidence in the case "changed the course of women's jurisprudence in the international institutions", shaped the tribunal's understanding of rape as both an individual and a group injury, and "allowed her fellow tribunal members and others to see the bigger picture" (Rackley, 2007, p. 90). Brenda Hale's exhortation in *Re D* about the need to consider the impact of domestic violence in child contact cases was taken up by the Court of Appeal in *Re L.*[29]

Feminist judges' persuasion of their colleagues may occur behind the scenes as well as in the authorship of leading judgments. For instance, the US Ninth Circuit Court of Appeals coined the "reasonable woman standard" in employment discrimination cases in a decision written by a male judge; but, according to Hon. Mary Schroeder, this would never have occurred if the court had been all male (Schroeder, 2002, p. 255). In Elaine Martin's survey of members of the US National Association of Women Judges, 77% of respondents agreed that women judges had an influence on how their judicial colleagues perceived cases involving women's issues; 51% agreed that their presence on the bench had made a difference in the number of judicial decisions by themselves and others that promoted gender fairness in the substantive law; 48% agreed that their presence on the bench had made a difference in male judges' sensitivity to the existence and consequences of gender-based discrimination; and 47% said that they made efforts to change traditional, stereotyped attitudes towards women among male judges and attorneys (Martin, 1993, pp. 170–1). Likewise, Justice Rosalie Abella, in paying tribute to Justice Claire L'Heureux-Dubé, noted that she had "consistently introduced the woman's voice to the judicial conversation" (Abella, 2004, p. 40).

At lower levels of the court hierarchy, where, as discussed above, a single judge may be bound by doctrine and precedent to reach a particular result, her judgment may nevertheless suggest the possibility of a different approach, point out injustices wrought by the current rules and/or call for legislative intervention to change those rules. As Brenda Hale notes, "The task of judging frequently requires a judge to uphold a law in the wisdom or justice of which [she] does not believe" (Hale, 2007, p. 17). Judges have "no right to opt in and out of particular cases in accordance with our conscientious objections to particular laws" (Hale, 2007, p. 17). But, short of resigning, a judge may indicate her dissent from the rule, while nevertheless being bound to apply it in the case before her. This form of 'dissent' may also influence the legislature, or the thinking of appellate court judges.

Once more, these aspects of feminist judging do not violate norms of judicial behaviour. A dissenting opinion cannot compromise fairness, impartiality or independence (indeed, as argued by L'Heureux-Dubé, it may enhance the latter), and will only have credibility to the extent that it presents legally acceptable alternative reasoning in the case at hand. When a feminist judge persuades other judges to adopt her view, they are presumably persuaded by the cogency of her construction of the case and the legal plausibility of her argument, rather than by any form of judicial impropriety. And when a single judge expresses her disagreement with the law that she is bound to apply, she nevertheless applies it, so that her decision is one made according to existing law.

Extra-judicial activities

Empirically, feminist judges appear to engage in a wide range of extra-curricular activities. These include law reform projects, participation in women judges' organisations, giving speeches and writing articles, and generally practising feminism in their professional lives. Unlike their day jobs, however, extra-curricular activities are clearly optional. While feminist judges may, and often will, become involved in a range of activities, they cannot reasonably be *expected* to do so. But if and when they do, they can, once more, reasonably be expected to practise their feminism consistently. That is, in the course their extra-curricular activities, feminist judges ought to (and in fact do) ask the woman question, challenge gender bias, seek to make improvements in women's lives, promote substantive equality, and support and encourage other women judges and lawyers. They encounter fewer institutional constraints in doing so than they do in relation to the task of judging, although some constraints do remain.

(i) Law reform. Feminist judges may become involved in particular law reform projects on an ad hoc basis or may be appointed to generalist law reform bodies. As argued above, whatever the matters under consideration, it would be reasonable to expect a feminist judge involved in law reform consistently to act and think as a feminist, to draw upon relevant feminist legal literature, and to exercise feminist choices in contexts where there may be scope for disagreement between feminists as to the best approach to be taken.

Brenda Hale has argued that law reformers by necessity must develop a reform 'agenda'—a point of view about what the law should be (Hale, 2007, pp. 5–6). Thus, she states that "in the Law Commission, I never had any qualms about describing myself as a feminist" (Hale, 2007, p. 13). On the other hand, a feminist judge may be challenged on the basis that her law reform commitments demonstrate unacceptable bias in favour of one group or another, and/or insufficient respect for and deference to the current law which she is bound to apply in her day-to-day judicial role. The implication here is that she cannot be trusted to judge independently, impartially and according to law. Yet unless there is actual proof of bias or persistent legal errors in her judgments, such accusations carry little weight.

Moreover, like appellate courts, law reform bodies are generally collegial, which means that the feminist law reformer may be outvoted, write a dissenting report,[30] persuade her colleagues to agree with her position, join with other colleagues who take a similar approach, or listen to other arguments and be persuaded by them.

As on an appellate court, force of reasoning is the key criterion, regardless of the source of the agreed position.[31]

(ii) Women judges' organisations. Women judges' organisations tend not to be explicitly feminist organisations,[32] and many of their members may not identify as feminists. However, they do espouse some feminist goals, and provide both an avenue for feminist judges to pursue their commitments, and a source of social and professional support and solidarity (see Martin, 1989, p. 76). The general aims of women judges' organisations tend to be threefold: to provide mutual support, encouragement and collaboration amongst women judges; to promote the appointment of women to the judiciary; and to promote women's equality, awareness of 'women's issues' in law, and justice for women litigants.[33] The US National Association of Women Judges (NAWJ), for example, provided the impetus for the creation of State and federal task forces to investigate gender bias in the courts, and has supported and assisted women running for State judicial office (Kessler, 1983; Martin, 1993, p. 168). Elaine Martin's research suggests that members of women judges' organisations are more likely than other women judges to adopt a 'representative role' both collectively and individually (Martin, 1993, p. 170), while other research has pointed to the importance in activating individual feminist projects of a supportive network of like-minded women who share feminist views (Martin, 1993, pp. 167–8; Rackley, 2006, p. 167).

One important feature of women judges' organisations, as Judith Resnik has noted, is that they provide a means by which women judges can collectively speak out about issues which it might be difficult for them to address as individuals (Resnik, 1988, p. 1931). This refers not only to the power and persuasiveness of a collective as opposed to an individual voice, but also to the fact that personal attacks resulting from feminist activity are obviated when the activity is undertaken by an organisation rather than being attributable to any individual. Further, the organisation can perform a legitimating role, suggesting that particular views and concerns are not wildly radical, judicially inappropriate, or held by a minority of one, but are in fact widely shared. It is difficult to see how any of the activities of women judges' associations in challenging gender bias, exposing injustices, promoting substantive equality and supporting other women could be described as in any way compromising judicial independence or creating a perception of partiality. Neither does membership of a women's organisation *per se* indicate partiality, other than towards the concept of women's equality.

(iii) Speeches and articles. Feminist judges are often invited to speak at women lawyer functions and to women law students, and they also give speeches and addresses at conferences, law schools and to the legal profession, which may then be published as journal articles. Several themes tend to be prominent in feminist judicial speeches: critiques of the current judicial appointment process and advocacy for the appointment of more women judges (e.g. Branson, 1997; Matthews, 1998; Gaudron, 1999, 2002; Hale, 2001; and see also Cruikshank, 2003, pp. 127–36); discrimination against women in the legal profession, including their own experiences of sexist/gender-biased/discriminatory treatment (e.g. Branson, 1997; Gaudron, 1999, 2003; see also Cruikshank, 2003, pp. 127–36; Batrouney, 2005); the

pioneering role of 'first women' in the legal profession (see, e.g. Batrouney, 2005); and social and legal injustices towards women (e.g. O'Shane, 1994; Gaudron, 1999; see also Cruikshank, 2003, pp. 127–36; Batrouney, 2005). In other words, in their speeches, feminist judges challenge gender bias, expose injustices, promote substantive equality (see especially L'Heureux-Dubé, 1997b, 1999, 2000b, 2002; Hale, 2001; and see also Cruikshank, 2003, pp. 127–36); discrimination against women in the legal profession, including their own experiences of sexist/gender-biased/discriminatory treatment (e.g. Branson, 1997; Gaudron, 1999, 2003; see also Cruikshank, 2003, pp. 127–36; Batrouney, 2005); the pioneering role of 'first women' in the legal profession (see, e.g. Batrouney, 2005); and social and legal injustices towards women (e.g. O'Shane, 1994; Gaudron, 1999; see also Cruikshank, 2003, pp. 127–36; Batrouney, 2005). In other words, in their speeches, feminist judges challenge gender bias, expose injustices, promote substantive equality (see especially L'Heureux-Dubé, 1997b, 1999, 2000c), and support other women. These occasions can also provide the opportunity for a judge to identify herself as a feminist (see, e.g. Thornton, 1996, p. 208; Gaudron, 1999; Hale, 2007), and/or to highlight the importance of feminist legal theory in exposing and analysing women's inequality before the law, and in informing their thinking and practice (e.g. O'Shane, 1994, p. 12; Gaudron, 1997).

Daphne Gilbert observes that Justice Claire L'Heureux-Dubé made similar arguments in her speeches and articles and in her legal judgments, but was more tempered in her judgments while speaking with more passionate conviction outside the court (Gilbert, 2003, p. 3). Speeches and articles do provide greater freedom in this respect, but they are not entirely free of constraint. Firstly, judges cannot express views on issues that might come before them in individual cases, as this would raise the possibility of apprehended bias. Notably, however, this renders the themes of feminist judicial speeches identified above relatively safe. Processes of judicial appointment, promotion of women, legal professional practices, personal experiences and the experiences of other women lawyers and judges, and historical topics are unlikely to be raised in individual cases coming before the courts. Injustices towards women may potentially be raised, but any problems of apprehended bias may be avoided by speaking in very general terms,[34] or by repeating views that the judge has already expressed judicially (e.g. L'Heureux-Dubé, 1997a, pp. 5–6; Gilbert, 2003, p. 3; Hale, 2007).

Secondly, the content of her speeches may expose the feminist judge to the same kinds of objections and accusations as noted above in relation to law reform activities—perhaps more so than in that context. For example after her speech on "Will Women Judges Really Make a Difference?", Bertha Wilson faced a chorus of criticism that she was "a feminist judge who had violated her own judicial oath of impartiality and was accordingly incapacitated from the execution of her judicial duties" (Rackley, 2007, p. 79). Similarly, an Australian judge's description of herself as a feminist at her swearing-in was greeted with "considerable consternation and comment" (Thornton, 1996, p. 208). Once again, however, despite the hysteria that extra-curial feminist pronouncements may attract, they are no more disqualifying than sexist, racist or homophobic jokes delivered by male judges as part of the more traditional after-legal-dinner repertoire, or, for example, than expressed judicial commitments to Christianity or individual rights. If bias is alleged, then its existence must be proved in the context of individual cases.

(iv) Other activities. Feminist judges can play an important role in mentoring, supporting and encouraging other women judges and lawyers (see, e.g. Sparks, 2004, p. 382). Specific forms of support might include practising affirmative action in the appointment of clerks/associates/research staff; encouraging women to apply for silk and for judicial appointments, and to re-apply if they are initially rejected;[35] publicly standing up to senior male bullies in the profession (e.g. Gaudron, 2002); and directly confronting apparently discriminatory practices. For example, Mary Gaudron relates that she tackled a particular State Solicitor General as to why he never had women juniors in the constitutional cases in which he appeared before the Australian High Court. He said that he did not know any good women barristers, whereupon she supplied him with a list, after which women did begin to appear alongside him in the court (Gaudron, 1999, p. 119).

Another day-to-day activity of the feminist judge can be drawing her male colleagues' attention to the fact that women have different perspectives and experiences which have previously been excluded from the law, and challenging their unconscious (or overt) gender bias. Judith Resnik notes that to hear their female colleagues speaking about their own experiences of subordination can be both disconcerting and enlightening for male judges and lawyers. They may come to realise that "If women judges do not escape the effects of being women, then no one can" (Resnik, 1996, pp. 971–2). Thus, for instance, the US task force reports which documented women judges' experiences of discrimination provided "male judges with a new awareness of women's oppression" (Resnik, 1996, p. 972). In addition, rather than behaving as 'one of the boys'—trying to emulate men as far as possible—the feminist judge can remind her colleagues that law does include the feminine, and in doing so, compel them to think twice about sexist language, assumptions and behaviour.[36]

Conclusion

I have argued in this essay that while it is unrealistic to make generalisations or to impose demands upon women judges as a whole, *feminist* judges both can and ought to make a difference. They *can* do so because there is an identifiable body of feminist judicial theory and praxis upon which they can draw (*contra* Solimine & Wheatley, 1995, p. 907), and further, because adopting a feminist approach and applying a feminist philosophy has been shown to be entirely permissible within the bounds of judicial propriety—that is, while observing the judicial norms of fairness, impartiality, independence, and decision-making according to law—in relation to many if not all aspects of judging. They *ought to* do so (at least in their judicial role, and ideally in their extra-curricular activities as well) because self-identification as a feminist involves a commitment to a community of belief, and thus gives rise to legitimate expectations on the part of other community members that that commitment will be put consistently into practice.

One final objection remains to be disposed of. It might be thought that my normative argument places an intolerable burden on feminist judges (and therefore would tend to discourage judges from identifying as feminists). Not only do feminist judges often face challenges, complaints, sniping and disrespect from non-feminist colleagues and other detractors inside and outside the legal profession when they act as feminists,[37] but now they will also face challenges, demands and criticism from feminist commentators when they do not act as feminists, or do so insufficiently.

Feminist expectations, however, need not (indeed *ought* not) be expressed in a way that would exacerbate feminist judges' experiences of being perpetually under scrutiny and potential attack. Feminist judges might reasonably expect that discussion and debate among feminists about feminist positions and approaches would be more considered and respectful, and more in the way of an ongoing dialogue, than the personalised attacks of anti-feminists. Moreover, they might also reasonably expect encouragement and support from other feminists in the face of such attacks, whether privately or, where possible, in the form of public statements or demonstrations of support and solidarity. As Cotterrell notes, communities of belief give rise to obligations of *mutual* support (2006, p. 72)—not unilateral expectations, but a concerted effort to put beliefs into practice, from wherever one might sit.

Acknowledgements

An earlier version of this essay was presented at the AHRC Research Centre for Law, Gender and Sexuality 'Gender Unbound' conference, Keele University, June 2007, and as part of the IRC Gender and Judging sessions at the LSA/RCSL Annual Meeting, Berlin, July 2007. I would like to thank all of those who gave useful feedback on the paper. I am particularly grateful to Helen O'Sullivan, Constance Backhouse and Brenda Hale for their comments on the paper and for permission to cite unpublished material.

Notes

[1] For a good, recent account of liberal feminist theory, see Munro (2007, pp. 14–23).

[2] Similarly, in relation to the appointment of Black judges, Justice Corinne Sparks has noted that "Having black skin does not necessarily mean that one will embrace racial consciousness. It does not mean that the person will be sensitive to racial issues or claim racial identity" (Sparks, 2004, p. 383).

[3] See, e.g. Junqueira (2003, p. 445), discussing the case of a woman judge who had a "horror" of feminist language.

[4] *R v. Lavallee* [1990] 1 SCR 852: Wilson J authored the majority opinion which allowed the admission of expert evidence on battered woman syndrome in support of a woman who had killed her partner after suffering prolonged abuse.

[5] *R v. Morgentaler* [1988] 1 SCR 30: in her concurring judgment, Wilson J held that Criminal Code provisions limiting access to abortions violated women's rights to life, liberty and security of the person contrary to s.7 of the Canadian Charter of Rights and Freedoms.

[6] For this reason, I refer throughout this essay to the feminist judge as 'she', although with the invitation that the feminine be read as incorporating the masculine.

[7] A point made by one of the participants in a conversation about 'Feminism and Judging', University of Westminster, 1 May 2007.

[8] Along similar lines, Hester Lessard refers to Justice L'Heureux-Dubé's advocacy of "an open minded, carefully considered, and dispassionately deliberate investigation of the complicated reality of each case" (Lessard, 2004, p. 136).

[9] Conversation on 'Feminism and Judging', as above n. 7.

[10] *Ibid.*

[11] See *R v. RDS* [1997] 3 SCR 484.

[12] Though see Hale (2007). She adopts Cass Sunstein's identification of four different approaches to judging in the US Supreme Court (p. 4), and professes herself to be a 'minimalist' (p. 24). Minimalists "may be either conservative or liberal, willing to nudge the law in one direction or another. But they prefer nudges to earthquakes. They refuse to promote a broad agenda. Their distinguishing feature is that they believe in narrow, incremental decisions, not broad rulings that the nation may later have cause to regret. By their very nature, minimalists are not too sure that they are right" (p. 5).

[13] Society of Legal Scholars Annual Conference, Durham University, 11 September 2007.

[14] *Symes v. Canada* [1993] 4 SCR 695. For a discussion of this and the following cases, see Boivin (2003).

[15] *Moge v. Moge* [1992] 3 SCR 813.

[16] *R v. Seaboyer* [1991] 2 SCR 577.

[17] *R v. Osolin* [1993] 4 SCR 595; *R v. Carosella* [1997] 1 SCR 80.

[18] *R v. Ewanchuk* [1999] 1 SCR 330.

[19] *R v. RDS* [1997] 3 SCR 484.

[20] *Ibid.*, as discussed in Boivin (2003, p. 99).

[21] *Re D* [1993] 2 FLR 1.

[22] *R v. J* [2005] 1 All ER 1.

[23] *Parkinson v. St James and Seacroft University Hospital NHS Trust* [2002] QB 266.

[24] For Gaudron, see *Australian Iron & Steel v. Banovic* [1989] 168 CLR 165; *Street v. Queensland Bar Association* [1989] 168 CLR 461; Gaudron (1997); Gaudron (1999, pp. 117–8); and Tate (2006). For L'Heureux-Dubé, see *Egan v. Canada* [1995] 2 SCR 513; *Gosselin v. Quebec (Attorney-General)* [2002] 4 SCR 429; Gilbert (2003); Sheehy (2004b, p. 25); Sheehy and Boyle (2004, pp. 270, 275); M. Young (2004); and McIntyre (2004, p. 314).

[25] *Gonzales v. Carhart* [2007] 127 SCt 1610 (concerning the Constitutional validity of a legislative ban on so-called 'partial birth' abortions).

[26] *Ledbetter v. Goodyear Tire & Rubber Co.* [2007] 127 SCt 2162 (concerning the question of whether the applicant's pay discrimination claim was time-barred, even though she only became aware of the discrimination long after it had commenced).

[27] *R v. Lavallee* [1990] 1 SCR 852.

[28] *The Prosecutor v. Jean-Paul Akayesu* [1998] Case No. ICTR-96-4-T.

[29] *Re D (Contact: Reasons for Refusal)* [1998] 1 FCR 147; *Re L (A Child) (Contact: Domestic Violence)* [2000] 4 All ER 609.

[30] See, e.g. the 'Minority View with Regard to Certain Aspects of the Equality Act' in Australian Law Reform Commission (1994, ch. 16).

[31] Unlike courts, however, law reform bodies do not have the last word, but rely on their recommendations being accepted by politicians. This may introduce another kind of institutional constraint on the pursuit of a feminist agenda, which is beyond the scope of this essay to explore.

[32] The best known women judges' organisations are the US National Association of Women Judges (NAWJ, established 1979), and its extension, the International Association of Women Judges (IAWJ, formed in 1991): see http://www.iawj.org. The UK Association of Women Judges was founded more recently in 2003.

[33] See, e.g. United Kingdom Association of Women Judges, 'Response to DCA Consultation Paper 11/03', 6 November 2003, Annex 1, accessed at http://www.dca.gov.uk/consult/supremecourt/responses/sc160.pdf; and International Association of Women Judges at http://www.iawj.org/what/what.asp.

[34] For example the following from Mary Gaudron: "Confidence in the law is shaken every time a judge makes a statement that implies women or members of some minority group in our society are less deserving of the law's protection than others . . . Regrettably, judges and lawyers have provided sufficient evidence of their insensitivity to the situation of women for many women to believe that the courts and establishment lawyers simply do not serve the interests of women and, thus, to that extent do not serve the interests of justice" (Gaudron, 1999, pp. 119–20).

[35] Conversation on 'Feminism and Judging', as above n. 7.

[36] *Ibid.*

[37] Perhaps the best-known example is the extraordinary reaction to Justice L'Heureux-Dubé's judgment in the *Ewanchuk* case (*R v. Ewanchuk* [1999] 1 SCR 330), which included an official complaint and a wholly unprecedented personal attack in the press by the judge whose decision she had criticised (see, e.g. Backhouse, 2003, pp. 172–5; McIntyre, 2004); but this is far from being the only example (see, e.g. Hunter, 2004, 2006).

References

Abella, R.S. (2004) Tribute, in: E. Sheehy (Ed.) *Adding Feminism to Law: The Contributions of Justice Claire L'Heureux-Dubé* (Toronto, Irwin Law).

Allen, D.W. & Wall, D.E. (1993) Role orientations and women State Supreme Court justices, *Judicature*, 77, pp. 156–65.

Anderson, E. (2001) *Judging Bertha Wilson: Law as Large as Life* (Toronto, University of Toronto Press).

Australian Law Reform Commission (1994) *Report No. 69, Part II—Equality Before the Law: Women's Equality* (Sydney, ALRC).

Backhouse, C. (2003) The chilly climate for women judges: reflections on the backlash from the *Ewanchuk* case, *Canadian Journal of Women and the Law*, 15, pp. 167–93.

Backhouse, C. (2007) Madam Justice Bertha Wilson and the politics of feminism (unpublished paper on file with author).

Baker, W. (1996) Women's diversity: legal practice and legal education—a view from the bench, *University of New Brunswick Law Journal*, 45, pp. 199–208.

Bartlett, K.T. (1990) Feminist legal methods, *Harvard Law Review*, 103, pp. 829–88.

Batrouney, J. (2005). The contribution that the Hon. Mary Gaudron QC has made to women and the law, Conference Honouring Mary Gaudron's Contribution to Australian Law, 5 March, University of Melbourne, available at: http://www.womenlawyers.org.au

Berns, S. (1999) *To Speak as a Judge: Difference, Voice and Power* (Aldershot, Ashgate).

Bingham, T. (2005) The judges: active or passive?, *Proceedings of the British Academy*, 139, pp. 55–72.

Boivin, M. (2003) Les principes féministes en action: l'oeuvre judicaire de l'Honorable Juge Claire L'Heureux-Dubé ou 'Voir Juste, Voir Clair/e', *Canadian Journal of Women and the Law*, 15, pp. 73–101.

Boyd, S.B. (2004) Contextualizing the best interests of the child: Justice L'Heureux-Dubé's approach to child custody and access law, in: E. Sheehy (Ed.) *Adding Feminism to Law: The Contributions of Justice Claire L'Heureux-Dubé* (Toronto, Irwin Law).

Boyle, C. (1985) Sexual assault and the feminist judge, *Canadian Journal of Women and the Law*, 1, pp. 93–107.

Branson, C. (1997) Running on the edge: address to Women Lawyers' Association of New South Wales, Sydney, 15 October, available at: http://www.womenlawyers.org.au

Cain, P.A. (1988) Good and bad bias: a comment on feminist theory and judging, *Southern California Law Review*, 61, pp. 1945–55.

Canadian Bar Association Task Force on Gender Equality in the Legal Profession (1993) *Touchstones for Change: Equality, Diversity and Accountability* (Ottawa, CBA).

Cotterrell, R. (2006) *Law, Culture and Society: Legal Ideas in the Mirror of Social Theory* (Aldershot, Ashgate).

Cruikshank, E. (Ed.) (2003) *Women in the Law: Strategic Career Management* (London, Law Society).

Davis, S. (1993) Do women judges speak 'in a difference voice?' Carol Gilligan, feminist legal theory, and the Ninth Circuit, *Wisconsin Women's Law Journal*, 8, pp. 143–73.

Davis, S., Haire, S. & Songer, D.R. (1993) Voting behaviour and gender in the US Courts of Appeals, *Judicature*, 77, pp. 129–33.

Derrida, J. (1990) Force of law: 'The mystical foundation of authority', *Cardozo Law Review*, 11, pp. 920–1045.

DuBois, E.C., Dunlap, M.C., Gilligan, C.J., MacKinnon, C.A. & Menkel-Meadow, C.J. (1985) Feminist discourse, moral values, and the law—a conversation, *Buffalo Law Review*, 34, pp. 11–87.

Gaudron, M. (1997) Speech to launch Australian Women Lawyers, Melbourne, 19 September, available at: www.womenlawyers.org.au

Gaudron, M. (1999) A happy coincidence of self-interest and the public interest: equality of opportunity for women at the Victorian Bar, *Australian Feminist Law Journal*, 12, pp. 117–20.

Guadron, M. (2002) Speech for Women Lawyers Association of New South Wales 50th anniversary gala dinner, Sydney, 13 June, available at: http://www.womenlawyers.org.au

Gaudron, M. (2003) Highlights from the summer twilight reception in honour of Justice Mary Gaudron, High Court of Australia, Patron of Australian Women Lawyers, Sydney, 25 January, available at: http://www.womenlawyers.org.au

Gilbert, D. (2003) Unequalled: Justice Claire L'Heureux-Dubé's vision of equality and section 15 of the *Charter*, *Canadian Journal of Women and the Law*, 15, pp. 1–27.

Gilligan, C. (1982) *In a Different Voice* (Cambridge, MA, Harvard University Press).

Graycar, R. (1995) The gender of judgments: an introduction, in: M. Thornton (Ed.) *Public and Private: Feminist Legal Debates* (Melbourne, Oxford University Press).

Greenhouse, L. (2007) Oral dissents give Ginsburg a new voice on court, *New York Times*, 31 May.

Hale, B. (2001) Equality and the judiciary: why should we want more women judges, *Public Law*, pp. 489–504.

Hale, B. (2005) Making a difference? Why we need a more diverse judiciary, *Northern Ireland Legal Quarterly*, 56, pp. 281–92.

Hale, B. (2007) Maccabaean lecture in jurisprudence 2007: a minority opinion? Lecture to the British Academy, London, 13 November.

Hunter, R. (2002) Talking up equality: women barristers and the denial of discrimination, *Feminist Legal Studies*, 10, pp. 113–30.

Hunter, R. (2004) Fear and loathing in the Sunshine State, *Australian Feminist Studies*, 19, pp. 145–57.

Hunter, R. (2005) *Women's Experience in Court: The Implementation of Feminist Law Reforms in Civil Proceedings Concerning Domestic Violence*, JSD thesis, Stanford University.

Hunter, R. (2006) The high price of success: the backlash against women judges in Australia, in: E. Sheehy & S. McIntyre (Eds) *Calling for Change: Women, Law, and the Legal Profession* (Ottawa, Ottawa University Press).

Hunter, R. (2007) Consent in violent relationships, in: R. Hunter & S. Cowan (Eds) *Choice and Consent: Feminist Engagements with Law and Subjectivity* (Abingdon, Routledge-Cavendish).

Junqueira, E.B. (2003) Women in the judiciary: a perspective from Brazil, in: U. Schultz & G. Shaw (Eds) *Women in the World's Legal Professions* (Oxford, Hart Publishing).

Kessler, G. (1983) NAWJ: the value of sisterhood on the bench, *Trial*, 55 (August), p. 55.

Kobayashi, A. (1998) Do minority women judges make a difference?, *Canadian Journal of Women and the Law*, 10, pp. 199–212.

Lakeman, L. (2004) A feminist view of the Supreme Court from the anti-rape frontline, in: E. Sheehy (Ed.) *Adding Feminism to Law: The Contributions of Justice Claire L'Heureux-Dubé* (Toronto, Irwin Law).

Lawrence, S. (2004) Feminism, consequences, accountability, *Osgoode Hall Law Journal*, 42, pp. 583–601.

Lessard, H. (2004) Backlash and the feminist judge: the work of Justice Claire L'Heureux-Dubé, in: E. Sheehy (Ed.) *Adding Feminism to Law: The Contributions of Justice Claire L'Heureux-Dubé* (Toronto, Irwin Law).

L'Heureux-Dubé, C. (1997a) Making a difference: the pursuit of a compassionate justice, *Canadian Journal of Family Law*, 14, pp. 103–27.

L'Heureux-Dubé, C. (1997b) Making equality work in family law, *UBC Law Review*, 31, pp. 1–15.

L'Heureux-Dubé, C. (1999) Conversations on equality, *Manitoba Law Journal*, 26, pp. 273–98.

L'Heureux-Dubé, C. (2000a) The dissenting opinion: voice of the future?, *Osgoode Hall Law Journal*, 38, pp. 495–517.

L'Heureux-Dubé, C. (2000b) The search for equality: a human rights issue, *Queens Law Journal*, 25, pp. 401–15.

L'Heureux-Dubé, C. (2000c) A conversation about equality, *Denver Journal of International Law and Policy*, 29, pp. 65–75.

L'Heureux-Dubé, C. (2001) Outsiders on the bench: the continuing struggle for equality, *Wisconsin Women's Law Journal*, 16, pp. 15–30.

Martin, E. (1989) Differences in men and women judges: perspectives on gender, *Journal of Political Science*, 17, pp. 74–85.

Martin, E. (1993) The representative role of women judges, *Judicature*, 77, pp. 166–73.

Martin, E. & Pyle, B. (2000) Gender, race, and partisanship on the Michigan Supreme Court, *Albany Law Review*, 63, pp. 1205–36.

Matthews, J. (1998) Women judges: the great wall, Address to Women Lawyers Association of New South Wales, 22 July, available at: http://www.womenlawyers.org.au

McGlynn, C. (2003) Book review: Ellen Anderson, *Judging Bertha Wilson, Feminist Legal Studies*, 11, pp. 307–10.

McIntyre, S. (2004) Personalising the political and politicizing the personal: understanding Justice McClung and his defenders, in: E. Sheehy (Ed.) *Adding Feminism to Law: The Contributions of Justice Claire L'Heureux-Dubé* (Toronto, Irwin Law).

Menkel-Meadow, C. (1986) The comparative sociology of women lawyers: the 'feminization' of the legal profession, *Osgoode Hall Law Journal*, 24, pp. 897–918.

Mossman, M.J. (2004) Inequalities and social context, in: E. Sheehy (Ed.) *Adding Feminism to Law: The Contributions of Justice Claire L'Heureux-Dubé* (Toronto, Irwin Law).

Munro, V. (2007) *Law and Politics at the Perimeter: Re-Evaluating Key Debates in Feminist Theory* (Oxford, Hart Publishing).

Murdoch, I. (1970) *The Sovereignty of Good* (London, Routledge & Kegan Paul).

Omatsu, M. (2005) The fiction of judicial impartiality, in: G. MacDonald, R.L. Osborne & C.C. Smith (Eds) *Feminism, Law, Inclusion: Intersectionality in Action* (Toronto, Sumach Press).

O'Shane, P. (1994) Launch of the *Australian Feminist Law Journal*, August 29, 1993, The University of Melbourne, *Australian Feminist Law Journal*, 2, pp. 3–12.

O'Sullivan, H. (2007) *The Right to Silence at Trial: A Critique and a Call for a New Approach*, PhD thesis, Griffith University (embargoed until 15 December 2008).

Ptacek, J. (1999) *Battered Women in the Courtroom: The Power of Judicial Responses* (Boston, Northeastern University Press).

Rackley, E. (2006) Difference in the House of Lords, *Social & Legal Studies*, 15, pp. 163–85.

Rackley, E. (2007) Judicial diversity, the woman judge and fairy tale endings, *Legal Studies*, 27, pp. 74–94.

Resnik, J. (1988) On the bias: reconsideration of the aspirations for our judges, *Southern California Law Review*, 61, pp. 1877–944.

Resnik, J. (1996) Asking about gender in courts, *Signs*, 21, pp. 952–90.

Rush, S.E. (1993) Feminist judging: an introductory essay, *Southern California Review of Law and Women's Studies*, 2, pp. 609–32.

Schroeder, M.M. (2002) Judging with a difference, *Yale Journal of Law and Feminism*, 14, pp. 255–61.

Schultz, J. (2001) Can women judges help make civil sexual assault trials more therapeutic?, *Wisconsin Women's Law Journal*, 16, pp. 53–66.

Sheehy, E. (Ed.) (2004a) *Adding Feminism to Law: The Contributions of Justice Claire L'Heureux-Dubé* (Toronto, Irwin Law).

Sheehy, E. (Ed.) (2004b) Introduction, *Adding Feminism to Law: The Contributions of Justice Claire L'Heureux-Dubé* (Toronto, Irwin Law).

Sheehy, E. & Boyle, C. (2004) Justice L'Heureux-Dubé and Canadian sexual assault law: resisting the privatization of rape, in: E. Sheehy (Ed.) *Adding Feminism to Law: The Contributions of Justice Claire L'Heureux-Dubé* (Toronto, Irwin Law).

Sherry, S. (1986) Civic virtue and the feminine voice in constitutional adjudication, *Virginia Law Review*, 72, pp. 543–616.

Solimine, M.E. & Wheatley, S.E. (1995) Rethinking feminist judging, *Indiana Law Review*, 70, pp. 891–920.

Sparks, C. (2004) Justice L'Heureux-Dubé: dimensions of a quintessential judicial leader, in: E. Sheehy (Ed.) *Adding Feminism to Law: The Contributions of Justice Claire L'Heureux-Dubé* (Toronto, Irwin Law).

Sullivan, R. (2004) The era of concealed underlying premises is over: L'Heureux-Dubé J.'s contributions to statutory interpretation, in: E. Sheehy (Ed.) *Adding Feminism to Law: The Contributions of Justice Claire L'Heureux-Dubé* (Toronto, Irwin Law).

Tate, P. (2006) 10th Ethel Benjamin commemorative address, Dunedin, 2 September, available at: www.womenlawyers.org.au

Thornton, M. (1996) *Dissonance and Distrust: Women in the Legal Profession* (Melbourne, Oxford University Press).

Van Marle, K. (2004) To revolt against present sex and gender images: feminist theory, feminist ethics and a literary reference, *Stellenbosch Law Review*, 15, pp. 247–67.

Weil, S. (1977) *The Simone Weil Reader*, G.A. Panchias (Ed.) (New York, McKay).

Westergren, S. (2004) Gender in the Courts of Appeals revisited: the data since 1994, *Georgetown Law Journal*, 92, pp. 689–708.

Wilson, B. (1990) Will women judges really make a difference?, *Osgoode Hall Law Journal*, 28, pp. 507–22.

Young, C.F.L. (2004) Taxing times at the Supreme Court of Canada: the contributions of Justice L'Heureux-Dubé to a better understanding of the application of the *Charter* to the income tax system, in: E. Sheehy (Ed.) *Adding Feminism to Law: The Contributions of Justice Claire L'Heureux-Dubé* (Toronto, Irwin Law).

Young, M. (2004) Travels with Justice L'Heureux-Dube: equality law abroad, in: E. Sheehy (Ed.) *Adding Feminism to Law: The Contributions of Justice Claire L'Heureux-Dubé* (Toronto, Irwin Law).

What a difference difference makes: gendered harms and judicial diversity

ERIKA RACKLEY
Durham Law School, Durham, UK

ABSTRACT *Taking the UK Ministry of Justice's ongoing quest to ensure a more diverse judiciary as its starting point and backdrop, this paper establishes the House of Lords' decision in* Secretary of State for the Home Department v. K (FC); Fornah (FC) v. Secretary of State for the Home Department [2006] *as a lens through which to explore the 'difference' of the woman judge and, in particular, the developing jurisprudence of Baroness Hale—the first (and only) female law lord in the UK. It argues that Baroness Hale's candid recognition and articulation of the gendered nature of the experiences and violence in Fornah's story reveals not only the difference difference (in whatever form) might make to understandings of the judge, judging and justice but also the importance of recognising the transformative potential of judicial diversity to create a space in which difference is celebrated and valued on its own terms, a place where difference can truly make a difference.*

Introduction

> My Lords . . . the answer in each case is so blindingly obvious that it must be a mystery to some that either of them had to reach this house. (Baroness Hale in *Secretary of State for the Home Department v. K (FC); Fornah (FC) v. Secretary of State for the Home Department* [2006] 83)

Since her elevation to the House of Lords in January 2004, it has become increasingly apparent that while she is far from "trouble with a capital H" (Hardcastle, 2004) Baroness Hale is nevertheless "just a bit different" from her exclusively male colleagues (Hale, 2004a). Indeed, the combination of her pioneering achievement, her candid exposure of the inheresnt sexism in her profession (Verkaik, 2003), and her willingness to talk about "clothes, cooking and childcare" (Hale, 2002) which secured her place as one of the "Women We Loved in 2003" (Addley, 2003) continues to confirm her status as not only one of the most interesting feminists alive today (Anon, 2005) but also "one of our more thoughtful" law lords (Anon, 2004).

The decision in *Secretary of State for the Home Department v. K (FC)*; *Fornah (FC) v. Secretary of State for the Home Department* is a case in point.[1] Baroness Hale's explicit recognition of gender-related and gender-specific persecution—her difference, if you like—haunts the unanimous ruling. Put another way, gendered difference is both the method and the subject of the appeal. This is not unproblematic. While the world may have "woken up to the fact that women as a sex may be persecuted in ways which are different from the ways in which men are persecuted" (Baroness Hale, *Fornah* [2006] 86), in the context of adjudication the mere suggestion of difference—particularly in relation to the woman judge—remains contentious. The existence or otherwise of a 'different' judicial voice (however so articulated) is, more often than not, rejected as a "dangerous myth" (O'Connor, 1991, p. 1553) that threatens to lure the unwary toward the quagmire of essentialism while, at the same time, going to the heart of Herculean understandings of the judge and judging. So viewed, the woman judge is a threat to the aesthetic norm; her presence on the bench is an inescapable irritant, simultaneously confirming and disrupting its established masculinity. As a result, while calls—in both the UK and beyond—for judicial diversity grounded in the importance of equal opportunities or democratic legitimacy abound (Thomas, 2005), arguments located in difference (whatever that might mean) have largely fallen silent.

And yet, perhaps the irritant potential of the woman judge is no bad thing. In fact some might ask—what's so great about Herculean understandings of the judge and judging anyway? Maybe the detached, disembodied, impassive judicial superhero has had his day; the aesthetic image of the Herculean judge is increasingly understood as not only unattainable but also undesirable (Rackley, 2006a). If so, then the presence of difference on the bench provides us with an opportunity to reassess both what it is we want from our judges and what it means to judge. Put another way, it is because the woman judge is 'different' that we both look for and—more importantly—*find* difference (Rackley, 2006b). So viewed, difference brings into sharp relief not only the extent to which prevailing images of the judge are enmeshed in notions of sameness and uniformity but also attributes of the judge and judging currently hidden beneath his superhero's clothes.

However this is not to suggest that all—or indeed any—women judges speak with a 'different voice' akin to the elusive (and currently derided) voice of the idealised, Gilligan-inspired lawyer and judge (although there may be similarities in tone).[2] Nor is it to fetishise Baroness Hale's difference *as a woman* over other aspects of her identity—for example, her academic background, her time as a law commissioner, her judicial training—or other personal characteristics—her feminist credentials (Hale, 2007), her experiences as a mother and grandmother and so on. Rather my point is this. Properly understood, the promise of judicial difference (however defined) lies in its ability to render contingent particular but dominant forms of judicial reasoning—that is the incorporation of difference on the bench exposes the extent to which the privileging of particular knowledges, the flattening of difference and the suppression of polytonality both affect and effect women, judging, and the delivery of justice. In so doing, judicial difference acts as a catalyst for disruption; impacting upon the legal monotony, destabilising its taken-for-granted assumptions and uncovering alternative ways of seeing, understanding, and judging and the possibility of true judicial diversity.

Taking the UK Ministry of Justice's ongoing quest to ensure a more diverse judiciary as its starting point and backdrop, this paper utilises the House of Lords' decision in *Fornah*—described by one commentator as a decision bearing "all the hallmarks of Britain's first woman law lord" (Anon, 2006)—as a lens through which to explore the 'difference' of the woman judge and, in particular, the developing jurisprudence of Baroness Hale—the first (and only) female law lord in the UK. To this end *Fornah* is illustrative rather than definitive. The paper argues that Baroness Hale's candid recognition and articulation of the gendered nature of the experiences and violence in Fornah's story reveals not only the difference difference (in whatever form) might make to the understandings of the judge, judging and justice but also the importance of recognising the transformative potential of judicial diversity to create a space in which difference is celebrated and valued on its own terms, a place in which difference can truly make a difference.

Appointing difference

Ever since John Griffith identified the judiciary in England and Wales as a largely homogenous group, possessing "a unifying attitude of mind, a political position, which is primarily concerned to protect and conserve certain values and institutions" (Griffith, 1997, p. 7), the class, age, education, sex, race and, more recently, sexuality of the judiciary have been subject to vigorous scrutiny.[3] While the judiciary in England and Wales is more diverse than it has ever been with almost twice as many women and people from ethnic minority groups working in, and being appointed to, it than there were ten years ago, current figures suggest we are in danger of having what Brenda Hale has described as a "pale male judiciary" for some time yet (2005b, p. 281). Although just over 25% of the judiciary as a whole is female, women make up less than 11% of full-time judges. Moreover, just 11 women sit in the High Court and above alongside 98 men; put another way just over 91% of the senior judiciary is male.[4] Following the retirement of Elizabeth Butler-Sloss as President of the Family Division, none of the Heads of Division are (or have been) female. Judges from a non-white ethnic minority background fare even worse. Linda Dobbs' hope that her appointment to the High Court in 2004 "would be the first of many" has not yet been realised (BBC News, 2004). Non-white ethnic minority groups remain significantly underrepresented in both the senior judiciary and the judiciary as a whole, comprising just 1.8% and 4% respectively.[5] Clearly, as the previous Lord Chancellor, Lord Falconer, observed there is "still more to do if we are to achieve a judiciary that better reflects the society it serves" (DCA Press Notice, 2006).

Unsurprisingly then judicial diversity—or lack thereof—has, for a number of years, been fairly consistently high on the UK's political agenda.[6]

> Achieving judicial diversity is a priority because it makes a real and positive difference to the administration of justice. We need to harness the talent and ability of all those who would make good judges, so that we can be sure that

> the best are being appointed whatever their background. The public needs to have confidence in judges who more closely reflect the diversity of the nation, and who have a real understanding of the problems faced by most people. (DCA Press Notice, 2005)

True to his word, the Falconer-era brought with it a number of key changes (as part of the Labour Government's wider programme of constitutional reform) designed to encourage and meet the needs of a more diverse judiciary. These included allowing for a reduction in the time spent as advocate before qualifying for judicial appointment, opportunities for job sharing, career breaks, a mentoring scheme and, most significantly, legislative provisions establishing an independent Judicial Appointments Commission responsible for nominating candidates for appointment by (or on the recommendation of) the Lord Chancellor.[7]

And yet, one might well ask: what is all the fuss about? *Why* should we want a more representative judiciary? Is it simply that there *ought* to be more women judges, just as there ought to be more women in Parliament or managing directors of FTSE 100 companies (Equal Opportunities Commission, 2006), not to mention more male nurses and primary school teachers (a kind of numerical aestheticism)? Or, alternatively, maybe the formal adherence to principles of fairness and equal opportunities is a mechanism to ensure the judiciary's survival? Perhaps judicial diversity is necessary in order to maintain public confidence in, and to ensure the legitimacy of, the judiciary as a whole? The difficulty is, however, that none of these proffered rationales draw on any advantage in the woman judge *per se*. But should they? Surely the *woman* judge has something to offer beyond simply evening up the numbers at the table? How, if at all, might her presence make a difference?

Enter Baroness Hale: the first—and so far only—lady law lord. Unsurprisingly perhaps, she believes "the case for increasing diversity on the Bench, not only in gender and ethnicity, is not just a fashionable and self-interested prejudice. It is overwhelming" (Hale, 2003). Importantly, her motivation is transformative rather than simply curative. A more diverse judiciary, she suggests, will not only meet the demands of democratic legitimacy and equal opportunities—increasing public confidence through a shrewd use of human resources which addresses the disadvantages of the current judiciary—but also, through the incorporation of a variety of perspectives, will make a difference to the decisions made:

> I would like to think that a wider experience of the world is helpful: knowing a little about bearing and bringing up children must make some difference ... [although] there have been some wonderful family judges who have never changed a nappy or cooked a fish finger in their lives. (Hale, 2001a, p. 501)

Nevertheless, crucially although Baroness Hale believes women lawyers and judges have "moved on" from an understandable reluctance to "acknowledge or claim the right to be different" (Hale, 2002, p. 12), her relationship with 'difference' remains somewhat prickly. Answering the question why we should want more women judges, she suggests that her academic career, her reforming inclinations and her "tendency to go native" are "at least as influential" in relation to her jurisprudence as her gender (Hale, 2001a, p. 500).

> We should not expect women judges to 'make a difference' in the sense that they are likely to make different decisions from men ... We are all lawyers first and men or women second ... But if it were as simple as that, why should having more women on the bench be expected to increase public confidence in its decision? Window dressing is important, as every retailer knows, but isn't it necessary also to improve the products on sale? The difference is more subtle. (Hale, 2003)

Her support for a more diverse judiciary is not, therefore, grounded in an understanding that women judges speak in a 'different voice' or that men and women 'judge' differently: "the great majority of judgments I have written or spoken [Hale contends] could just as easily have been written or spoken by a man" (Hale, 2003). Rather it lies in an understanding that the perspectives and experiences of women judges *as women* necessarily inform their judgments and that "the experience of leading those lives should be just as much part of the background and experience which shapes the law as the experience of leading men's lives has been for centuries" (Hale, 2003). Lady Justice Arden has made a similar point.

> The point I am making is that men and women often bring different perspectives to bear on a problem ... It is that potential for different perspectives that men and women often have that in my view has the potential to enrich judicial decision-making. I am not saying that other under-represented groups do not have different perspectives too, but women are by far the largest group under-represented in the judiciary. (Arden, 2008)

Put another way, Baroness Hale and Lady Justice Arden's understanding of the importance of difference is grounded in the recognition that who the judge *is* matters. As Sandra Berns has noted, it matters both in terms of "the kind of story ultimately told, and for the way that story reaches the law and the law reaches that story" (1990, p. 8).

This is deeply subversive. It explodes a paradox underlying current discourses on adjudication where on the one hand women judges are viewed as desirable in order to broaden the range of perspectives on the bench, thus making the judiciary more representative, while on the other judges are *supposed* to be without perspective (even if we no longer *really* believe this to be true), thus suggesting there is little need for a representative judiciary. As traditional understandings of the judge and judging—a fairy tale of one "almost superhuman in wisdom, in propriety, in decorum and in humanity" (Gall, 1996) able to apply the law in a neutral and detached way—lie in ruin, the presence of difference on the bench challenges us to reconsider our adjudicative expectations; to confront our Herculean demons in order to let go of the superhero and embrace the [(wo)man] judge (Rackley, 2002). So understood, difference—found in the distinctiveness of perspective and experience—is not an end in itself but rather a route to engendering diverse perspectives on adjudication, justice and law. Put simply, as Baroness Hale suggests, there *is* more to difference than simply window dressing; its strategic subtlety not only masks its true irritant potential but also the extent to which it can really 'make a difference'. In revealing previously unimagined adjudicative alternatives, it throws a spotlight onto the ordinary or normal, reorientating our focus away from difference itself and onto that which difference is different to; it moves the spotlight away from the prefix to its subject, from the *woman* judge to the woman *judge* and, in so doing, allows for and, more importantly, increases the possibility that one day judicial diversity might render this, and all other, descriptive prefixes superfluous.

Judging gender

Zainab Esther Fornah grew up in Freetown, the capital of Sierra Leone. Her childhood was a happy one:

> I had a nice life with my brothers and my mother and father . . . The only difficult thing I had to face was that my aunts used to come from the village to see my father and tell him it was time for me to join the secret society. That meant it was time for me to be cut, to be circumcised. (Walter, 2006)

Female Genital Mutilation (FGM)[8] is performed on the overwhelming majority of girls in Sierra Leone.[9] It typically takes the form of Type II FGM (commonly known as 'excision') which involves the excision of the prepuce and clitoris together with partial and total excision of the labia minora (WHO, 2000). It is often performed in very crude conditions by older women—members of secret societies—and causes excruciating pain as well as serious short- and long-term ill-effects including excessive bleeding, infection, urine retention, increased risk of fistula, sexual dysfunction, complications in pregnancy and childbirth, psychological damage and death. Although FGM is performed worldwide,[10] including (despite legislation prohibiting it) the UK,[11] in Sierra Leone the practice of FGM is particularly intractable:[12]

> [I]t is a rite of passage from childhood to full womanhood, symbolised by admission of the initiate to these secret societies. Even the lower class of Sierra Leonean society regard uninitiated indigenous woman as an abomination fit only for the worst sort of sexual exploitation. Because of its totemic significance the practice is welcomed by some women and accepted by almost all. In society as a whole the practice is generally accepted where it is not approved, and the authorities do little to curb or eliminate it. (*Fornah* [2006] 6).

Zainab Fornah is, therefore, somewhat unusual, her intact state the result of her father's rejection of what he understood as an 'evil' practice. In a newspaper interview she described how her father protected her from it: he "would give them excuses, and say that he would bring me one day . . . but he didn't want me to go . . . and said I didn't have to do it" (Walter, 2006). But then the war came. Zainab was just 12 when, like many girls and young women in Sierra Leone at that time, she was abducted and repeatedly raped by rebel soldiers. By the time the war was over and she returned to Freetown, her family had been killed. The abuse she had suffered during the war meant that it was impossible for her to remain in Freetown: "Everyone knew I had been taken to the bush, and they shouted and pointed at me in the streets" (Walter, 2006). And yet, she was scared to return to her father's village as this meant she would have to join the 'secret society'—to be cut. With the help of an uncle from America she flew to England where she claimed asylum.[13]

Article 1A (2) of the 1951 Geneva Convention Relating to the Status of Refugees defines a refugee for the purposes of the Convention as any person who

> owing to well-founded fear of being persecuted for reasons of race, religion, nationality, membership of a particular social group or political opinion, is outside the country of nationality and is unable or, owing to such fear, is unwilling to avail himself of the protection of that country ...[14]

It was common ground in *Fornah* that FGM "constitutes treatment which would amount to persecution within the meaning of the Convention and that if [Fornah] was ... a member of a particular social group the persecution of her would be for reasons of her membership of that group" ([2006] 25). This is unsurprising. Asylum claims based on fear of FGM have been recognised worldwide.[15] FGM has also been condemned as unconscionable, cruel, degrading, and discriminatory in numerous national and international instruments, declarations, resolutions, pronouncements, guidelines and recommendations (Fordham & Cassels, 2007).

> On this basis, we must conclude that FGM, which causes severe pain as well as permanent physical harm, amounts to a violation of human rights, including the rights of the child, and can be regarded as persecution. The toleration of these acts by the authorities, or the unwillingness of the authorities to provide protection against them, amounts to official acquiescence. Therefore, a woman can be considered a refugee if she or her daughters/dependents fear being compelled to undergo FGM against their will; or, she fears persecution for refusing to undergo or to allow her daughters to undergo the practice. (UNHCR memorandum, Female Genital Mutilation, 10 May 1994, in Fordham & Cassels, 2007, p. 347)

What was at issue then was whether Zainab Fornah's well-founded fear of persecution was "for reasons of ... membership of a particular group"—the most problematic of the five Convention grounds. Put another way was she, according to the Convention, a member of a particular social group—however defined? Opinions on this varied greatly. The Secretary of State, while granting her limited leave to enter the UK, rejected her claim to asylum on the grounds that "girls who were at risk of being subjected to FGM" did not constitute a social group for the purposes of the Convention.[16] This was subsequently overturned by an Adjudicator who found that "young, single Sierra Leonean women, who are clearly at considerable risk of enforced [FGM]" could in fact be seen as a social group for the purposes of the Convention. On appeal to the Immigration Appeals Tribunal it was held that neither "young, single Sierra Leonean women" nor the more specific "young Sierra Leonean women who [had] not undergone female genital mutilation" could (on the reasoning of the House of Lords in *Islam v. Secretary of State for the Home Department;*

R v. Immigration Appeal Tribunal, Ex p Shah [1999]) be properly regarded as a particular social group under the Convention. While in no way condoning or justifying the practice of FGM, this decision was supported by the Secretary of State and confirmed by a majority in the Court of Appeal.

Fornah appealed.[17] The House of Lords unanimously held that she qualified for protection under the Convention as a "member of a particular social group"—variously defined as either "all women in Sierra Leone" (Lord Bingham and Baroness Hale: 31 and 114, respectively) or somewhat more narrowly as "uninitiated or intact indigenous females women in Sierra Leone" (Lords Hope, Rodger and Brown: 58, 80 and 119, respectively). In so doing, the law lords "convincingly dispel the myth that FGM is simply a custom performed by women on women, and provide a powerful recognition that the practice constitutes a blatant breach of human rights in male-dominated societies" (Cragg, 2006): "[p]atriarchal societies have often recruited women to be the instruments of the continued subjection of their sex" (Baroness Hale, *Fornah* [2006] 93). Moreover, despite its linguistic similarity to male circumcision

> [t]he contrast ... is obvious: where performed for ritualistic rather than health reasons, male circumcision may be seen as symbolising the dominance of the male. FGM may ensure a young woman's acceptance in Sierra Leonean society, but she is accepted on the basis of institutionalised inferiority. (Lord Bingham, 31)

Put simply, the law lords in *Fornah* recognise and, importantly, articulate, the multi-layered gendered harm of FGM, as a form of gender-specific persecution. Their identification of it as a "very cruel expression of male dominance" and "extreme expression of the discrimination to which all women in Sierra Leone are subject" effectively establishes gender as an identifying characteristic of a particular social group for the purposes of the Convention (Lord Bingham, 31).

But what of Baroness Hale? To what extent, if any, did having a Lady amid the Lords make a difference to the Lords' unanimous decision in *Fornah*? Or, put another way, what difference, if any, did difference make?

Recognising harm

Like other human rights instruments of its time, the Refugee Convention reflects the concerns and conceptions of persecution and harm of the immediate post-Second World War period. Significantly, gender (or indeed sex) is not listed alongside "race, religion, nationality, membership of a particular social group and political opinion" as a reason for persecution which automatically gives rise to a claim for refugee status under the Convention. Traditionally, this has meant that women (and others) have found it difficult to utilise the protection of the Convention: "the refugee definition has been interpreted through a framework of male experiences, which has meant that many claims of women and of homosexuals have gone unrecognised" (UNHCR, 2002, p. 5; Crawley, 2001). Moreover, limited understanding or acknowledgement of the specific ways in which women are persecuted—honour killings, Sati, domestic violence, rape, FGM and so on—has, critics suggest, enabled governments to "hide behind narrow definitions to avoid their responsibility for crimes against women" (Kennedy, 2005, col. 856).

However more recently, in both academic commentary and international debate, it has not only been accepted that gender-specific and/or related harms fall within the remit of the Convention (usually through the use of the 'particular social group' provision) but that "the text, object, and purpose of the Refugee Convention *require* a gender-inclusive and gender-sensitive interpretation" (Baroness Hale, *Fornah* [2006] 84). This is not least because states who are party to the International Covenant on Civil and Political Rights and the Convention of the Elimination of All Forms of Discrimination against Women as well as the Refugee Convention are now obliged to interpret the latter in line with the commitment to gender equality contained therein. Coupled with the groundbreaking decisions of the House of Lords in *Islam* and *Shah* [1999] (allowing the asylum claims of women who, having been forced by their husbands to leave their homes in Pakistan, feared that if they returned they would be falsely accused of adultery and persecuted for sexual immorality, the penalty for which might be death by stoning or flogging) and the Court of Appeal in *P and M v. Secretary of State for the Home Department* [2004] (accepting a claim for asylum by a young Kenyan Kikuyu woman who feared her father would force her to undergo FGM) it seemed the time for undervaluing or ignoring gender-specific persecution had past. Sadly, the decision of the majority of the Court of Appeal in *Fornah* [2005]—a decision which "made all the right noises about how awful FGM is" before taking "sanctuary in a mean and narrow interpretation of the law"—bucked this trend (Kennedy, 2005, col. 856).

In dismissing Fornah's appeal, Auld and Chadwick LLJ concluded "female genital mutilation of young, single and uncircumcised Sierra Leonean women" did not constitute persecution "for reasons of" their membership of a "particular social group" on a number of "technocratic" (Kennedy, 2005, col. 856) grounds including the fact that

> the practice [of FGM], however repulsive to most societies outside Sierra Leone, is . . . clearly accepted and regarded by the majority of the population of that country, both men and women, as traditional and part of the cultural life of its society as a whole. (Auld LJ, *Fornah* [2005] 44)

As a result, far from ostracising them, FGM leads to "full acceptance by Sierra Leonean society of those young women ... into adulthood". Thus, while FGM clearly constitutes persecution for the purposes of article 3 of the ECHR, it is not, at least in the circumstances in which it was practised in Sierra Leone, discriminatory as required by the Convention (44). In so arguing, the majority of the Court of Appeal appears seduced by the arguments of the cultural relativists. Reluctant to follow through their recognition of FGM as a "repulsive" practice on the grounds that it is part of the "tradition" and "cultural life" of Sierra Leonean society (44), they come dangerously close to resorting to what Martha Nussbaum describes as the "worst option of all" when seeking to balance respect for cultures and human rights:

> To say that a practice endorsed by tradition is bad is to risk erring by imposing one's own way on others who surely have their own ideas of what is right and good. To say that a practice is alright wherever local tradition endorses it as right and good is to risk erring by withholding critical judgment where real evil and real oppression are surely present. To avoid the whole issue because the matter of proper judgment is so fiendish difficult is tempting, but perhaps the worst option of all. (Nussbaum, 1995).[18]

However the responses of Auld and Chadwick LLJ to Fornah's position are interesting for another reason. Referring to the Court of Appeal's "appalling" decision in a debate on FGM in the legislative body of the House of Lords, Helena Kennedy argues

> If anything, [*Fornah*] argues for more women judges in our courts. It is cases like these which highlight problems of gender issues still continuing in our courtroom because the men involved do not realise that their own mindset is often what determines their approach to law. (Kennedy, 2005, col. 856)[19]

Really? Certainly, the majority of the Court of Appeal in *Fornah*, while recognising FGM as a gendered harm fails to fully understand or locate this harm within the gendered context in which it takes place. Their focus on the practices and traditions of the community belies an individualistic understanding of the practice of FGM which is incompatible with the broader, group focused conception of harm or persecution required by the Convention. In so doing, as the dissent of Arden LJ acknowledges, they fail to recognise that "the effect of FGM is to identify a social group" and to mark out those who are not part of that group for persecution:

> the mere fact that Sierra Leonean society accepts FGM does not mean that the prospectively adult women in that society cannot constitute a particular social group for the purposes of the refugee convention. (*Fornah* [2005] 63)

And yet, while there is clearly a difference in approach and the ultimate decision between the male and female members of the Court of Appeal [the conventions of legal writing, whereby Lord *and* Lady Justice becomes simply 'LJ', obliterating the "stigmata" of Lady Justice Arden's sex (Berns, 1999, p. 203)], it is not immediately apparent that this necessarily points to, as Kennedy suggests, the need for more *female* judges per se, rather than, say, judges who are more attuned to the limitation of their own experiences and common sense (Graycar, 1995). We should be wary of the temptations of gender essentialism, of any claim to a 'female', or indeed 'male', judicial voice (Kennedy, 2005, col. 856; Hale, 2001a, p. 501). After all, as Arden LJ states: "If you had a woman judge a case and a man judge a case you would be likely to have the same conclusion on the case" (Smith-Spark, 2004). Although, presumably, the Court of Appeal's decision in *Fornah* is the exception that proves the rule?

Interestingly in light of Kennedy's claim, and somewhat unusually, *Fornah* met with two female judges as it progressed through the courts: Lady Justice Arden in the Court of Appeal and Baroness Hale in the House of Lords. Given the poor representation of women in the UK judiciary (especially at senior levels), this is no mean feat. It is not often that we are able to compare the decision-making of two senior *female* judges in the same case (and, of course, it is impossible to do so in the House of Lords). As a result, it is tempting to compare and contrast similarities in, say, outcome (they both found for Fornah) and differences in, say, their definitions of the particular social group to which she belongs. To comment on the fact that while Arden LJ would have limited it to "*prospectively* adult women, that is those women who have not yet undergone FGM" (*Fornah* [2005] 61), Baroness Hale favoured the broader group of all "Sierra Leonean women belonging to those ethnic groups where FGM is practised" ([2006] 114). Or, alternatively, to contrast Baroness Hale's explicit articulation of the gendered harm expressed through the practice of FGM with the measured more limited narrative of Arden LJ's lone dissent in the hope of reaching some, inevitably vague conclusions, as to their 'difference' (if any and however defined) both to each other and their male colleagues.

However, while such a comparison is perhaps interesting, it is ultimately, at best, a distraction and, at worst, a theoretical dead end. We must be careful not to become bewitched by their difference. It is because Arden LJ and Baroness Hale are women that we both look for and, more importantly, *find* difference. However, getting our attention in this way is not without its pitfalls. In embracing Baroness Hale and Arden LJ as *women* judges or even as (women) judges we risk looking for and then endowing their judgment and decision-making with feminine traits instead of closely scrutinising what they are really doing. Put another way, in our hunt for difference (in whatever form) we risk overlooking and stifling the potential impact of difference on judicial diversity.

So understood, that Arden LJ (perhaps unusually) comes to a different *conclusion* to her male colleagues is relatively unimportant (Belleau & Johnson, 2004). Judicial difference, Arden suggests, is found as much (if not more) in the process rather than the end of judgment (2008). Thus, while her lone dissent gets our attention, its persuasive success lies not in its manifestation as, or articulation of, difference *per se* but rather in its effects; that is in the ability of her narrative (as with all dissenting judgments) to challenge the majority's story and weaken its hold on our collective imagination. Put another way, her 'difference' lies in the fact that she hears and tells a different story (rather than simply the fact that it has a different ending) and, more specifically, in the potential of her counter-narrative to open up new avenues for exploration and alternative understandings of the judge and judging.

After all, if visibility (in the sense of different endings) were to be a necessary requirement of difference where would this leave Baroness Hale? True, in many ways her opinion in *Fornah* displays some, by now, familiar characteristics. Most notably, her deliberate recognition—and, importantly, articulation—of the particular "gender-related and gender specific persecution" raised by the case ([2006] 83). Gender not only tops and tails her opinion but runs throughout. Consider, for example, her easy identification of FGM as a gendered harm at its outset, its purposeful gender(ed)-focus evidenced in her lengthy and detailed description of what FGM involves and her strategic juxtaposition in her conclusion of the everyday reality faced by many women worldwide and the gender-biased nature of the protection offered by the Convention:

> [The resolution of this case] is by no means purely of academic interest to these women or to the many others in the world who flee similar fears. They are just as worthy of the full protection of the Refugee Convention as are the men who flee persecution because of their dissident political views. (115)

Contrast this with Lord Rodger's slightly less comfortable acceptance of the "gender specific" nature of the harm (74). Here gender is isolated securely in double-quotes, less it taint his subsequent remarks and coupled with an immediate clarification—"being a woman" the "causa sine qua non" of being a victim in such cases—the archaic Latinate legal term, presumably, a linguistic antidote or response to the new fangled idioms required by the recognition of so-called gender-issues (74).

However, semantic pedantries acknowledged and put aside, what is more interesting about the House of Lords' decision in *Fornah* is the *similarity* between Baroness Hale's and the other law lords' opinions. Consider, for example, Lord Bingham's rejection of the emphasis put by the majority of the Court of Appeal on the fact that FGM is carried out by women: "Most vicious rituals are in fact perpetuated by those who were themselves subject to the ritual as initiates and see no reason why others should not share the experience" (31) with Baroness Hale's assertion that "it cannot make any difference that [FGM] is practised by women upon women and girls. Those who have already been persecuted are often expected to perpetuate the persecution of others, as any reader of *Tom Brown's Schooldays* knows" (110). And Lord Hope's description of the "initiation ritual" as a "process of sexual separation" and the interrelationship between sexual discrimination and patriarchy (53–4) with Baroness Hale's blunt listing of the purposes of FGM as "to lessen the woman's sexual desire, maintain her chastity and virginity before marriage and her fidelity within it, and possibly to increase male sexual pleasure" ... which, she suggests, have been "translated into power social purposes" (93).

So viewed, her opinion isn't all that different. What difference there is is perhaps more a matter of style than substance—of discursive narrative compared to restrained legal reasoning (as traditionally understood)—and as such is maybe as much, if not more, reflective of Baroness Hale's background as an academic and law commissioner than her gender. Furthermore, while clearly her typically contextualised, gender-aware approach infused the law lords' opinions (compare, for example, Lord Bingham's gender-infused, context laden opinion with the narrowly legalistic judgments of Auld or Chadwick LLJ), no less than three of her four colleagues were more persuaded by Arden LJ's dissenting formulation of the definition of the relevant social group for the purposes of the Convention than by Baroness Hale's broader approach (Lords Hope, Rodger and Brown: 56, 74, 119 respectively).

That said, the unanimous decision of the House of Lords nevertheless clearly has (or, just as importantly, is seen to have) Baroness Hale's fingerprints all over it: "Although all five judges agreed ... few would doubt that Lady Hale has brought to the highest court in the land a bracing new approach to women's rights" (Anon,

2006; Tsang, 2006). Moreover, in stark contrast to the apocalyptic fears voiced on her appointment, the influence and impact of her "unique perspective" (Lord Hoffmann, *R v. G* [2008] 36) on the jurisprudence of the House of Lords has been seen as a good thing:

> [Lady Hale's] success should encourage the Lord Chancellor's slow progress in widening the gene pool of judges by looking for candidates—women and men, and in particular those from minorities—who can offer the right combination of intellectual excellence and diverse experience to the court that shapes English law. (Anon, 2006)

This insight is not particularly novel. It is something female judges have known for a while. Bertha Wilson made a similar point back in 1990 in her lecture exploring whether women judges "will really make a difference":

> women view the world and what goes on in it from a different perspective from men ... [and that] women judges, by bringing that perspective to bear on the cases they hear, ... play a major role in introducing judicial neutrality and impartiality into the justice system. (Wilson, 1990, p. 515)

Likewise, Beverley McLachlin more recently put it bluntly thus: "we need more women on our Benches ... because we need the perspectives that women can bring to judging" (in Hale, 2005a, p. 1); a view which is echoed in Baroness Hale's albeit slightly more tentative claim on her appointment to the House of Lords that "[b]eing a woman doesn't necessarily make a difference when you're making judgments but we are different and it's that more than anything else that will make a difference" (Brenda Hale in Pears, 2004).[20]

Whichever way you put it, the message is clear: the incorporation of difference on the bench subtly changes and, ultimately, improves the judicial product (Hale, 2004b). As the decision in *Fornah* shows, a truly diverse judiciary is not simply apposite (on the grounds of, say, equal opportunities or democratic legitimacy) but rather essential if we are to realise the best we possibly can in terms of justice, judgments and judging. However difference alone is not enough. What we need is more *diversity*. Put another way, while the presence of difference on the bench gets (for whatever reason) our attention, it is in fact only the beginning of the story. Where difference might take us? Now that's the start of a whole new adventure.

Toward an understanding of judicial diversity: concluding remarks

In its consultation paper *Increasing Diversity in the Judiciary* the Department for Constitutional Affairs (now the Ministry of Justice) defines diversity as: "The presence among a group of individuals of a wide variety of backgrounds, cultures, opinions, styles, perspectives, values and beliefs" (DCA, 2004b, p. 57). According to this definition judicial diversity simply requires the presence of a miscellaneous—albeit strategic—assortment of difference or dissimilarity on the bench appointed on 'merit', without regard to 'irrelevant' factors such as age, disability, gender, ethnicity, marital status, political affiliation, religion or belief, sexual orientation, gender identity (p. 8). While it remains to be seen how this, at best, somewhat optimistic and, at worst deliberately naïve belief in the reciprocity of merit and diversity plays out (p. 8), it is clear that this pragmatic understanding of diversity is significantly flawed (Rackley, 2007, p. 86).

Put simply, diversity is not about letting people in but about letting go. It challenges the complacency and normative superiority of the status quo: "majority groups are not entitled to retain more cultural status and recognition than others; they must therefore let go of some of their privilege, however painful such a letting go may feel" (Cooper, 2004, p. 35). So understood, the politics of diversity require more than simply tolerating of the presence of varied perspectives and distinctive backgrounds within a given group—"toleration implies disapproval or dislike. We do not tolerate things we like or endorse" (Weeks, 1993, p. 206). Rather, diversity compels us to create a space in which difference is celebrated and valued on its own terms (Cooper, 2004, p. 7). In so doing, diversity demands we "look away from that which stands out as different in order to be able to evaluate the mainstream, the common and the 'normal'" (Cooper, 2004, p. 7); to look not at the unusual but instead at the mundane or taken for granted and, in so doing, to embrace difference not as "intrinsic in the 'different' person, but rather the product of comparison" (Minow, 1989–90, p. 3).

Thus, properly understood, judicial diversity is not simply about ensuring that a strategic assortment of individuals of varying ages, sex, race, class, culture, and so on live 'happily ever after'—a strategic evening up of the numbers on the bench to ensure a kind of numerical aestheticism. Nor is it about securing the resigned acceptance by the status quo of the inclusion of difference as a political necessity—a strategy for survival, albeit with the tacit assurance that nothing will really change. Rather, diversity requires the usual to be transformed by the remarkable and the extraordinary to become the norm. It is as much about looking at that which difference is different to—the everyday or mundane—as it is about looking for difference itself.

So understood, judicial diversity is a process or means to an end, rather than an end in itself. Put another way, once difference is understood as "not merely 'out there' but [as] created through the ways we [or the judiciary] works" (Archer, 2004, p. 470) a focus on that which is different—both in the sense of *being* aesthetically atypical and *doing* judging differently—reveals the contingency of traditional accounts of legal reasoning and the possibility of alternative and diverse adjudicative voices, which are not necessarily (but may be) feminine and/or feminist in intonation. Put simply, difference provides us with an opportunity to test our assumptions about the judge and judging—to consider not only what is different to the judicial norm but the norm itself.

Perhaps, then, Sandra Berns is right—maybe the whole idea of difference and, in particular, "of a different voice is part of the problem" that threatens to "seduce" us away from what is really going on and what is really important in the context of judicial diversity (1998, p. 13). Maybe, like the sun, we should not—if we wish to avoid disorientating blindness—look directly at or for difference but rather explore its impact on those that it is different to. Put simply, instead of looking for the difference or otherwise of Arden LJ and Baroness Hale, our attention should rather be focused on norm—on Lord Justices Auld and Chadwick together with Lords Bingham, Hope, Rodger and Brown—and the impact the presence of difference has on them. To ask the question: do *male* judges make a difference? This might make for an interesting comparison. For example, while the majority of the Court of Appeal remain bound by their grid-like reasoning—the lure of "the aesthetic of bright-line rules, absolutist approaches, and categorical definitions" (Schlag, 2002, p. 1051), where law is predictable, stable, certain, solid, boundaried, coherent, and determinate—the law lords embrace the strategic importance of context and strategic detachment in decision-making. Following, one assumes, the lead of Baroness Hale toward the 'obvious' conclusion (indeed, how could they not?), Lords Bingham, Hope, Rodger and Brown utilise the seductive unbounded energy of law "on a mission" (Schlag, 2002, p. 1072) in order to make some small part of Fornah's story their own. In so doing, they let her experiences penetrate them fully, recognising that true detachment and effective judging is grounded in connection and contextualised engagement (Albom, 1997, p. 103).

So viewed, judicial diversity ultimately subverts that which it is said to reinforce; it utilises the presence of difference on the bench as a means of exploring aspects of judging often overlooked in conventional accounts of adjudication (rather than confining its potential as an end in itself). It requires us to let go of difference and embrace diversity; put simply, to consider where difference might take us and, in so doing, begin to re-imagine what it is we want from our judiciary and what it means to be a judge. If this means that there will be more decisions from the House of Lords like *Fornah*—where the transformative potential of difference captures our imagination—this may be no bad thing.

Notes

[1] Hereinafter *Fornah* [2006]. This paper concentrates exclusively on the facts and decision in relation to Zainab Fornah. *Fornah* was joined, on appeal to the House of Lords, with the case of *K* involving an Iranian national who had fled Iran following the arrest of her husband and having been raped and insulted by the Revolutionary Guards there. Her asylum claim—grounded in a fear of persecution as a member of a particular social group (her husband's family)—as well as issues of causation was successful, on appeal, to the House of Lords. For a discussion of the facts and decision in relation to K's appeal and Baroness Hale's criticism of the process of dividing families into "primary" and "secondary" members as "inherently sexist" see further, Chaudhry (2007).

[2] The extent to which women judges speak in a 'different voice'—although perhaps intuitively attractive—remains hotly disputed among both legal academics and professionals: see, e.g. Freenan (2007), Malleson (2003), Kay and Sparrow (2001), Sisk *et al.* (1998), Davis (1992–93), Martin (1993) and Belleau and Johnson (2005).

[3] See generally, Schultz and Shaw (2003), Moran (2006), Freenan (2007), Nicolson (2005), Darbyshire (2007) and Thomas (2005) in the UK; Thornton (1996) in Australia; Kay and Brockman (2000) in Canada; and Kruse (2001) in the US.

[4] Figures taken from the Judiciary of England and Wales website as at 1 April 2008, available at: http://www.judiciary.gov.uk/keyfacts/statistics/diversity_stats_annual/2007.htm (accessed 10 July 2008).

[5] *Ibid.* See further, Abbas (2005). There are no government figures available in relation to other indicators of diversity, for example, age, sexuality, educational background, disability or religion,

however see further Sutton Trust Briefing Note (2005) on the educational background of the senior judiciary, DCA (2005a) on disability, and Moran (2006) on sexuality.

[6] On 9 May 2007 the responsibilities of the Department for Constitutional Affairs (DCA) transferred to the new Ministry of Justice and Jack Straw was appointed Lord Chancellor and Secretary of State for Justice. In a speech at the Lord Mayor's annual judges dinner in July 2007 he confirmed the new department's continuing commitment to securing a more diverse judiciary (Straw, 2007). See in particular DCA (2003, 2004a, 2004b, 2004a, 2005b) and further http://www.dca.gov.uk/judges/diversity.htm (accessed 10 July 2008).

[7] Section 64 of the Constitutional Reform Act 2005 establishes that the JAC "must have regard to the need to encourage diversity in the range of persons available for selection for appointments" (although cf. Dyer, 2008). On the Judicial Appointments Commission see further http://www.judicialappointments.gov.uk/ (accessed 10 July 2008).

[8] In this paper I use the term 'Female Genital Mutilation' (FGM) in line with the House of Lords, however I recognise (with Baroness Hale) that increasingly the practice is being referred to internationally as 'Female Genital Cutting' (*Fornah* [2006] 90). On the issues raised by FGM more generally see further Nussbaum (1999, pp. 118–29), FORWARD (2002), The Female Genital Cutting Education and Networking Project, available at: http://www.fgmnetwork.org/index.php (accessed 26 September 2007); the Debate on 'Female Genital Mutilation' in the House of Lords on 8 December 2005 (HL Hansard, vol. 676, col. 844–68); Atoki (1995) and Bibbings (1995).

[9] Estimates put incidences of FGM in Sierra Leone at between 80 and 90%. It is practised (for social/cultural, as opposed to religious, purposes) by all ethnic groups except Krios who are located primarily in the western region and in Freetown (US Department of State, 2001).

[10] The World Health Organisation estimates that between 100 million and 140 million girls and women have undergone some form of FGM and that about three million more do so each year (WHO, 2006, p. 2).

[11] Some estimates suggest that there are 3,000–4,000 new cases in the UK per year (www.ipu.org). Under the Female Genital Mutilation Act 2003 (which replaced the Prohibition of Female Circumcision Act 1985) it is an offence to "excise, infibulate or otherwise mutilate the whole or any part of a girl's labia majora, labia minora or clitoris" (s1(1)) [unless it is a surgical operation necessary for the 'girl's' (which includes 'woman') (s6(1)) physical or mental health, or related to labour or child birth (s1(2))] and also to aid, abet, counsel or procure a person to do the relevant act outside the UK (s3). As of 2005, there have been no prosecutions under this Act (Lord Bassam, HL Hansard, vol. 676, col. 866–8, 8 December 2005).

[12] No law prohibits FGM in Sierra Leone and efforts by NGOs to eradicate it are actively resisted by the women's secret societies (Bowers, 2007; IRIN, 2005). Following the House of Lords' decision in *Fornah*, Zainab Fornah was criticised by Septimus Kaikai, Sierra Leone's information minister, in a interview for the BBC for what he described as a "deliberate and conscious and premeditated attempt by individuals to malign and besmear the reputation, integrity and character of a government and its people" (BBC News, 2006).

[13] Although the practical importance of Fornah's case was mitigated slightly by the Secretary of State's recognition that article 3 of the ECHR prevented her return to Sierra Leone, the case was not moot. The case was acknowledged as important not only in relation to the stronger protections Zainab Fornah will enjoy as a refugee but also in relation to the subsequent use of UK jurisprudence in relation to the convention's reach (*Fornah* [2006] 1; Chaudhry, 2007).

[14] As amended by the 1967 Protocol.

[15] See, e.g. *Yale v. Secretary of State for the Home Department* [2000]; *P and M v. Secretary of State for the Home Department* [2004] (England and Wales); *In re Kassindja* [1996]; *Abankwah v. Immigration and Naturalization Service* [1999]; *Mohammed v. Gonzales* [2005] (US); *RRT N97/19046* [1997]; *GZ 220.268/0-XI/33/00* [2002] (Austria); *Re B(PV)* [1994]; *Khandra Hassan Farah* [1994] (Canada).

[16] As discussed by Auld LJ in *Fornah v. Secretary of State for the Home Department* [2005] 5–7 (herein after *Fornah* [2005]).

[17] Remarkably the appeal permission grounds had to be drafted pro bono after the Legal Services Commission deemed the appeal unarguable (Tsang, 2006).

[18] See further Nussbaum (1999), Okin (1998), Harris-Short (2003), Gunning (1991–92).

[19] Rights of Women (2007) make a similar point. Welcoming the decision of the House of Lords they go on to argue: "decisions like these show the importance of having a judiciary and legal system that is representative of society as a whole and that there needs to be much more done to ensure that more women, and Black and Minority Ethnic (BME) women in particular, reach senior positions in the legal profession and judiciary" (p. 6).

[20] This view is by no means unanimous among all women judges (see, for example, O'Connor, 1991; Anon, 2000).

References

Abbas, Tahir (2005) *Diversity in the Senior Judiciary—A Literature Review of Research on Ethnic Inequalities* (London, Commission for Judicial Appointments).

Addley, Esther (2003) The women of the year, *Guardian*, 19 December.

Albom, Mitch (1997) *Tuesdays with Morrie* (Time Warner, paperback edition, 2003).

Anon (2000) Butler-Sloss is content to be a unisex judge, *The Times*, 21 November.

Anon (2004) Brief encounters, *Daily Telegraph*, 10 June.

Anon (2005) Women: The Feminist, *Guardian*, 6 May.

Anon (2006) In praise of ... Lady Hale of Richmond, *Guardian*, 20 October.

Archer, Louise (2004) Re/theorizing 'difference' in feminist research, *Women's Studies International Forum*, 27, pp. 459–73.

Arden, Mary (2008). Address to the Association of Women Barrister' Annual General Meeting, 3 June.

Atoki, Morayo (1995) Should female circumcision continue to be banned?, *Feminist Legal Studies*, 3(2), pp. 223–35.

BBC News (2004) High Court gets first black judge, 2 September.

BBC News (2006) S Leone anger at FGM asylum in UK, p. 19 October.

Belleau, Marie-Claire & Johnson, Rebecca (2004) La dissidence judiciaire: réflexions préliminaires sur les émotions, la raison et les passions du droit/Judicial dissent: early reflections on emotion, reason and passion in law, Marie-Claire Belleau & François Lacasse (Eds) *Claire L'Heureux-Dubé à la Cour suprême du Canada, 1987–2002* (Québec, Wilson & Lafleur), pp. 699–719.

Belleau, Marie-Claire & Johnson, Rebecca (2005) Les femmes juges feront-elles véritablement une difference? Réflexions sur leur presence depuis vingt ans à la Cour suprême du Canada, *Canadian Journal of Women and Law*, 17(1), pp. 27–39.

Berns, Sandra (1999) *To Speak as a Judge—Difference, Voice and Power* (Dartmouth, Ashgate).

Bibbings, Lois S. (1995) Female circumcision: mutilation or modification?, in: Jo Bridgman & Susan Millns (Eds) *Law and Body Politics—Regulating the Female Body* (Dartmouth, Aldershot), pp. 151–70.

Bowers, Emily (2007) Sierra Leone: FGM practitioners sway elections in Sierra Leone, *Women's eNews*, 9 July.

Chaudhry, Mehvish (2007) Particular social groups post *Fornah*, *Journal of Immigration, Asylum and Nationality Law*, 21(2), pp. 137–46.

Cooper, Davina (2004) *Challenging Diversity: Rethinking Equality and the Value of Difference* (Cambridge, Cambridge University Press).

Cragg, Stephen (2006) Legislation update, *The Times*, 24 October.

Crawley, Heaven (2001) *Refugees and Gender: Law and Process* (Bristol, Jordans).

Darbyshire, Penny (2007) Where do English and Welsh judges come from?, *Cambridge Law Journal*, 66(2), pp. 365–88.

Davis, Sue (1992–93) Do women judges speak 'in a different voice'? Carol Gilligan, feminist legal theory, and the Ninth Circuit, *Wisconsin Women's Law Journal*, 8, pp. 143–73.

Department for Constitutional Affairs (2003) *Constitutional Reform: A New Way of Appointing Judges*, CP 10/03 July.

Department for Constitutional Affairs (2004a) *Increasing Diversity in the Judiciary*, CP 25/04 October.

Department for Constitutional Affairs (2004b) *Summary of Responses to the Consultation Paper*, January.

Department for Constitutional Affairs (2005a) *Report on Progress Against the DCA's Action Plan on Disability Equality and Judicial Appointment*, December.
Department for Constitutional Affairs (2005b) *Responses to DCA Consultation Paper*, March.
Department for Constitutional Affairs Press Notice (2005) *Judges to come from Wider Pool of Applicants*, 13 July.
Department for Constitutional Affairs Press Notice (2006) *Continued Increase in Minority Ethnic and Female Judicial Appointments*, 31 January.
Dyer, Clare (2008) First 10 high court judges under new diversity rules, *Guardian*, 28 January.
Equal Opportunities Commission (2006) *Sex and Power: Who Runs Britain?* (Manchester, Equal Opportunities Commission).
Fordham, Michael & Cassels, Tom (2007) Case for the intervener in *Zainab Esther Fornah (Appellant) v. Secretary of State for the Home Department (Respondent) and UNHCR (Intervener)* (House of Lords), *International Journal of Refugee Law*, 19(2), pp. 293–359.
FORWARD (2002) *Female Genital Mutilation: Information Pack* (London, FORWARD).
Freenan, Dermot (2007). Women judges: gendering judging, justifying diversity, Paper presented at *Keele Law School Seminar*, Keele, UK, 18 April, 2007.
Gall, Gerald (1996) *The Canadian Legal System*, Canadian Judicial Council (1998) *Ethical Principles for Judges* (Ottawa, Canadian Judicial Council).
Graycar, Regina (1995) The gender of judgments: an introduction, in: Margaret Thornton (Ed.) *Public and Private: Feminist Legal Debates* (Australia, Oxford University Press), pp. 262–82.
Griffith, J.A.G. (1997) *The Politics of the Judiciary* (5th edn). (London, Fontana Press).
Gunning, Isabelle (1991–92) Arrogant perception, world-travelling and multicultural feminism: the case of female genital surgeries, *Columbia Human Rights Law Review*, 23, pp. 189–248.
Hale, Brenda (2001a) Equality and the judiciary: why should we want more women judges?, *Public Law*. Aut, pp. 489–504.
Hale, Brenda (2002) Judging women and women judging, *Counsel*, August, pp. 10–2.
Hale, Brenda (2003) Equality in the judiciary: a tale of two continents, 10th Pilgrim Fathers' Lecture.
Hale, Brenda (2004a) The lady and their lordships, *Independent Review*, 29 March.
Hale, Brenda (2004b) The unique perspective of women judges on the law, Bar Law Reform Lecture at the Inner Temple, London.
Hale, Brenda (2005a) Making a difference? Why we need a more diverse judiciary, *Northern Ireland Legal Quarterly*, 56(3), p. 281.
Hale, Brenda (2005b) Law maker or law reformer: what is a law lady for?, *Irish Jurist*, XL, pp. 1–16.
Hale, Brenda (2007) Maccabaean lecture in jurisprudence 2007: a minority opinion?, Lecture to the British Academy, London, 13 November.
Hardcastle, Ephraim (2004) Editorial, *Daily Mail*, 13 January.
Harris-Short, Sonia (2003) International human rights law: imperialist, inept and ineffective? Cultural relativism and the UN Convention on the Rights of the Child, *Human Rights Quarterly*, 25, pp. 130–81.
IRIN Web Special (2005) *Razor's Edge—The Controversy of Female Genital Mutilation*.
Kay, Fiona & Brockman, Joan (2000) Barriers to gender equality in the Canadian legal establishment, *Feminist Legal Studies*, 8(2), pp. 169–98.
Kay, Herma H. & Sparrow, Geraldine (2001) Workshop on judging: does gender make a difference?, *Wisconsin Women's Law Journal*, 16, pp. 1–14.
Kennedy, Helena (2005) Debate on female genital mutilation, *HL Hansard*, col. 844–68, 8 December.
Kruse, B. (2001) Luck and politics: judicial selection methods and their effect on women on the Bench, *Wisconsin Women's Law Journal*, 16, p. 67.
Malleson, Kate (2003) Justifying gender equality on the Bench: why difference won't do, *Feminist Legal Studies*, 11(1), pp. 1–24.
Martin, Elaine (1993) Women on the Bench: a different voice?, *Judicature*, 77, p. 126.
Minow, Martha (1989–90) Making all the difference: three lessons in equality, neutrality, and tolerance, *De Paul Law Review*, 39, p. 1.
Moran, Leslie (2006) Judicial diversity and the challenge of sexuality: some preliminary findings, *Sydney Law Review*, 28(4), p. 565.

Nicolson, Donald (2005) Demography, discrimination and diversity: a new dawn for the British legal profession?, *International Journal of the Legal Profession*, 12(2), pp. 201–28.

Nussbaum, Martha (1995) Introduction, in: Martha Nussbaum & J. Glover (Eds) *Women, Culture, and Development: A Study of Human Capabilities* (Oxford, Clarendon Press), pp. 1–34.

Nussbaum, Martha (1999) *Sex and Social Justice* (Oxford, Oxford University Press).

O'Connor, Sandra (1991) Portia's progress, *New York University Law Review*, 66, pp. 1546–58.

Okin, Susan Moller (1998) Feminism, women's human rights, and cultural differences, *Hypatia*, 13(2), pp. 32–52.

Pears, Christen (2004) The trouble with women in wigs, *The Northern Echo*, 8 January.

Rackley, Erika (2002) Representations of the (woman) judge: Hercules, the Little Mermaid and the vain and naked Emperor, *Legal Studies*, 22(4), pp. 602–24.

Rackley, Erika (2006a) Difference in the House of Lords, *Social and Legal Studies*, 15(2), pp. 163–85.

Rackley, Erika (2006b) When Hercules met the happy prince: re-imagining the judge, *Texas Wesleyan Law Review*, 12, pp. 213–32.

Rackley, Erika (2007) Judicial diversity, the woman judge and fairy tale endings, *Legal Studies*, 27(1), pp. 74–94.

Rights of Women (2007) Focus on women, *Rights of Women Policy Newsletter*, p. 6.

Schlag, Pierre (2002) The aesthetics of American law, *Harvard Law Review*, 115, pp. 1047–115.

Schultz, Ulrike & Shaw, Gisela (Eds) (2003) *Women in the World's Legal Professions* (Oxford, Hart Publishing).

Sisk, Gregory C. *et al.* (1998) Charting the influences on the judicial mind: an empirical study of judicial reasoning, *New York University Law Review*, 73(5), pp. 1377–500.

Smith-Spark, Laura (2004) Where are all the women judges?, *BBC News Online*, Friday 15 October.

Straw, Jack (2007). Speech to Lord Mayor's annual judges dinner, 17 July.

Sutton Trust Briefing Note (2005) *The Educational Backgrounds of the UK's Top Solicitors, Barristers and Judges*.

Thomas, Cheryl (2005) *Judicial Diversity in the UK and Other Jurisdictions—A Review of Research, Policies and Practices* (London, Commission for Judicial Appointments).

Thornton, Margaret (1996) *Dissonance and Distrust: Women in the Legal Profession* (Oxford, Oxford University Press).

Tsang, Linda (2006) Lawyer of the week, *The Times*, 28 November.

UNHCR (2002) UNHCR Guidelines on *Gender-Related Persecution*, 7 May

US Department of State (2001) *Sierra Leone: Report on Female Genital Mutilation (FGM) or Female Genital Cutting (FGC)*, 1 June.

Verkaik, Robert (2003) Hitting out: the judge who refused to be retiring about sexism in her lodgings, *Independent*, 18 September.

Walter, Natasha (2006) Flight from the knife, *The Guardian*, 18 October.

Wilson, Bertha (1990) Will women judges really make a difference?, *Osgoode Hall Law Journal*, 28, pp. 507–22.

Weeks, J. (1993) Rediscovering values, in: J. Squires (Ed.) *Principled Positions: Postmodernism and the Rediscovery of Value* (London, Lawrence and Wishart), p. 189.

World Health Organisation (2000) *Female Genital Mutilation—Fact no 241*, June.

World Health Organisation (2006) *Progress in Sexual and Reproductive Health Research*, 72, pp. 1–8.

Case list

Abankwah v. Immigration and Naturalization Service [1999] 185 F 3d 18 (2d Cir).

Fornah v. Secretary of State for the Home Department [2005] EWCA Civ 680.

GZ 220.268/0-XI/33/00, unreported, 21 March 2002.

Islam v. Secretary of State for the Home Department; R v. Immigration Appeal Tribunal, Ex p Shah [1999] AC 629.

Khandra Hassan Farah, 13 July 1994, IRB Refugee Division. (Toronto) T93-12199 and 12197.

Mohammed v. Gonzales [2005] 4000 F 3d 785 (9th Cir).

P and M v. Secretary of State for the Home Department [2004] EWCA Civ 1640.

R v. G [2008] UKHL 37.

Re B (PV) [1994] CRDD No 12, 10 May 1994.

Re Kassindja [1996] 21 I & N Dec 357.

RRT N97/19046, unreported, 16 October 1997.

Secretary of State for the Home Department v. K(FC); Fornah (FC) v. Secretary of State for the Home Department [2006] UKHL, 46; [2007] 1 AC 412.

Yale v. Secretary of State for the Home Department, 19 January 2000, unreported.

Judging gender: difference and dissent at the Supreme Court of Canada

MARIE-CLAIRE BELLEAU* & REBECCA JOHNSON**
*Faculty of Law, Université Laval, Canada
**Faculty of Law, University of Victoria, Canada

ABSTRACT *Over 25 years ago, Justice Bertha Wilson asked "Will women judges really make a difference?" Taking up her question, we consider the place of difference in gender and judging. Our focus is on those 'differences of opinion' between judges that take the form of written and published judicial dissent. We present and interrogate recent statistics about practices of dissent on the Supreme Court of Canada in relation to gender. The statistics are provocative, but do not provide straightforward answers about gender and judging. They do, however, pose new questions, and suggest the importance of better theorizing and exploring the space of dissent.*

1. Introductory observations

In a controversial 1990 speech, Justice Bertha Wilson, the first woman judge of the Supreme Court of Canada, posed a question that has occupied many theorists of law: "Will women judges really make a difference?" (Wilson, 1990). With the benefit of 25 years with women judges on Canada's highest court, it is worth returning to Justice Wilson's question. But in asking about judges, gender and difference, we want to foreground a particular kind of difference often present for appellate judges: a 'difference of opinion'. All judges grapple constantly with the unavoidable tension at the heart of law—a tension between the demands of stability and responsive change (Fitzpatrick, 2001). But the grappling is intensified for appellate judges, who bring multiple skills and divergent life experiences to bear on a single case. Working as a group to do justice in ways that best resolve the tensions between the demands of universality and particularity, appellate judges can and do disagree about the shape of the world *as it exists*, and about the ways that the world *should* be legally ordered.

And in the resolution of these disagreements, judges sometimes find themselves in the space of dissent.

Here, we want to take up the link between gender difference, and those differences of opinion between appellate judges that ultimately take the form of written and published dissenting judicial opinions. In what follows, we first make some preliminary remarks on the Supreme Court of Canada and its practices of judicial dissent (Part 2). We present some recent statistics about these practices of dissent on the Supreme Court of Canada in relation to gender (Part 3). We then interrogate these statistics, troubling their ability to provide straightforward answers about gender and judging. We end by asking questions about difference in identity and in dissent (Part 4).

2. The Canadian Supreme Court and practices of judicial dissent

The Supreme Court of Canada is the country's court of final appeal in all areas of law (it is not a court of uniquely constitutional or federal jurisdiction). There are nine judges on the court, each of whom is appointed by the Prime Minister, and has lifetime tenure. The Court has a large measure of control over its docket, generally granting leave only to those appeals it deems to raise questions of national importance, on the average hearing about 80 cases per year. The judges sit in uneven numbered benches of nine, seven, or five judges. Unlike in France, where written opinions appear as if unanimous and anonymous, opinions of the Canadian Supreme Court are generally issued in the name of specific judicial authors. Like many Commonwealth countries, Canada has moved away from a history of *seriatim* judgements (where each judge is required to give his or her own written reasons) towards a model where individual judges sign on to opinions authored by other judges.

Each written opinion addresses two matters: result and reason. The first of these—*result*—is something that can generally be expressed in binary form. Someone wins, and someone loses. But it is not enough for a judge to pronounce the 'yes or no' of a result. The judge must also give *reasons*. The reasons tell us *how* the thinking process proceeded from the facts to the outcome, *why* certain outcomes are desirable, justifiable or inevitable. Reasons are "the primary mechanism by which judges account to the parties and to the public for the decisions they render" (*R v. Walker* [2008] para 19).

In situations where an appellate court produces a unanimous opinion, reason and result move together. That unanimous opinion may bear the authorial imprint of one of the judge's names, or it may be issued under the 'nom de plume' of 'The Court'. While the proportion shifts over time, it has been common for unanimity to be achieved in only 50% of the Supreme Court's judgements (McCormick, 2000). It is often the case that differences emerge between judges—differences that make unanimity impossible. In such situations, the case will result in the production of multiple texts: a majority opinion (a text supported by more than half the judges hearing the case), and one or more dissenting or concurring opinions.

A terminological note is in order here, as the identification of a text as dissenting or concurring depends on the distinction between result and reason. Where the minority judges disagree with the *result* reached by the majority, the opinion is a dissenting one. Where, however, the minority judges agree with the result but disagree with the majority *reasons*, the opinion is a concurring one. In English, the word 'concur' means 'to agree', but in law, the concurrence is a form of disagreement. This is perhaps more evident for francophone than anglophone readers, since in French, the terms dissent and concurrence are rendered as 'dissidences sur les résultats' and 'dissidences sur les motifs'. This linguistic marking better exposes the distinction between reason and result, and puts emphasis on the dissenting nature of both types of opinion. The central point for the empirically minded is that, for the purposes of statistical analysis, the concurrence can be problematic. It straddles categories: it can be counted with the majority on the 'result', but with the dissent on the 'reasoning' (Belleau *et al.*, 2008; McCormick, 2005–2006).

Dissenting and concurring opinions, like their majority counterparts, seek to persuade the readers to understand the world in a specific way. While a dissent is not, strictly speaking, 'the law', the fact that the substance of the dissenting opinion is produced by a *judge* is a matter of some significance. This makes a dissenting opinion significantly different from other attempts to persuade or convince. A dissenter has the ability to force the majority to respond, to answer, to explain, to shift or to accommodate. The words of a dissenting opinion are a direct *challenge*, and the majority may feel required to enter into dialogue. And even where a majority does not respond directly, the very fact of the dissent often means that the majority reasons must be written differently than they would have been in its absence.

Certainly, some dissents have sufficient force to become part of the 'canon' of law (Primus, 1998; Krishnakumar, 2000). Some, with time, successfully bring about change in the law: courts may explicitly revisit particular problems, expressly overturning the law, and adopt what had formerly been a dissenting view.[1] Other dissents have brought about change in a more direct fashion: those with legislative power may be persuaded to propose statutory changes in line with those suggested in a dissent.[2] As judicial texts, dissents are a form of dialogue with a number of legal and non-legal communities, and these forms of conversation can matter in important ways (Sheehy, 2004). United States constitutional law theorist Cass Sunstein (2003) has gone so far as to claim that "societies need dissent".

Of course, to say societies need dissent is not to say that dissent must take the form of written judicial opinions. Certainly, such an assertion would not have universal resonance, since the published dissenting judicial opinion is *not* a feature of all legal regimes (Mastor, 2005). Neither has it been an unchanging feature where it has operated. The forms and manners and magnitude of judicial dissent have varied across time and location, with judges feeling, at various historical junctures, more or less pressure to speak with a unified voice (Kolsky, 1995; Post, 2001). There is a rich debate about value (and risks) of judicial dissent, with some seeing it as assuring the integrity of the justice system, and others suggesting it undermines the legitimacy and authority of the Court (Belleau & Johnson, 2004). While there are persistent debates about how much is too much, dissent is accepted, by the legal and non-legal communities alike, as inherent in the Canadian judicial tradition. It is a practice in which all judges engage.

3. Gender and dissent on the Supreme Court of Canada

But of course, to say that 'all judges dissent' is to skate over variations in dissenting practice, and differences in the significance of particular dissenting opinions. Some judicial reputations have been solidified through the power of canonical dissents, and some judges are even reputed to be dissenters. The two of us were formerly law clerks to Madame Justice Claire L'Heureux-Dubé, the second woman appointed to the Supreme Court, and indeed, its first Francophone woman. We were well aware that our own judge was frequently in dissent, and that she was popularly referred to as "The Great Dissenter". Our scholarly interest was piqued, however, by the observation of court-watching political scientists that it was not simply *our* judge: they observed that Justices Bertha Wilson and Beverley McLachlin also showed heightened propensities to dissent (Morton *et al.*, 1994; McCormick, 2000).

As part of a larger research project considering gender and dissent, we began collecting and compiling data on our Supreme Court Justices, and their individual patterns of decision-making. We wondered how, if at all, the gender of a judge might be visible in either 'voting' practices (how often the judge was with the majority on result or reasons) or practices of 'authorship' (how often the judge was the author of an opinion, majority or otherwise). As other scholars had indicated, with respect to the first three women on the Court, the pattern was quite striking.

Consider Table 1, in which Justice Wilson serves as the anchor point for some comparative data on gender and dissent. Listed are the 15 Supreme Court Justices (with dates of appointment) whose tenure intersected with that of Bertha Wilson. We thus include judges who were already on the Court when the first woman judge was appointed, as well as those who arrived after her, but before her retirement in 1990. This gives us a context for examining the first three 'trailblazer' women against the male judges with whom they sat.

For each of the 15 judges included in Table 1, we list first the total number of divided cases in which that judge participated during their tenure on the court.[3] The next three columns provide a proportionate breakdown of the 'voting' practices of that judge in those divided cases: how frequently did the judge join the majority, and how often was the judge with the concurrence (agreeing with result but differing with respect to the majority reasons), or with the dissent (disagreeing with the majority result). The final column provides an indicator of 'authorial labour' in the divided cases. That is, how often was the judge a named author of one of the opinions, whether majority, dissenting or concurring.

If we consider only these 15 judges and their participation in non-unanimous cases, we have judges, on the average, with the majority 56.6% of the time. We can see that judges expressed their disagreement through the form of a concurrence 25.7% of the time, and in the form of a dissent 15% of the time. Disagreement, that is, was nearly twice as likely to be expressed through concurrence as through dissent. We also see that, on the average, judges were producing a written opinion in just over a third of the divided cases they heard.

A discussion of the numbers in Table 1 cannot help but begin with the observation that the first three women judges (who were at that time also the *only*

Table 1. *Divided judgements and 'the Wilson cohort'*

Justice (date of appointment)	Divided cases heard (nominal)	With majority (%)	With concurrence (%)	With dissent (%)	Took part in writing (%)
Average	**298**	**56.6**	**25.7**	**15**	**35.8**
L'Heureux-Dubé ♀ 15 April 1987	531	35.6	31.5	28.1	42.7
Wilson ♀ 4 March 1982	250	40.4	32.4	23.2	55.2
McLachlin ♀ 30 March 1989	555	53.1	23.6	19.6	43.8
Sopinka 24 May 1988	382	54.2	25.7	17.3	46.1
La Forest 16 January 1985	467	54.8	30.4	12	38.8
Lamer 28 March 1980	502	54.9	29.1	13.4	44.5
McIntyre 1 January 1979	183	55.8	23.5	16.4	37.2
Stevenson 17 September 1990	70	57.1	28.8	14.3	25.7
Beetz 1 January 1974	134	57.5	29.1	11.1	22.4
Dickson 26 March 1973	229	59.4	27.9	12.2	39.3
Estey 29 September 1977	107	61.7	17.8	17.8	42.1
Gonthier 1 February 1989	506	62.6	21.3	12.5	17.2
Chouinard 24 September 1979	86	65.1	20.9	12.8	16.3
Cory 1 February 1989	397	68	19.4	9.8	35.5
Le Dain 29 May 1984	70	68.8	24.3	5.7	30

women) top the list of judges 'most likely to disagree'. Their position at the top of the table makes it nearly impossible not to re-invoke the question posed in the title of Justice Wilson's controversial speech. One could be forgiven for ironically responding with the observation that, whether or not women judges will make a difference, it appears that they will certainly differ.

The chart affirms that the label "The Great Dissenter" was indeed an apt one for Claire L'Heureux-Dubé, who agreed with the majority opinion in only 35% of the 531 divided cases she heard (against an average of 56.6%). Justice L'Heureux-Dubé dissented in 28.1% of the cases she heard, which is nearly double the average rate of dissent. Bertha Wilson, on the court for fewer years, participated in 250 divided cases, voting with the majority 40.2% of the time. She was with the concurrence 32.1% of the time and with the dissent 22.5% of the time. The profile of 'disagreement' here is particularly interesting. Justice Wilson's disagreement was more likely to take the form of concern with majority 'reasons' than with majority 'results'. In fact, if one focuses only on the concurrences, it is Justice Wilson who tops the chart, suggesting that the label "The Great Concurrer" might have been aptly applied to her. While the divergence from the majority is not as stark for Justice McLachlin as for the other two women judges, she nonetheless appears third on this table. But we see here that she, unlike Justice Wilson, concurred at a rate below the group average, and dissented at a rate above. Of the 555 divided cases heard by Justice McLachlin, on the other hand, disagreement was more likely to take the form of dissent than concurrence.

Looking at those judges whose tenure intersected with the initial arrival of a woman at the Supreme Court, we can see that the three first women judges have the highest levels of dissents. It is difficult to avoid the conclusion that gender is linked to certain differences in the process of decision-making. And yet, does such a conclusion risk suggesting a certain form of essentialism in relation to women and the act of judging (Harris, 1990)? Do these statistics show us that women judges have a shared perspective on the world, a perspective that would stem, by necessity, from their feminine essence? Can one conclude that women judges speak in a "different voice" (Gilligan, 1982; Belenky *et al.*, 1986)? Not necessarily.

Other studies of these first three women judges indicate that the phenomenon of gendered dissent does not operate in a 'predictive' sort of way. Though the first three women were each dissenting at rates higher than the average, McCormick (2000) also noted that they did not dissent as a unified block (McCormick, 2000). Morton *et al.* (1994), in their study of the first ten years of *Charter* jurisprudence, made a similar observation. The three women, they said, were as likely to disagree with their female as with their male colleagues. Indeed, each of the three women was located as the outlier in one of three different quadrants inside a matrix assessing support for/opposition to left/right policies on 'criminal justice' and 'court party' issues. The authors used the expression 'court party' to describe a specific set of organised societal interests, those which exhibit a preference for non-traditional modes of political action such as litigation. They used it to include feminism, Aboriginal claims, linguistic and other minorities, environmentalism, gay rights, peace and disarmament. Justice Bertha Wilson expressed strong support for both court party and criminal rights claims; Justice Claire L'Heureux-Dubé showed strong support for court party claims but equally strong opposition to criminal rights claims; and now Chief Justice Beverley McLachlin showed strong opposition to court party claims and moderate support for criminal rights claims. Certainly, the heightened rates of gendered dissent do not allow us to predict from the judge's gender *how* the judge will vote.

But if there seems to have been no self-evident agreement between the first three women on the substantive content of particular issues, it is also interesting to refocus on what they *did* have in common: a higher than average number of occasions on which they seemed to either see something differently from the majority, or have a different explanation for why a given result should be reached. Further, it is not just that the first three women disagreed more often in terms of their 'votes'. In Canada, the first three women did a lot of writing. Returning to Table 1, note that each of the first three women did a significant amount of authorial work in the context of the divided cases. The three women, along with Justices Sopinka and Lamer, fill out the top five places in that column. Justice Wilson is, however, far in front. She produced a written opinion in 55% of the divided cases she heard. While Justices McLachlin and L'Heureux-Dubé did not generate authored opinions at quite the same rate, given the number of cases they heard, they too generated a significant number of authored divergent opinions. Just as one measure of that magnitude, note that, between 1982 and 1999, the first three women judges (representing three of the 23 judges to have sat on the court during that period of time) produced 455 of the total 1,272 written dissenting/concurring opinions produced by the entire court during that period of time: 13% of the judges generated 35.8% of the dissenting texts. It appeared to be not simply that the women were more likely to disagree, but also that they were more likely to express their disagreement through written reasons.

How, then, can one understand this unusual portrait of dissent and gender in the trailblazer women? Is it the case that what these women judges had in common was a substance or an essence or a feminine nature, or rather that, as the first women in a new space, they were positioned distinctively in relation to the majority and to the discursive practices which formed the centre of judicial power? They seem to have had a greater propensity than average to perceive and, later, to understand differently from the majority what had been presented to the court. But again, these women did not always share the same perspective, but rather they shared a positioning that left them seeing something different, or having a different view about how a common result should be better understood.

4. Complicating the picture

Since 1999, there have been changes to the judicial roster. Both Bertha Wilson and Claire L'Heureux-Dubé have retired, and Beverley McLachlin is now the first female Chief Justice of the Supreme Court. Four additional women have been appointed: Louise Arbour in 1999 (she stepped down in 2004), Marie Deschamps in 2002, and both Rosalie Abella and Louise Charron in 2004. In January 2008, Justice McLachlin was thus the Chief Justice of a court on which four of the nine judges were women. What do more recent data suggest about this seeming relationship between gender and dissent? In Table 2, we offer a portrait of judicial dissent that incorporates the new appointees. Here, arranged from the least to the most dissenting, one can see the individual practices of disagreement for all 26 judges who sat on the court between 1982 and 15 June 2007.

The first observation is that, even with the new additions to the court, the first three women remain at the top of the chart. The next four, however, are distributed more broadly amongst their judicial peers. It is hard to draw conclusions at this relatively early stage for each of these judges, particularly Justices Abella and Charron. It may be that the lower rates of dissent are reflective of the ways those judges

Table 2. *Divided judgements: Judges of the Supreme Court, 1982–2007*

Justice	Divided cases heard (nominal)	With majority (%)	With concurrence (%)	With dissent (%)	Took part in writing (%)
Average	**243.8**	**60.6**	**19.6**	**16.8**	**34.0**
L'Heureux-Dubé ♀	531	35.6	31.5	28.1	42.7
Wilson ♀	250	40.4	32.4	23.2	55.2
McLachlin ♀	555	53.1	23.6	19.6	43.8
Sopinka	382	54.2	25.7	17.3	46.1
La Forest	467	54.8	30.4	12	38.8
Lamer	502	54.9	29.1	13.4	44.5
LeBel	166	55.4	15.1	24.7	39.8
McIntyre	183	55.8	23.5	16.4	37.2
Stevenson	70	57.1	28.8	14.3	25.7
Beetz	134	57.5	29.1	11.1	22.4
Bastarache	235	58.7	13.6	25.1	41.3
Dickson	229	59.4	27.9	12.2	39.3
Deschamps ♀	109	60.6	10.1	23.9	33
Estey	107	61.7	17.8	17.8	42.1
Fish	82	62.2	9.8	25.6	22
Gonthier	506	62.6	21.3	12.5	17.2
Major	384	64	14.3	19.5	24.7
Chouinard	86	65.1	20.9	12.8	16.3
Abella ♀	65	66	10.8	21.5	30.8
Arbour ♀	108	67.6	10.2	14.8	37
Cory	397	68	19.4	9.8	35.5
Le Dain	70	68.8	24.3	5.7	30
Binnie	221	72.4	7.2	16.3	28.5
Iacobucci	420	72.9	14.3	10.2	24.8
Charron ♀	63	73	7.9	14.3	28.6
Rothstein	19	73.7	10.5	15.8	36.8

participate, but it is also the case that judges have shown shifts in their patterns of dissent over time. Some judges (like Justice Wilson) generated more dissent the longer they were on the Court while other judges (like Justice Sopinka) started as great dissenters, but produced increasingly less dissent the longer they were on the Court. Justice Louise Arbour remains at the lower end of dissent. However, she sat on the Court for only five years before stepping down to become the United Nations High Commissioner for Human Rights. Again, it is unclear that the relatively low rate of dissent would have persisted in the context of a longer judicial career.

A further complexity resides in the reality that dissent, like difference itself, is deeply relational (Minow, 1990). A dissent has meaning only in the context of the majority against which it stands in opposition. This poses a difficulty. Does a shift in a judge's pattern of dissent represent a shift in how that judge thinks, or, rather, a shift in how the majority decides? Does it represent an increasing willingness by the majority to be persuaded by the voice of a colleague once seen as a dissenter?

Or does it represent a shift in the dissenter (a movement by the dissenter towards the majority)?

For example, in the context of Canadian discourse about multiculturalism, Justice John Sopinka was considered the first ethnic appointment because of his Ukrainian background. The pattern of his dissent rates was similar to Chief Justice Laskin, who was the first Jewish appointee. That is, like Laskin, Sopinka showed a very high dissent rate for the first half of his time on the Bench, followed by a sharp decline in the second half (McCormick, 2000).[4] Overall, the average dissent rates of both Justices Sopinka and Laskin met that of the Court as a whole.

One might wonder what trends pressed Laskin and Sopinka's dissent rates down. In the case of Justice Laskin, did his appointment as Chief Justice give him greater success in influencing the members of his court, change his point of view on law and the decision-making process, or lead him to see his role differently? In the case of Justice Sopinka, can the result be explained by the natural evolution in a judge coming to the bench from practice, slowly getting accustomed to the norms followed by judges rather than by advocates? In either event, it is also interesting to compare the trajectory of Justice Sopinka with that of Justice Beverley McLachlin. The two judges were appointed at around the same time, but Justice McLachlin showed an *increase* in dissent over that same period of time (up to 1999 and before she became Chief Justice). In this, her profile is akin to that of the other first two trailblazing women, who also showed an increasing trajectory of dissent over their careers. In the case of McLachlin, is it also noteworthy that, since becoming Chief Justice, her dissent rate has decreased, again, possibly due to a shifting interest in unanimity.

Gender does not seem to be operating as a random variable, but neither does it seem to be operating in a self-evident fashion. There are further questions that need asking. For instance, whether individual dissenters (male or female) are engaged in group or solo projects: Justice McLachlin, for instance, tended to dissent in conjunction with others judges, while L'Heureux-Dubé was very frequently a lone dissenter, sometimes managing to convince one other judge to join her (Joseph, 2006). Taking these statistics into account, can it be that Justice McLachlin succeeds more often than before to sway the votes of her colleagues thus reaching a majority? The statistics alone cannot fully capture the full dynamics operating in judicial decision-making. Dissent is something that necessarily emerges out of a context, and shifts in the context matter hugely.

In understanding gender and dissent, there is another point that is important to foreground. Rates of dissent differ across the male judges, with some, like Justice Iacobucci, showing up at the very lowest end, while others, like Justice LeBel, produce a significant proportion of dissenting judgements. While the statistics suggest that gender (as a marker of 'outsider status'?) is operating in some fashion worthy of further interrogation, they also remind us that the practice of dissent is not the exclusive providence of one gender, or of any judge. Dissent as a phenomenon certainly predates the arrival of women on the court; each generation of judges has had its (male) dissenters of renown.

In the Canadian context, Bora Laskin, Canada's first Jewish appointment to the Supreme Court, was also renowned as a great dissenter. But such an observation draws us back to another question: 'Why focus on gender'? The decision to focus on gender as the primary source of difference is certainly one worthy of scrutiny. One should notice, for example, that our seven women judges share not just gender, but also whiteness. There has not yet been a single First Nations judge, or judge of colour in the history of our Supreme Court, and thus whiteness is something shared both by the women, and by *all* our judges. Such an important commonality can be obscured by attention to gender difference. Critical race theorists and postcolonial feminist critics have long cautioned against an approach to gender that proceeds as if the perspective of white, Western middle-class heterosexual women were the viewpoint of all women (Spelman, 1988 ; Rajan & Park, 2000).

In making visible labels of identity, we seek to remain conscious of the risk of misapprehending as 'gendered' differences that which may find root in other sources. For marking out identity through labels does send one right to the centre of highly political debates: what identities do we privilege, what is the deemed content of those identities, and how do we know we have correctly determined which identities get attached to which bodies? In Canada, for example, debates about identity and judgement have been fierce not only around 'gender', but also around language (French/English) and culture— nationalism/cultural difference, sometimes articulated as 'the Quebec question' (Belleau, 1999). What becomes visible if we problematise the singular focus on gender, and ask also about how the judges can be identified on these two additional dimensions? Such questions force an additional level of nuance and difficulty into debates about identity and difference.

An account of judicial difference requires similar nuance, because judicial opinions matter not only for their results, but also for their reasons. The statistics, while making visible some of the variations in patterns of voting and writing, tell us very little about the substance of the disagreements, the shape of the written reasons, or the context in which the conflicts emerged. To further flesh out our snapshot of gendered judicial judgement, we would need to know more about each of these additional dimensions of dissent. Where dissent is theorised as a space of difference, there are additional questions that arise. How do judges work in the space of dissent? How do they articulate an alternative vision of 'the real', re-describe the facts, re-draw the boundary between the legal and the social, and challenge how we think about law itself? What does the dissenting judicial text seem to require/desire of us as readers? What questions do they ask us? In what directions do they point? What courses of action do they suggest? How do they focus our attention in some places and not in others? How do they articulate and disarticulate 'reality', rendering visible the voices and values which are muted or absent in the opposing reasons? Do judges do all this differently when writing in dissent, or in majority?

Posing such questions makes visible another important dimension of the relational nature of dissent: dissent, in and of itself, it is not necessarily 'progressive' or 'reactionary'. That is, dissents can lean in the direction of change, as well as pull towards a status quo. Dissents are written in relation to majority opinions, whatever their political leaning. Thus, it is unsurprising that dissent itself can seem more or less risky given both institutional factors internal to the Court, and socio-political complexity external to the Court (Smyth, 2004). In the face of large scale social unrest, judges may feel more strongly the need to speak with a more unified voice than they might feel in periods of relative calm. Similarly, there are issues and moments in which Courts will conclude that a unanimous front (and indeed, the authorial label of 'The Court' rather than any of its single judges) is demanded by the interests of justice *and* politics (Belleau *et al.*, 2008).[5]

Here, we find it interesting to note that, at the current political juncture, we see evidence of both the Canadian and United States Supreme Courts moving away from patterns of the past 20 years towards an increased incidence of unanimity. Chief Justice McLachlin, while affirming the right to dissent, explained that she and her colleagues are attempting to "reduce the unnecessary differences" (Guly, 2006, p. 22). Chief Justice John Roberts of the Supreme Court of the United States was reported to say that he "wants the Justices to speak with one voice as much as possible, to decide cases 9 to 0, with no pesky dissents or concurrences" (Holding, 2007, p. 34). McCormick's work (2000) shows that historically, since 1982, the Supreme Court achieved unanimity in between 40% and 50% of its case load. In 2006, under Chief Justice McLachlin (whose dissent rate was number three of the most frequent dissenters since 1982), the Court produced 70% unanimous judgements (Gully, 2006). Again, there is a puzzle here: one of the top dissenters on the Court until the late 1990s, Justice McLachlin is now the Chief of a Court which is producing higher rates of unanimous judgement, a court in which rates of dissent and concurrence seem to be dropping. In the light of this specific historical juncture, the practices of dissent for the most recent appointees would have to be explored against the context of the particular year. For example, given the proportion of dissent in that year, are the judges at the low or high end of dissent? Certainly, the fact that dissent has sometimes had a gendered face suggests that there are reasons to think seriously about the current reduction in dissenting judgements (and particularly in concurrences).

5. Conclusion

Professor Peter McCormick, observing the high level of gendered dissent on the Canadian Supreme Court, suggested that women judges occupied the periphery, and that they passively assisted law's development and application. They were not, he suggested, taking an active part in the determination of the law: "The women members of the Supreme Court are not being absorbed—but the price they are paying for this is that they are being left outside the dominant decision-making coalitions" (McCormick, 2000, p. 138). Professor McCormick captures a common preoccupation with majority decision-making, a preoccupation we have sometimes shared, but one which often places women judges on the sidelines.

We argue that it is important to resist the tendency to think of dissent as a space of failed possibilities, as evidence of marginal status either of the dissenting judges or of the different point of view that they attempt to raise. With Professor Diana Majury, we are of the opinion that concurrences and dissents must be the objects of a more positive theorisation (Majury, 2000, paras 28–31). Dissents make manifest the struggles about difficult concepts and hard negotiations regarding how we live in the world.

Even if dissents do not constitute 'the law', they provide an authorised judicial space for the articulation and exploration of angles of visions whose public expressions are sometimes denied, concealed or silenced. Indeed, in certain contexts, it may be useful and even fundamental that courts do not deliver unanimously 'the good and clear answer'. Indeed, there are contexts when the best guarantee for justice rests in the articulation of arguments in conflict and not on a specific result. In cases where dissent allows the explanation of arguments, it is fundamental to the legitimacy of the judicial project and, consequently, to justice itself. Dissent then supersedes greatly the failure of possibilities.

The heightened proportion of times that women judges find themselves in dissent should be understood not predictively, and not as a conclusion about who or what women 'are'. It should, however, serve as a disruption to our traditional ways of theorising judicial judgement. It should encourage us to ask more about the space of dissent. Gilles Deleuze affirms that the thinking process "is the invention of new concepts and possibilities out of the experience of friction", the friction between what we think that we know and the unpredictable events that disturb these knowledges (Connolly, 2002, p. 94). The unpredictable event, the "strange encounter", creates the moment of friction which opens the space for translation and changes of thought. Dissent often functions exactly in this manner—as a friction—a "strange encounter" which opens the space for novel ways of conceptualising or advancing on the path towards justice.

Justice Wilson asked if women judges would really make a difference. We believe that the answer is an unequivocal 'Yes'. For us, the experience of friction is in the recognition that a considerable part of difference is located in an impressive production of dissenting opinions. For decades, authors have been asserting that "the role of the judge must be re-imagined as one in which women and members of other currently underrepresented groups can comfortably and constructively occupy" (Rackley, 2002, p. 624). We suggest that it is worth thinking about the ways women and other members of under-represented groups within the judicial body already occupy their role as judges in a constructive way, both as majority decision-makers and when speaking from the space of dissent. Those of us who observe courts of justice must study what these judges do and say in this space of dissent. Heightened rates of dissent should lead us not to consternation but to exploration.

In response to the question originally asked by Justice Wilson, we would add two variations on a theme: "What difference does gender make?" or, again, "What difference does difference make?" We know that the places where women judges differ are not always around women. Judges' differences of opinion do not always concern issues that are self-evidently about gender. Men and women judges both dissent. The higher production level of dissent expressed by at least the first three women judges tell us perhaps more about difference itself than about the 'identity' of those particular judges. We can't say gender does not matter because in dissent we can see that women do occupy the space of difference. Gender, like dissent, matters. Currently, dissent does point us in the direction of identity. However, identity does not predict dissent and dissent does not predict identity. Indeed, dissent and identity both exceed their own predictive value.

Dissenting opinions open the space to imagine and construct a more complete vision of law, and also of humanity. The friction caused by the statistics concerning the first women judges and their levels of dissent allows us to imagine the role of judges in a way that affirms the importance of the space of dissent, the necessity of conceiving the expression of dissent as a masterpiece of the adjudication process in the context where multiple points of view must be articulated, recognised and considered seriously. The 'different point of view' opens the space in the decisional process producing sometimes a particular result by influencing the law with a unanimous or majority opinion issued from this alternative perspective. Clearly, the simple articulation of a novel perspective does not always lead to a specific result. However, the expression of difference is important for many reasons. It reveals and recalls the importance of multiple perspectives in the adjudication process. It does not presuppose that a privileged voice exists to render judgement. The presence of multiple voices opens the space to the other judges so that they consider the structure or the specificity of their own decisional process. The expression of difference is significant in the process that leads to judgement. Consequently, the judicial bench must be composed of members with varied experiences from which judges can be inspired. These judges—women judges, visible minority judges, judges from a variety of social classes, judges with physical disabilities—will not share 'essential' perspectives but they bring an important diversity of approaches to the decisional process. It is thus possible to anticipate that one of the impacts of diversity on the bench will lead to a corresponding increase in the numbers of experiences and perspectives added to the decisional process. The space of judicial dissent is one worthy of closer examination.

Acknowledgements

The authors wish to thank the Social Sciences and Humanities Research Council of Canada for funding their research on dissenting opinions at the Supreme Court of Canada. They are also grateful for the research assistance of Julie Banville, Christine Joseph, Anik Lamontagne, Sara-Dawn Schenk, Andrew Tomilson and Christina Vinters.

Notes

[1] So, for example, the famous dissent in *Plessey v. Ferguson* [1896] 163 US 537, would move to the centre in *Brown v. Board of Education of Topeka* [1954] 347 US 483. Note that a dissent may be adopted expressly, or in a quiet fashion; for example, in the 1995 equality trilogy cases (*Egan v. Canada* [1995] 2 SCR 513; *Miron v. Trudel* [1995] 2 SCR 418, and *Thibaudeau v. Canada* [1995] 2 SCR 627). Justice L'Heureux-Dubé articulated a new approach to equality problems. At the time, the other judges on the court made no comment on her approach. That is, in the context of the judges mutually referring to each other's reasons in the trilogy of equality cases, for the purposes of expressing both agreement and disagreement, the other judges said *nothing* of the test being proposed by Justice L'Heureux-Dubé. They did not adopt her test, nor did they reject it. The silence was deafening. However, by the time the *Law v. Canada (Minister of Employment and Immigration)* [1999] 1 SCR 497 was decided in 1999, the test was incorporated by the unanimous court.

Perhaps a strategy of silence may be deployed where an idea is sufficiently new that judges simply need time and space to think.

[2] In the Canadian context, for example, Parliament introduced a set of legal reforms dealing with the disclosure of sexual assault victims' private records. Legislators can make real that which is imagined in the space of dissent. See *R v. O'Connor* [1995] 4 SCR 411, and s. 276(3) of the *Canadian Criminal Code*.

[3] Chief Justice McLachlin is the only one of the 15 who is still on the Court. For her, we have given the numbers up to 15 June 2007. There are of course some clear limits to the comparative work one can do with the data captured in Table 2. For one thing, the table does not reflect a stable time period. Though each of these judges served with Justice Wilson, they did not all sit together. Justice LeDain, for example, retired five years before Justice McLachlin was appointed. And (Chief) Justice McLachlin, unlike 14 of the judges on the chart, is still a sitting justice and still in the process of hearing new cases. Table 1 portrays the differences in the decision-making practices of multiple judges situated over overlapping yet different streams of time.

[4] See McCormick (2000), Table 7.1 at p. 113 and Table 8.1 at p. 133. Between 1963 and 1973, Bora Laskin's average rate of dissent was 69% compared to the Court's average of 34. 2% (McCormick, 2000, Table 5.1 at p. 65). He became Chief Justice of the Supreme Court of Canada in 1973. His dissent rates dropped to 54.1% (Court's average of 37.3%) between 1973 and 1978 (McCormick, 2000, Table 6.1A at p. 90) and to 24.3% (a rate lower than the Court's average of 34.2%) (McCormick, 2000, Table 6.1B at p. 91).

[5] Note that this was done, for example, with the *Daigle* case (*Tremblay v. Daigle* [1989] 2 SCR 530, an important case from the province of Québec concerning an injunction obtained by a father to prevent the mother from having an abortion) and with the *Quebec Secession Reference* (*Reference re Secession of Quebec* [1998] 2 SCR 217, a case asking questions to the Supreme Court of Canada about the possibility of the unilateral secession of the province of Québec from Canada). Here, arguably, having the judgement authored by a man or woman (or a Québec or non-Québec judge) would itself have carried additional political questions into the text.

References

Belenky, M.F., Clinchy, B.M., Goldberger, N.R. & Tarule, J.M. (1986) *Women's Ways of Knowing: The Development of Self, Voice, and Mind* (New York, Basic Books, Inc).

Belleau, M.-C. (1999) L'intersectionalité: feminisms in a divided world (Quebec-Canada), in: D. Lacombe & D. Chunn (Eds) *Law as a Gendering Practice* (London, Oxford University Press).

Belleau, M.-C. & Johnson, R. (2004) La dissidence judiciaire: réflexions préliminaires sur les émotions, la raison et les passions du droit/Judicial dissent: early reflections on emotion, reason and passion in law, in: M.-C. Belleau & F. Lacasse (Eds) *Claire L'Heureux-Dubé à la Cour suprême du Canada, 1987–2002* (Québec, Wilson & Lafleur).

Belleau, M.-C., Johnson, R. & Vinters, C. (2008) Voicing an opinion: authorship, collaboration and the judgments of Justice Bertha Wilson, *Supreme Court Law Review*, p. 20.

Connolly, W.E. (2002) *Neuropolitics: Thinking, Culture, Speed* (Minneapolis, University of Minnesota Press).

Fitzpatrick, P. (2001) *Modernism and the Grounds of Law* (Cambridge, Cambridge University Press).

Gilligan, C. (1982) *In a Different Voice: Psychological Theory and Women's Development* (Cambridge, MA, Harvard University Press).

Guly, C. (2006) Beverley McLachlin: 'A model judge', *Canadian Lawyer.*

Harris, A.P. (1990) Race and essentialism in feminist legal theory, *Stanford Law Review*, 42, pp. 581–616.

Holding, R. (2007) In defence of dissent, *Time Magazine*, p. 34.

Joseph, C. (2006) All but one: solo dissents on the Supreme Court of Canada, *Osgoode Hall Law Journal*, 44, pp. 501–25.

Kolsky, M. (1995) Justice William Johnson and the history of the Supreme Court dissent, *Georgetown Law Journal*, 83, pp. 2069–98.

Krishnakumar, A.S. (2000) On the evolution of the canonical dissent, *Rutgers Law Review*, 52, pp. 781–817.

Majury, D. (2000) The charter, equality rights, and women: equivocation and celebration, *Osgoode Hall Law Journal*, 40, pp. 297–336.

Mastor, W. (2005) *Les opinions séparées des juges constitutionnels* (Aix-en-Provence, Presses universitaires d'Aix-Marseille).

McCormick, P. (2000) *Supreme at Last: The Evolution of the Supreme Court of Canada* (Toronto, James Lorimer & Company Ltd).

McCormick, P. (2005–2006) The Choral Court: separate concurrence and the McLachlin Court, 2000–2004, *Ottawa Law Review*, 37, pp. 1–33.

Minow, M. (1990) *Making All the Difference: Inclusion, Exclusion and American Law* (Ithaca, Cornell University Press).

Morton, F.L., Russell, P.H. & Riddell, T. (1994) The Canadian Charter of Rights and Freedoms: a descriptive analysis of the first decade, 1982–1992, *National Journal of Constitutional Law*, 5, pp. 1–60.

Post, R. (2001) The Supreme Court opinion as institutional practice: dissent, legal scholarship, and decisionmaking in the Taft Court, *Minnesota Law Review*, 85, pp. 1267–384.

Primus, R.A. (1998) Canon, anti-canon, and judicial dissent, *Duke Law Journal*, 48, pp. 243–303.

Rackley, E. (2002) Representations of the (woman) judge: Hercules, the little mermaid, and the vain and naked Emperor, *Legal Studies*, pp. 602–24.

Rajan, R.S. & Park, Y.-M. (2000) Postcolonial feminism/postcolonialism and feminism, in: H. Schwarz & S. Ray (Eds) *A Companion to Postcolonial Studies* (Oxford, Blackwell Publishing).

Sheehy, E. (Ed.) (2004) *Adding Feminism to Law: The Contributions of Justice Claire L'Heureux-Dubé* (Toronto, Irwin Law Inc).

Smyth, R. (2004) What explains variations in dissent rates? Time series evidence from High Court. (Australia), *Sydney Law Review*, 26, pp. 221–40.

Spelman, E.V. (1988) *Inessential Woman: Problems of Exclusion in Feminist Thought* (Boston, Beacon Press).

Sunstein, C.R. (2003) *Why Societies Need Dissent* (Cambridge, MA, Harvard University Press).

Wilson, B. (1990) Will women judges really make a difference?, *Osgoode Hall Law Journal*, 28, pp. 507–22.

Cases

Brown v. Board of Education of Topeka [1954] 347 US 483.
Egan v. Canada [1995] 2 SCR 513.
Law v. Canada (Minister of Employment and Immigration) [1999] 1 SCR 497.
Miron v. Trudel [1995] 2 SCR 418.
Plessey v. Ferguson [1896] 163 US 537.
Quebec Secession Reference (Reference re Secession of Quebec) [1998] 2 SCR 217.
R v. O'Connor [1995] 4 SCR 411.
R v. Walker [2008] SCC 34.
Thibaudeau v. Canada [1995] 2 SCR 627.
Tremblay v. Daigle [1989] 2 SCR 530.

Gender, race, bias and perspective: OR, how otherness colours your judgment

REG GRAYCAR
Sydney Law School, The University of Sydney, Australia

ABSTRACT *This discussion considers assumptions about judges and judging and suggests that despite what is sometimes perceived as increasing diversity on the bench and in the legal profession, outsider decision makers' membership of the jurisprudential community is still marked by 'otherness'. The argument draws upon my ongoing interest in the law's concern with the concepts of 'objectivity', 'neutrality' and 'perspective'. I argue that the legal system is inherently suspicious of 'otherness' and most specifically so when 'others' occupy positions of 'judgement'. The consequence is to render decisions made by 'otherised' judges liable to attack for bias in a way that decisions made by insiders simply are not. The argument is illustrated by a review of a number of challenges made on the ground of 'bias' or recusal motions to judges whose failure to match the white Anglo hetero-normative standard of 'the judge' is seen as a limit on their ability to be 'impartial'. The examples used range across many jurisdictions, from Australia, Canada, the US and a challenge to the impartiality of a decision of the International Criminal Tribunal for the former Yugoslavia (ICTY).*

The project I discuss in this paper is an ongoing project that I return to from time to time: I feel that I can never consider it more than a work in progress as I keep finding new examples. It concerns an overarching theme in feminist engagements with law, and that is, how the concepts of 'bias', 'partiality' and 'perspective' are connected, via notions of 'otherness', to 'outsider' judges and other legal decision makers.[1] This particular incarnation of the ongoing project started life in 2002 as a critical reflection for a festschrift to mark the retirement of Justice Claire L'Heureux-Dubé from the Supreme Court of Canada,[2] on which she had served for 15 years, a period in which that court developed an equality jurisprudence that is widely considered the most sophisticated in the world.

The argument I make is that the legal system is inherently suspicious of 'otherness' and most specifically so when 'others' occupy positions of 'judgment'. The consequence is to render decisions made by judges seen as 'other' liable to attack for bias in a way that decisions made by insiders are not. By other, here I mean people who are other than white, male, able bodied, heterosexual etc. To put it another way, there is simply no corresponding assumption—indeed, it would probably be considered absurd in legal circles to assume—that white male decision-makers will be 'blinded' by their race or their gender. Nor does it ever seem to be assumed that white people are not in a position to fairly impose judgment on non-white people.[3] Whiteness or maleness are not viewed as impediments to impartiality precisely because they are not recognised as *positions* as all, but the treatment of decision-makers who are racialised as 'other' (of whom, of course, we have very few in Australia), or the response to decisions that make explicit reference to gender, race or unequal race relations (at least if made by 'others'), reveals a very different set of assumptions. It is in this context that we see the term 'bias' invoked in challenges (often by way of recusal, or judicial review applications) to the decision making authority of that person.

It is now more than ten years since the decision of the Supreme Court of Canada in *RDS v R*,[4] and it is with that case that I will start this discussion. The lead judgment was written by Justices Claire L'Heureux-Dubé and Beverly McLachlin (now McLachlin CJ).[5] However, lest the focus on this case suggest that this is a peculiarly Canadian phenomenon, I will refer to some other cases, including one from the international law arena,[6] and another from the United States.[7] In earlier work[8] I have also discussed a number of analogous Australian cases. I will conclude with some preliminary questions about how (if at all) we might begin to think about moving away from this devaluing of legal system outsiders into a more genuinely diverse way of engaging with law and legal problems.

R v. RDS[9]

The facts of the case are fairly straightforward and involved events in what is effectively a children's court. Judge Corinne Sparks, a provincial court trial judge in Nova Scotia (and at that time, the only African-Canadian woman judge in the province—note the use of adjectives to qualify the word 'judge'), was hearing the case of a 15-year-old black youth who was alleged to have interfered with the arrest of another youth.[10] He was charged with unlawfully assaulting a police officer and resisting arrest. While delivering an oral judgment (as is customary in the lower courts) dismissing the case against him,[11] having found that the prosecution had not proved its case beyond reasonable doubt, the judge said:

> I am not saying that the Constable has misled the Court although police officers have been known to do that in the past. And I am not saying that the officer overreacted, but certainly police officers do overreact, particularly when they are dealing with non-white groups ... I believe that probably the situation in this particular case is the case of a young police officer who overreacted. And I do accept the evidence of [*RDS*] that he was told to shut up or he would be under arrest. It seems to be in keeping with the prevalent attitude of the day.[12]

The prosecution successfully argued in the Nova Scotia Supreme Court that these comments gave rise to a reasonable apprehension of bias,[13] a decision confirmed by a majority of the Nova Scotia Court of Appeal.[14] The Supreme Court of Canada overturned this decision,[15] though not exactly overwhelmingly. The actual decision was 6:3; but the six was really four and two. L'Heureux Dubé and McLachlin JJ wrote the lead judgment, with which two other judges concurred. Another two judges agreed that the decision should be reversed, but clearly felt that while the judge had not actually crossed it she had, as it were, come 'very close to the line'.[16] In dissent, three other judges would have affirmed the decision, that is, maintained the finding that the decision was tainted by the judge's bias.[17]

The court was assisted by two separate interventions, the first a joint intervention by the Women's Legal Education and Action Fund (known as LEAF) and the National Organization of Immigrant and Visible Minority Women of Canada; and the second by the African-Canadian Legal Clinic, the Afro-Canadian Caucus of Nova Scotia and the Congress of Black Women of Canada. I mention this, particularly the first joint intervention, because the collaboration between the LEAF women and the Visible Minority Women was itself quite significant in Canada. It followed a considerable period of introspection and reflection (not to mention conflict and controversy) about LEAF and about which 'women' it purported to speak for when it intervened in Supreme Court litigation on behalf of women.[18]

The dissenting judges[19] took a fairly standard formal equality approach, and what is of particular interest is the way in which they drew strategically upon some of the discourses of stereotyping for rhetorical purposes:

> It would be stereotypical reasoning to conclude that, since society is racist, and, in effect, tells minorities to 'shut up', we should infer that *this* police officer told *this* appellant minority youth to 'shut up'. This reasoning is flawed.[20]
>
> . . .
>
> Canadian courts have, in recent years, criticized the stereotyping of people into what is said to be predictable behaviour patterns. If a judge in a sexual assault case instructed the jury or him- or herself that because the complainant was a prostitute he or she probably consented, or that prostitutes are likely to lie about such things as sexual assault, that decision would be reversed.[21]

By contrast, in their joint judgment, Justices L'Heureux-Dubé and McLachlin stated:

> In our view, the test for reasonable apprehension of bias established in the jurisprudence is reflective of the reality that while judges can never be neutral, in the sense of purely objective, they can and must strive for impartiality. It therefore recognizes as inevitable and appropriate that the differing experiences of judges assist them in their decision-making process and will be reflected in their judgments, so long as those experiences are relevant to the cases, are not based on inappropriate stereotypes, and do not

> prevent a fair and just determination of the cases based on the facts in evidence.[22]

They drew heavily on Benjamin Cardozo's, *The Nature of the Judicial Process*[23] ... "where he affirmed the importance of impartiality, while at the same time recognizing the fallacy of judicial neutrality":[24]

> ... Cardozo recognized that objectivity was an impossibility because judges, like all other humans, operate from their own perspectives. As the Canadian Judicial Council noted in Commentaries on Judicial Conduct (1991), at p. 12, "[t]here is no human being who is not the product of every social experience, every process of education, and every human contact". What is possible and desirable, they note, is impartiality:
>
> True impartiality does not require that the judge have no sympathies or opinions; it requires that the judge nevertheless be free to entertain and act upon different points of view with an open mind.[25]

In a comment on some analogous issues, Martha Minow described the same phenomenon in a different, but perhaps equally apposite, manner: she described the ability to approach things with an open mind, as "the ability to be surprised".[26]

Returning to *RDS*, McLachlin and L'Heureux-Dubé went on to say that

> [J]udges in a bilingual, multiracial and multicultural society will undoubtedly approach the task of judging from their varied perspectives. They will certainly have been shaped by, and have gained insight from, their different experiences, and cannot be expected to divorce themselves from these experiences on the occasion of their appointment to the bench.[27]

In their view, this was essential, among other reasons, to ensure diversity on the bench:

> The reasonable person [*central to 'bias' doctrine*] ... is an informed and right-minded member of the community, a community which, in Canada, supports the fundamental principles entrenched in the Constitution by the *Canadian Charter of Rights and Freedoms.* Those fundamental principles include the principles of equality set out in s. 15 of the *Charter* ... The reasonable person must be taken to be aware of the history of discrimination faced by disadvantaged groups in Canadian society protected by the *Charter's* equality provisions. These are matters of which judicial notice may be taken.[28]

And in support of this, they referred to judgments from Provincial Courts of Appeal, both in Ontario and in Nova Scotia, where those courts had made comments acknowledging the widespread existence of racism.[29]

Not only was their reasonable person aware of disadvantage, but also, they pointed out, as a member of the local Nova Scotia community, someone who was aware of such issues as the extensive history of

> ... widespread and systemic discrimination against black and aboriginal people, and high profile clashes between the police and the visible minority population over policing issues. ... In *Nova Scotia (Minister of Community Services) v. SMS* (1992), 110 N.S.R. (2d) 91 (Fam. Ct.), it was stated at p. 108:
>
> [Racism] is a pernicious reality. The issue of racism existing in Nova Scotia has been well documented in the Marshall Inquiry Report (sub. nom. *Royal Commission on the Donald Marshall, Jr, Prosecution*). A person would have to be stupid, complacent or ignorant not to acknowledge its presence, not only individually, but also systemically and institutionally.

So in summary then, the majority judgment acknowledges the context and says it is necessary to put the case into that context (including what is widely known about the existence and impact of racism in Nova Scotia) in order to be impartial (though 'neutrality' is impossible). The dissent, by contrast, uses 'formal equality' discourse to insist that even the mention of race/colour is a form of impermissible stereotyping: '[a]ll witnesses must be placed on equal footing before the court'.[30] So in that construction, the aggrieved person is of course the white police officer who is the victim of inappropriate stereotyping, while the history of racism in the province, including its acknowledgment by other courts and by royal commissions etc., is considered strictly irrelevant as evidence in this case.

In the article I wrote for the Justice L'Heureux-Dubé festschrift,[31] I discussed a debate that that judgment had provoked in Australia, which resulted in two published papers by judges.[32] For the purposes of this article, I take just one comment from that debate, coming from Justice Mason, President of the New South Wales Court of Appeal, in a very thoughtful article responding to the other judge's article and use it as a springboard for the remaining part of my discussion. Justice Mason discussed his judicial colleague's critique of the L'Heureux-Dubé/McLachlin judgment in *RDS*, and also of an extra judicial comment made by Justice L'Heureux-Dubé, and commented as follows:

> Judges should not aspire to neutrality. When Judges have the opportunity to recognise inequalities in society, and then to make those inequalities legally relevant to the disputes before them in order to achieve a just result, then they should do so.[33]

Justice Mason said:

> If, in a judgment, a hypothetical female Aboriginal magistrate gives effect to her attitudes about police behaviour or systemic violence to women, we tend to sit up and take notice. The media will usually ensure publicity and there will be no lack of critical commentators. Similarly, a hypothetical white male judge who betrays a now controversial attitude about female sexual complainants can expect to be taken to task by a different section of the public.[34]

He pointed out: "the same forces are at work in each situation (regardless of our approval or disapproval of the suppositions revealed in the remarks of the two hypothetical judicial officers)".[35] This idea—that expressing a point of view (any point of view) that engages with issues of equality, whether for or against equality values, is inherently problematic—is central to my concern about the impact of otherness on the way judges are perceived. In a forum in the *Canadian Journal of Women and the Law* about the *RDS* case, Canadian Professor Constance Backhouse, calls this idea—that acknowledging and drawing attention to pervasive racism, or to the systemic disadvantages experienced by women, is the same as, or equivalent to (and equally impermissible for judges as) exhibiting sexism or racism—the "peas in a pod" approach.[36]

Of course, another remarkable thing about this comment is that it assumes that the notion that police treat indigenous or racialised people badly, or that there is systemic violence against women, is 'an opinion' or 'point of view' and, moreover, an opinion or point of view on a par with the belief that women lie about rape. But unfortunately, the first 'set of ideas' is concerned with a real social problem that flows from disadvantage and inequality; the second is simply the perpetuation of long held myths and stereotypes.

Another interesting thing about the judgments in the Nova Scotia Supreme Court, the Court of Appeal and even in the Supreme Court of Canada decision is the almost complete absence of discussion of the racial dynamics of the courtroom on that day.[37] Some of the secondary discussions tell us that most of the personnel in the court room that day were African-Canadian and this had an impact on the perception of the prosecutor on the day of the trial.[38] Backhouse has suggested that this erasure of racial identity makes it easier to slip into this 'peas in a pod' approach, that is, to treat a bias complaint about racism as the same thing as a bias complaint about anti-racism. And the same applies to gender:[39]

> This is a false parallelism, unless one assumes that we inhabit a world that is scrupulously egalitarian. If our society did treat all races and genders equally, then it would be manifestly unfair for judges and adjudicators to take either race or gender into account. However, . . . [w]e live in a society in which there is a great deal of documented evidence to suggest that, at least systemically, whites continue to hold a position of dominance over people of colour, and men continue to hold a position of dominance over women. When judges are perceived to possess perspectives that support and reinforce these imbalances, you have a problem. When judges are perceived to possess perspectives that consider such imbalances to be improper and needing alteration, you have something quite different.[40]

To illustrate her point Backhouse refers to a number of government sponsored inquiries, Royal Commission reports and the like, into either racism or sexism in parts of the Canadian justice system including, of course, the Royal Commission on the Donald Marshall Jr prosecution in Nova Scotia which was referred to in the judgment of the Supreme Court in *RDS*. While perhaps not as numerous, there are many counterparts to these in Australia,[41] and in the US perhaps the best known examples are the taskforces on gender bias or racial bias or both in the justice system.[42]

Surely if racism and anti-racism, sexism and anti-sexism, were equally bad and equivalent as social problems, we would have a shelf full of reports and inquiries into anti-racism, and into the problematic nature of equality-seeking activities more broadly. In fact, not only are there no such reports, but as Backhouse points out only too clearly, a contemporaneous development with the documenting of the disadvantage of some groups within the justice system is the tendency to challenge those small numbers of 'outsider' decision makers (such as Judge Sparks) who have been appointed to the judiciary on the grounds of 'bias'.[43] There are many such challenges, including one to Backhouse herself in her role as a human rights adjudicator.[44]

This issue—the use of challenges/recusal motions against outsider decision makers on the grounds of bias—is the one that I keep returning to as part of my interest in the marginalisation of women and other outsiders. And it is not a new issue. Derrick Bell has pointed out the unselfconscious way in which challenges have been made to racialised judges about the perceived difficulty of their being impartial in race discrimination cases.[45] He argues that in the US context: "Black judges hearing racial cases are eyed suspiciously and sometimes asked to recuse themselves in favour of a white judge—without those making the request even being aware of the paradox in their motions".[46] Similarly, the late Justice Leon Higginbotham once remarked when asked to recuse himself from a race discrimination case, "[B]lack lawyers have litigated in the federal courts almost exclusively before white judges, yet they have not urged that white judges should be disqualified on matters of race relations".[47] And Judge Constance Baker Motley, an 'African-American woman judge': notice how many adjectives I have to use? was asked to recuse herself and commented

> If background or sex or race of each judge were, by definition, sufficient grounds for removal, no judge ... could hear this case or many others by virtue of the fact that all of them were attorneys, of a sex, often with distinguished lawfirm or public service backgrounds.[48]

Of course, the very use of these adjectives of colour or gender or sexuality is a marker of otherness: we don't often refer to white male judges, but a woman judge, or a racialised judge or a gay judge is frequently marked by the use of an adjective as 'other'.[49] Some years ago, a national Australian newspaper reported a successful application for special leave to appeal to the High Court of Australia by an applicant for refugee status claiming that his sexuality was the cause of persecution, under the headline "Kirby grants gays a hearing".[50] I am still waiting to see a headline that says "White male heterosexual judge grants convicted rapist a hearing".

Lest you think that the cases I refer to, particularly the US cases from the 1970s, are old, and such things would not happen now, there are more recent examples. In a fascinating discussion of the *Bush v. Gore* litigation following the 2000 US election, Professor Sherilyn Ifill draws our attention to the fact that, for all the unorthodox behaviour of judges who played some role in that saga, right up to and including members of the Supreme Court, the only actual formal challenge on the ground of bias was against an African-American woman judge in one of the lower court hearings in Florida.[51] Ifill's discussion also draws our attention to the issue of recusal challenges against African-American judges, in the context of a judiciary that remains characterised by its lack of diversity.[52]

Also in the United States, in 2005, a department store facing a class action for racially profiling customers as potential shoplifters applied to have the judge recused from hearing the case.[53] The judge was not only an African-American woman, but she had been stopped by the police while driving a Jaguar and had appeared on television to discuss this incident. The defendant argued that this, combined with their perception that her decisions on preliminary matters were antithetical to them, demonstrated her inability to be impartial. That application was dismissed (as are most such applications) but their very existence is enough to indicate that the targets of such challenges are being marked for otherness. Indeed, the challenges serve a kind of disciplinary constraining function, and remind those whose racial or gender identities are indicated by adjectives where their white counterparts are not so described, of the tenuousness of their hold on their position. Can we think of an equivalent in a world where white male judges are not the subject of police harassment, or are not stopped when driving smart cars?

The final example I raise comes from the international law arena. The response to this 'bias' challenge may give us some cautious optimism that there are alternatives to the 'peas in a pod' approach.

In 1998 in the ICTY, a man called Anto Furundzija was convicted of several acts of torture, including, among other things, rape.[54] He appealed this conviction and among the grounds he raised in his appeal was the fact that the presiding judge, Judge Mumba, had, before her appointment to the ICTY, been a member (as a representative of her government, Zambia), on the UN Commission on the Status of Women.[55] One of the things that the Commission worked on was the issue of rape in war.

Furundzija argued that for this reason, Judge Mumba should have been disqualified from hearing his case. He argued that "an appearance was created that she had sat in judgment in a case that could advance and in fact did advance a legal and political agenda which she helped to create while a member of the UNCSW".[56] Of course, he did not argue that she was actually biased, but rather, that her involvement would cause a reasonable person to have an apprehension about her impartiality.

The appeals chamber rejected this ground and made a number of comments that are of particular interest to these concerns. First, they pointed out that Judge Mumba's involvement was as a representative of her country, rather than as an individual advocate;[57] but more interesting for our purposes is their view on the actual issues involved. The chamber said:

> Secondly, even if it were established that Judge Mumba expressly shared the goals and objectives of the UNCSW and the Platform for Action, in promoting and protecting the human rights of women, that inclination, being of a general nature, is distinguishable from an inclination to implement those goals and objectives as a Judge in a particular case. It follows that she could still sit on a case and impartially decide upon issues affecting women.[58]

After pointing out that the UNCSW's objectives "merely reflected the objectives of the United Nations", the appeals chamber could find "no reason why the fact that Judge Mumba may have shared these objectives should constitute a circumstance which would lead a reasonable and informed observer to reasonably apprehend bias".[59] They continued:

> To endorse the view that rape as a crime is abhorrent and that those responsible for it should be prosecuted within the constraints of the law cannot in itself constitute grounds for disqualification.

The appeals court also referred to, among other authorities, the decision in *R v. RDS* and echoed the sentiment of Justices L'Heureux Dubé and McLachlin by commenting: "Absolute neutrality on the part of a judicial officer can hardly if ever be achieved".[60]

Finally, the Appeals Chamber addressed the argument that had been made against Judge Mumba based upon her prior membership of the UNCSW. They drew attention to Article 13(1) of the Court's Statute, which provided that "[i]n the overall composition of the Chambers due account shall be taken of the experience of the judges in criminal law, international law, including international humanitarian law and human rights law", and discussed the extent to which her previous role with the UNCSW and her broader general experience would be relevant to the statutory qualifications. As they noted:

> The possession of this experience is a statutory requirement for Judges to be elected to this Tribunal. It would be an odd result if the operation of an eligibility requirement were to lead to an inference of bias. Therefore, Article 13(1) should be read to exclude from the category of matters or activities which could indicate bias, experience in the specific areas identified. In other words, the possession of experience in any of those areas by a Judge cannot, in the absence of the clearest contrary evidence, constitute evidence of bias or partiality.[61]

So what are we to make of these cases? How do we properly acknowledge the very real dynamics of racial or gender hierarchy in legal decision making? The minority dissenting judgment in *RDS*, or indeed the Australian judge's comments that I highlighted, would suggest that any recognition of racial difference is discriminatory and impermissible, and, likewise, to paraphrase the way this was dealt with in Furundzija, any acknowledgement of the gender-specific nature of a particular form of harm, such as rape in war, would give rise to a perception of bias. This presupposes that all references to race or gender hierarchy are racist or sexist and leaves no room for legal decision-making which seeks to recognise that racialisation and gender hierarchy impact upon people unequally and can negatively affect how people are treated and how their legal rights are infringed or upheld.

So my purpose in doing this work is to try to start a conversation about how we might try to identify when it is appropriate to explicitly take race or ethnic origin, gender, or sexuality into account and how, if at all, we might start to develop a language and a methodology for doing so effectively. As a start, we need to understand that attention to race or gender or sexuality may well be essential to understanding the context in which a legal dispute arises, rather than assuming that any such reference is impermissible. But to do that effectively, we need to draw a distinction between negatively stereotyping on the one hand, and constructively recognising differences and disadvantage in a way that is sensitive to discrimination and inequality, on the other. We also need to work very hard at unpacking what lies behind law's use of notions of 'common sense' which, of course, accords with dominant euro-centric and patriarchal views. By means of the processes of naturalisation and rendering whiteness and maleness and other sorts of privilege and entitlement invisible, common sense notions have for too long been insulated from criticism or critical evaluation. By contrast, outsider perspectives are treated as specialised, emotionally-based, agenda-driven and political. It seems to me that our project is to try to redraw those boundaries between the natural or the 'neutral' and the 'other'.

Acknowledgements

This discussion has benefited from the opportunity to discuss the ideas in a number of different forums including Cornell Law School; Columbia Law School; Washington College of Law, American University; Santa Clara Law School; CUNY Law School; Cleveland-Marshall Law School; University of Sydney Law School; and the Gender and Judging group at the Law and Society Association Conference, Berlin, 2007. I should also like to thank the many people who have made comments and suggestions or assisted in other ways over the years: these include Christine Chinkin, Ruthann Robson, Jenny Morgan, Jane Wangmann, Fleur Beaupert and Tiffany Hambley. Thanks also to the anonymous referees for their helpful suggestions.

Notes

[1] See Reg Graycar, The gender of judgments: an introduction, in: Margaret Thornton (Ed.) *Public and Private: Feminist Legal Debates* (Oxford University Press Australia and New Zealand, 1995); Reg Graycar, The gender of judgments: some reflections on 'bias' (1998) 32 *University of British Columbia Law Review* 1.

[2] Reg Graycar, Claire L'Heureux-Dubé: some reflections from Down Under, in: Elizabeth Sheehy (Ed.) *Adding Feminism to Law: The Contribution of Justice Claire L'Heureux-Dubé* (Irwin Law Inc., 2004), pp. 81–107.

[3] For an interesting discussion of the ways in which ascriptions (or in some cases the erasure) of racial identities is used, see Constance Backhouse, Bias in Canadian law: a lopsided precipice, in: Christine Boyle *et al.*, *R v. RDS*: an Editor's forum (1998) 10 *Canadian Journal of Women and the Law* 159 at 172–4.

[4] *RDS v. R* [1997] 3 SCR 484 ('*RDS*').

[5] At the time they were the only two women on the court; there are now four women among the nine judges of the Court: they are Chief Justice Beverley McLachlin, appointed to the Supreme Court of Canada on 30 March 1989 and appointed Chief Justice on 7 January 2000; Justice Marie Deschamps, appointed on 7 August 2002; Justice Rosalie Silberman Abella, appointed in August 2004; Justice Louise Charron, appointed on 30 August 2004: Supreme Court of Canada, Judges of the Court, Current Judges, available at: http://www.scc-csc.gc.ca/court-cour/ju/cju-jua-eng.asp (last accessed 8 October 2008).

[6] *Prosecutor v. Furundzija* (Appeals Chamber) Case No IT-95-17/1 (21 July 2000), (Judgment) ('Furundzija'): International Criminal Tribunal for Yugoslavia, ICTY Cases & Judgments, available at: http://www.un.org/icty/furundzija/appeal/judgement/index.htm (last accessed 25 January 2008).

[7] *Dillard's Inc. v. Michael J. Scott* [2005] 908 So.2d 93.

[8] See Graycar (1995), *op. cit.*, (1998), *op. cit.* See also Regina Graycar and Jenny Morgan, *The Hidden Gender of Law*, 2nd edition (Sydney, Federation Press, 2002), Ch. 4.

[9] For other discussions of this case, see Richard Devlin, We can't go on together with suspicious minds: judicial bias and racialized perspective in *R v RDS* (1995) 18 *Dalhousie Law Journal* 408; Boyle *et al.*, *op. cit.* at 159.

[10] The proceedings were heard at first instance in the Nova Scotia Youth Court: [1994] NSJ No 629, cited in *RDS* at [70], per Cory J.

[11] *R v. RDS*, Y093-168 (2 December 1994), cited in Devlin, *op. cit.* at 411 ('*R v. RDS* #1'). The judge issued supplementary reasons following the filing of the appeal to the Nova Scotia Supreme Court (Trial Division).

[12] *R v. RDS* #1, cited in *RDS* [1997] 3 SCR 484 at [4], per Major J, his emphasis omitted.

[13] *RDS v. R* [1995] NSJ No 184 (NSSC).

[14] *R v. RDS* [1995] 145 NSR (2d) 284 (NSCA).

[15] *RDS* [1997] 3 SCR 484. The main judgment was written by Justices McLachlin and L'Heureux-Dubé (with whom La Forest and Gonthier JJ agreed); Cory J wrote a separate concurring judgment (with which Iacobucci J agreed); Lamer CJ, Sopinka and Major JJ dissented.

[16] Iacobucci and Cory JJ at [52].

[17] Major and Sopinka JJ and Lamer CJ.

[18] For a discussion of some of the issues of LEAF and its 'representativeness', see Lise Gotell, Towards a democratic practice of feminist litigation?: LEAF's changing approach to charter equality, in: Rahda Jhappan (Ed.) *Women's Legal Strategies in Canada* (University of Toronto Press, 2002).

[19] Major J, with whose judgment Lamer CJ and Sopinka J agreed.

[20] RDS [1997] 3 SCR 484 at [9].

[21] *Ibid.*, at [16]

[22] *RDS* [1997] 3 SCR 484 at 29.

[23] Benjamin Cardozo, *The Nature of the Judicial Process* (New Haven, Yale University Press, 1921).

[24] RDS [1997] 3 SCR 484 at [34].

[25] *Ibid.*, at [34–5].

[26] Martha Minow, Stripped down like a runner, or enriched by experience: bias and impartiality of judges and jurors (1992) 33 *William and Mary Law Review* 1201 at 1214.

[27] RDS [1997] 3 SCR 484 at [38].

[28] *Ibid.*, at [46].

[29] See for example the decision of the Ontario Court of Appeal in *R v. Parks* [1993] 15 OR (3d) 324.

[30] Major and Sopinka JJ and Lamer CJ at [20].

[31] Graycar (1995), *op. cit.*

[32] David Ipp, Judicial impartiality and judicial neutrality: is there a difference? (2000) 19 *Australian Bar Review* 212; Justice Keith Mason, Unconscious judicial prejudice (2001) 75 *Australian Law Journal* 676. Justice Ipp criticised the judgment on the grounds that it undermined the concept of judicial neutrality.

[33] Mason, *op. cit.*, 676 at 678–9, quoting Justice Claire L'Heureux-Dubé, Reflections on judicial independence, impartiality and the foundations of equality (1999) 7 *CILJ Yearbook* 95 at 106.

[34] Mason, *op. cit.*, at 680.

[35] *Ibid.* Of course, in Australia, there is only one such easily identifiable woman, though there are probably many more of the latter type of judicial officer.

[36] Backhouse, *op. cit.*, at 175. Boyle *et al.*, *op. cit.*, at 160, opened the discussion: "At a time when some, albeit limited, progress is being made in diversifying the bench, the decision provides food for thought on theories of judicial impartiality as well as on the role of 'the other' and, in particular, the racialized 'other' in perceptions of impartiality. It invites consideration of judicial notice, the

appropriate use of generalizations in assessments of credibility, the meaning of 'evidence', the role of storytelling in the construction of 'facts', and the values that construct the reasonable person".

[37] Having read the Supreme Court judgments knowing something of the background, I was intrigued to have pointed out to me by students that the judge's racial identity was not mentioned until the last of the three separate judgments in the Supreme Court (by Cory J). Before the matter came to the Supreme Court, the only express mention of her racial identity was contained in the dissenting judgment of Freeman JA in the Nova Scotia Court of Appeal as follows:

> [61] In supplementary reasons for judgment filed after the appeal, and which do not play a part in it, Judge Sparks referred to the racial configuration of the court "which consisted of the accused, the defence counsel, the court reporter and the judge all being of African-Canadian ancestry".
>
> [62] The case was racially charged, a classic confrontation between a white police officer representing the power of the state and a black youth charged with an offence. Judge Sparks was under a duty to be sensitive to the nuances and implications, and to rely on her own common sense which is necessarily informed by her own experience and understanding.

[38] See, for example, Devlin, *op. cit.*, at 411.

[39] Backhouse, *op. cit.*, at 174–5.

[40] *Ibid.*

[41] On the disadvantage of women in the Australian legal system, see for example Australian Law Reform Commission, *Equality Before the Law: Women's Access to the Legal System, Interim Report No 67* (Sydney, ALRC, 1994); Australian Law Reform Commission, *Equality Before the Law: Justice for Women, Report No 69, Part I* (Sydney, ALRC, 1994); Australian Law Reform Commission, *Equality Before the Law, Women's Equality, Report No 69, Part II* (Sydney, ALRC, 1994); *Gender Bias and the Judiciary, Report by the Senate Standing Committee on Legal and Constitutional Affairs* (Canberra, Australian Government Publishing Service, 1994). Note also non-government initiatives, such as: Law Society of NSW, *Getting Through the Door is Not Enough: An Examination of the Equal Opportunity Response of the Legal Profession in the 1990s* (Law Society of NSW, 1993); *Equality of Opportunity for Women at the Victorian Bar* (Victorian Bar Council, 1998). See Rosemary Hunter & Helen McKelvie, Gender and legal practice (1999) 24 *Alternative Law Journal* 57; Keys Young, *Research on Gender Bias and Women Working in the Legal Profession, Report Prepared for the Department for Women* (Department of Women, 1995); and NSW Ministry for the Status and Advancement of Women, *Gender Bias and the Law: Women Working in the Legal Profession in NSW, summary report*, (March 1995). On racism, see for example Commissioner Ronald Wilson, *Bringing Them Home: Report of the National Enquiry into the Separation of Aboriginal and Torres Strait Islander Children From Their Families* (Sydney, Australian Government Publishing Service, 1997), full text available online at: http://www.austlii.edu.au/au/special/rsjproject/rsjlibrary/hreoc/stolen/; Commissioner Elliott Johnston, *National Report: Royal Commission into Aboriginal Deaths in Custody* (Canberra, Australian Government Publishing Service, 1991), available online at: http://www.austlii.edu.au/au/special/rsjproject/rsjlibrary/rciadic/. Note also conferences and events such as *Beyond Tolerance: A National Conference on Racism*, convened by the Human Rights and Equal Opportunity Commission (HREOC), Sydney Opera House, 12 and 13 March 2002, speeches and papers reproduced online at: http://www.humanrights.gov.au/racial_discrimination/conferences/beyond_tolerance/speeches.html.

[42] In the 1980s and 1990s, a majority of states and some of the Federal Circuit courts of appeal conducted task forces on Gender and/or Racial Bias in the Law: for an overview of task forces on gender and racial bias in the law and the history of the task force movement see Judith Resnik, Gender matters, race matters (1997) 14 *New York Law School Journal of Human Rights* 219; Myra C. Selby, Examining race and gender bias in the courts: a legacy of indifference or opportunity (1999) 32 *Indiana Law Review* 1167. For gender bias-specific commentary, see Barbara Allen Babcock, Introduction: gender bias in the courts and civil and legal education (1992–93) 16 *Stanford Law Review* 2143 at 2143–4; Kimberly A. Lonsway *et al.*, Understanding the judicial role

in addressing gender bias: a view from the Eighth Circuit federal court system (2002) 27 *Law and Social Inquiry* 205. More recently, studies of bias in the justice system have expanded to consider intersections between gender, race, and ethnicity. See, for example, Jay C. Carlisle, Synopsis of the report of the Second Circuit task force on gender, racial and ethnic fairness in the courts (1998–99) 19 *Pace Law Review* 431; the Final Report of the Pennsylvania Supreme Court Committee on Racial and Gender Bias in the Justice System, appointed in October 1999, contained a chapter on the intersection of racial and gender bias in which it was reported, inter alia, that "female litigants of color" experienced additional hurdles which were exacerbated by poverty and linked to the "gap in experience and understanding between middle-class Caucasian judges and poor minority litigants" (at 548): Interbranch Commission for Gender, Racial and Ethnic Fairness, available at: http://www.courts.state.pa.us/NR/rdonlyres/EC162941-F233-4FC6-9247-54BFE3D2840D/0/FinalReport.pdf (last accessed 8 October 2008).

[43] Her article outlines the spate of "lopsided" challenges against decision makers presumed to be biased because of their racialisation, or their purported "feminism": Backhouse, *op. cit.*, at 178–83. See also the discussion in Maryka Omatsu, The fiction of judicial impartiality (1995) 8 *Canadian Journal of Women and the Law* 528; and Graycar (1998), *op. cit.*, at 1. Interestingly, a number of white male judges have drawn attention to the existence of racism without incident: for some examples, see *R v. Parks* [1993] 15 OR (3d) 324 at 342 (per Doherty JA); and from Australia, *B and R and Separate Representative* [1995] FLC 92-636 (Family Court, Full Court). The present Chief Justice of the High Court of Australia, Gleeson CJ, once endorsed criticism of the defence of provocation on the grounds that, with respect to this defence, "the law's concession to human frailty was very much, in its practical application, a concession to male frailty": *Muy Ky Chhay* [1994] 72 A Crim R 1 at 11 (NSW Court of Criminal Appeal).

[44] Backhouse recounts how in 1993, when she held a part-time appointment as a human rights adjudicator, she was successfully removed from a sex discrimination case for bias because she had been one of 120 complainants in a systemic discrimination case against a university: *Great Atlantic & Pacific Co of Canada v. Ontario (Human Rights Commission)* [1993] 13 OR (3d) 824 (Gen Div). She further notes that "bias challenges for 'feminist' perspectives have also affected the Supreme Court of Canada", given that in the early 1990s both Justice Bertha Wilson and Justice Beverley McLachlin had complaints of bias lodged against them by the conservative women's organisation, REAL Women of Canada. In both instances, "feminist perspective" or "feminist ideology" were said to negate the judge's "impartiality" or to undermine "the integrity of the court": Backhouse, *op. cit.*, at 180. Note also the controversy that followed the decision of the Supreme Court of Canada in *R v. Ewanchuk* [1999] 1 SCR 330; Ed Ratushny, Speaking as judges: how far can they go? (2000) 11 *National Journal of Constitutional Law* 293 at 387–401 provides an excellent overview of the vituperative response (particularly on the part of Justice McClung) that followed Justice L'Heureux-Dubé's judgment in Ewanchuk. The complaints that followed from that are discussed in the chapter referred to in note 2 above.

[45] Derrick Bell, *Faces at the Bottom of the Well: The Permanence of Racism* (New York, Basic Books, 1993).

[46] *Ibid.*, at 113.

[47] *Pennsylvania v. Local Union 542, International Union of Operating Engineers* 388 F Supp 155, at 177 (Ed Pa, 1974), per Higginbotham J.

[48] *Blank v. Sullivan & Cromwell* 418 F. Supp. 1 (SDNY 1975).

[49] See Graycar (1998), *op. cit.*, 1 at 2–3 where I suggest that, when we talk about judges, adjectives are almost invariably used only to indicate that a judge is NOT white, male, or heterosexual; we rarely use those descriptions, while 'women', 'African-American or African-Canadian', 'Aboriginal', or 'gay' are commonly used indicators of 'difference'.

[50] Benjamin Haslem, Kirby grants gays a hearing, *The Australian*, 24 October 2002, p. 3.

[51] Sherilyn Ifill, Do appearances matter?: judicial impartiality and the Supreme Court in Bush v Gore (2002) 61 *Maryland Law Review* 606 at 639–41. The judge whose disqualification was sought, Judge Nikki Clark, denied President Bush's recusal motion, as did the Federal Court of Appeals on appeal.

[52] *Ibid.*, especially at 642–5.

[53] *Dillard's Inc. v. Michael J. Scott* [2005] 908 So.2d 93.

[54] *Furundzija* (Trial Chamber) Case No IT-95-17/1 (10 December 1998), (Judgment): International Criminal Tribunal for Yugoslavia, ICTY Cases & Judgments ('Furundzija'), available at: http://www.un.org/icty/furundzija/trialc2/judgement/index.htm (last accessed 8 October 2008).

[55] *Prosecutor v Furundzija* (Appeals Chamber) Case No IT-95-17/1 (21 July 2000), available at: http://www.un.org/icty/furundzija/appeal/judgement/index.htm (last accessed 8 October 2008).

[56] *Ibid.*, at 169.

[57] *Ibid.*, at 199.

[58] *Ibid.*, at 200.

[59] *Ibid.*, at 202.

[60] *Ibid.*, at 203.

[61] *Ibid.*, at 200–5. There is a remarkable resonance here with an earlier Australian case in which an Aboriginal adjudicator, appointed to a human rights hearing body, was recused on the ground that she had indicated that her daughter had been refused service in a bar the subject of a complaint: *Koppen v. Commissioner for Community Relations* [1986] 67 ALR 215. This case was discussed in Graycar (1995), *op. cit.*, (1998), *op. cit.*; Graycar and Morgan, *op. cit.*

Thinking about gender and judging

Sally J. Kenney

Abstract *Reviewing the work of three political scientists who studied women judges provides an opportunity for rethinking the concept of gender and how to do gender-based research. Scholarship on women judges sometimes veers toward an essentialist view of women and gender differences, despite empirical evidence to the contrary. A close reading of this early work reveals some essentialist missteps but also offers strong examples of research across many methodologies that should serve as exemplars for current research across disciplines. If we move beyond the question of whether women decide cases differently from men, using sex as a variable, like other gender-based research strategies, can provide useful feminist insights.*

1. Introduction

How should we think about gender differences in ways that are theoretically sophisticated, empirically true, and do not lead to women's disadvantage? Political scientists who study women judges have been grappling with this problem for 30 years. Carefully examining the body of work of three pioneering scholars, Beverly Blair Cook, Elaine Martin and Sue Davis, yields insights beyond the particular subject matter and helps us to understand sex and gender more generally. Legal academics, sociologists, historians, and other scholars are increasingly studying gender and judging across jurisdictions and legal systems (Schultz & Shaw, 2003). Yet rarely does that work incorporate the insights of political scientists—a pity since political scientists advance gender theory, apply social science research methods, and understand judicial selection as a political process. Overlooking this early relevant work contributes to two problems in contemporary research. First, although she frequently functions as a straw woman, educational psychologist Carol Gilligan's work as applied to the question of whether women judges reason in a different voice has come to define *the* feminist approach to gender and judging and hampers our ability to theorise effectively about difference. Second, this dominance worsens rather than recedes over time. As new scholars take up questions of gender and judging, rather than build on their predecessors, many fall into the same predictable trap of essentialism. Even some of the later work of the three scholars I consider in depth falls into essentialism. Therefore, this essay argues that the earliest work in the field offers insights that repay careful consideration.

In this essay, I review the work of Beverly Blair Cook, Elaine Martin and Sue Davis. These three scholars are exemplary in at least four ways relevant to contemporary scholars. They theorise gender as a social process rather than treat sex as an essential difference. They investigate sex differences empirically rather than assume them. They treat women as a varied group and see feminism as something women (as well as some men) espouse to different degrees (if at all). They investigate gender beyond the question of whether women judges decide cases differently from men. Their work spans different research methods. My analysis is not confined to one approach; rather, I shall show how each methodological approach can illuminate the production of gender. Similarly, scholars have produced deeply flawed work within each method. I begin by defining my concepts of sex and gender and discuss sex as a variable. I then examine scholarship that treats sex as a variable: first, women judges in the political opportunity structure, second, judges' attitudes as inputs to decisions, and third, sex differences in judicial decisions, in general, in cases on sex discrimination, and in cases of divorce.

2. Sex and gender

Sex, meaning biological sex differences, has dropped from the lexicon, in favour of gender, making the distinction more confused than ever. Most feminists now theorise gender as a social process rather than an essential dichotomous difference, and use the word as both an adjective—gendered—as well as a verb. While gender differentiation is ubiquitous, which activities or attributes become the basis of differentiation vary, even within different groups (classes or races) of the same society at the same time, as well as across time and cultures. Gender differentiation thus does not flow inevitably from sex differences; rather it is the process by which we attach meaning to sex differences, most often to devalue whatever society associates with women (Chamallas, 2003). We must explore the construction of and asserted content of gender differences empirically rather than assume them (Kenney, 1996). Using gender to mean a sex binary may distort and conceal as much as it illuminates. Scientists have shown repeatedly that women differ as much from other women as they do from men, whether the attribute is strength, mathematical reasoning ability, or the ability to calm toddlers. The categories are overlapping bell curves not two non-intersecting wholes. Regardless of this fact, even though studies often find no differences, scholars continue to look for them and assume they are merely masked rather than address squarely what these inconsistent findings mean for gender theory.

3. Sex as a variable

Although postmodernism leads feminists to be sceptical of binaries such as male and female, not all attempts to use sex as a variable are misguided. Evidence does occasionally show differences worthy of feminists' attention. In some cases we are right to question the sample size from which a sex difference is declared. Findings based on a few trial judges in Wisconsin, a few women agonising over abortion in Massachusetts, or even all judges in Michigan at one point in time do not prove essential sex differences. The problem is not the finding, but the meanings attached to it. If we abandoned the search for the essential sex difference that persists across time and place, we might be able to say some more interesting things about gender differences with empirical support. Rather than discovering an essentially different voice, we might uncover tendencies particular to a cohort. Why is it, for example, that we can generalise about baby boomers, or the approach of German judges on the International Court of Human Rights or European Court of Justice, in ways that do not lead to the same sort of essentialising we see when we find sex differences? If we could find a way to talk about tendencies and overlaps—if sex were one variable among many—feminist scholars might not have to be so worried about essentialism.

Besides the dangers of overgeneralisation that lead to claims of a false dichotomy, such research may wrongly claim sex to be the explanation when sex masks other determinants. President Carter, for example, appointed more judges to the federal bench than all other presidents combined and a higher percentage of women judges than any other president until President Clinton. If one finds sex differences among federal judges, it may merely be an artefact of the appointing president. But if one avoids this second pitfall by controlling for party, ideology, even such things as experience as a prosecutor versus experience as a public defender, then one is left with the concept of sex as a residual variable. Such an approach is at odds with a growing tendency to think of gender intersectionally within feminist theory.[1] Identity categories work in many intersecting ways that are patterned if not true for all members of the group. Not all black women think alike, but black women lawyers who went to law school in the 1970s were likely to have had many common experiences. By stripping away class, race, sexual orientation, to drill down to the core of what constitutes sex differences, one inevitably approaches sex as a biological category (one that feminists reject) instead of gender as a social process, a process that is intersectional, not just something that happens to women who are otherwise privileged. If using sex as a variable has a number of limitations, it also has great utility for feminist scholars when done well.

3.1. *Women judges in the political opportunity structure*

Unfortunately, comparisons between men and women continue to expose unfairness. Such an approach has radical implications for thinking about merit and the best process for choosing judges. By comparing the treatment of women lawyers considered (or not) for judgeships, and studying women's progress (or lack thereof) up the hierarchy, we can document differential treatment because of sex, the doctrinally simplest form of sex discrimination which, unfortunately, remains pervasive. The first political scientist to study women judges was Beverly Blair Cook and she did so at a time when women in political science, as well as research on gender, were both unwelcome. Although Cook came from a strong judicial behaviour background,[2] her use of sex as a variable is not reductive; she explored gender as a social process.

In her 1980 chapter, "Political Culture and Selection of Women Judges in Trial Courts", Cook laid a foundation for future scholars by identifying every woman who has ever served as a judge on state or federal courts in the United States. Cook wrestled with how to think about the position of these women she will come to call tokens. Anticipating feminist standpoint theory, she recognised feminist consciousness does not flow inevitably from women's experience (1980b, 49) and that women who do operate in the world of men may not be advocates for women or even themselves. As she considered the obstacles to feminist consciousness and advocacy, Cook implicitly assumed that women's difference exists and would have an impact but for these systemic barriers. She would later look for evidence of these hypothesised latent differences empirically.

Before she did so, Cook sought to explain the variation in the number of women in different jurisdictions. Some states had no women judges while California had 20. Differences in state subcultures provided some explanatory power for these differences. She found the size of the court mattered enormously but the method of selection did not. In an earlier study, Cook documented women's exclusion from higher prestige courts, and the efforts of judges to shunt women into special jurisdictional courts dealing with family and juvenile law (1978b). How many women should we expect to be serving on the bench given the pool of eligibles, assuming no discrimination? Between 1920 and 1970, states varied as to whether 1 or 5% of lawyers were women and 1–10% of trial court judges were women. She hypothesised that as the number of eligible women increases, we might expect the number of women judges to increase.

Cook traced the 12 chances Florence Allen—the first woman on the Ohio Supreme Court and the first woman on any federal appeals court and the only woman on a federal appeals court for 32 years (she sat on the Sixth Circuit)—had to be appointed to the US Supreme Court (1980a). Cook effectively documented Allen's exclusion from the group of insiders most eligible for appointment: close friends of the president, champions of the New Deal (particularly Roosevelt's court-packing plan), and senators. As the social movement that produced suffrage waned and elites turned against unmarried women partnered with other women, such as Florence Allen (Faderman, 2000), homophobia may also have played a role (Organ, 1998, pp. 228, 242). In 1982, Cook compared Florence Allen's 12 unsuccessful attempts to reach the Supreme Court to the process that yielded the first woman Supreme Court justice, Sandra Day O'Connor. Cook set their credentials against other Supreme Court justices and found elite education, politically active and connected families, and comfort if not affluence in both Allen and O'Connor's background, as in nearly all of the justices. Noting that only eight of 101 male justices were unmarried, Cook contrasted Allen's unmarried status (without remarking on her two lengthy partnerships with women) with O'Connor's marriage, three children, and break from work when her children were small, making her life experiences closer to the experience of most American women than Allen's and therefore more acceptable to her appointing authorities. Cook plotted women's groups' first involvement in the process in recommending three women candidates for the Arthur Goldberg vacancy. The first formal project to place women on the federal bench was the National Women's Political Caucus's project which began in 1977. Cook showed how the American Bar Association's Standing Committee's evaluations of potential women nominees thwarted women's progress and echoed the views of many, such as Chief Justice Burger, that no qualified woman existed. When President Reagan gave the committee O'Connor's name in 1980, the committee had reluctantly accepted the viability of women candidates and had its first woman member, who also became the chair.

In her 1984 article entitled "Women Judges: A Preface to Their History", Cook argued that only when three factors have been achieved will women's numbers rise: an increase in the number of judicial positions to be filled, an increase in the numbers of eligible women, and an increase in the number of gatekeepers positively inclined to give women fair consideration, although she also recognised the importance of the pressure exerted by a strong feminist movement. Cook ultimately rejected the 'trickle up' argument: that women will automatically increase their numbers on the bench as their numbers in the legal profession rise. Instead, she carefully documented the factors that thwart women's proportional representation. A significant finding was that the larger the size of the court, whether they are superior and municipal courts as a whole, federal appellate courts, or state supreme courts, the greater the likelihood of a woman member. She documented the admission of women to the bar, their progress, the number of women Supreme Court clerks and law professors, noting the importance of serving as a clerk or working in a prestigious law firm for being on the fast track for high judicial office. She also documented the interval between a state's admission of women to the bar and appointment of women to the state trial court supreme court (104 years for Iowa, which admitted the first woman to the bar, 110 years for Missouri, which took the longest, the average being 50). Vital gatekeepers, such as the law professors who suggest law clerks to Supreme Court justices, do not recommend women in proportion to their increasing numbers.

Although her earlier findings found women appointed proportionate to their representation in the legal profession, by 1984, Cook found a disparity between the numbers of women judges we might expect based on the number of women lawyers of 50%, and found the transition from non-attorney to attorney judges to have reduced the proportion of women serving. She traced the career paths of women judges. Contrary to her earlier finding that the method of selection did not affect the proportion of women judges, Cook found women more likely to find a place on the bench through appointment rather than election and that having women on appointing panels increases the number of women chosen. Women have the best chance of serving on a state bench in a large state with an elective system, strong party organisations, and weak interest groups, under Democratic Party hegemony. Political scientists will continue to explore whether the type of selection system affects the numbers of women selected (Alozie, 1996; Cook, 1988; Bratton & Spill, 2002).

After Beverly Blair Cook, Elaine Martin is the political scientist with the most sustained body of work on women judges. Like Cook, she used sex as a variable to see if presidents use different criteria for choosing men and women judges. In 1982, Martin explored the disparate impact[3] of using the criterion of being well known by senior judges as the basis for choosing judges. Her survey found that 43% of the women felt that they would not have been considered under the previous system rather than merit selection because they lacked the political influence and credentials. Carter was looking for women with a profound commitment to 'equal justice under the law' and 90% of the women he appointed had accepted pro bono work or worked for legal aid, and 90% had shown a demonstrable commitment to feminism. If Carter's women judges behaved differently than men once on the bench, it might well be because he carefully chose them from among feminists rather than because of either an essential female difference or from having experienced life as a woman. Martin may not be prepared to second the National Women's Political Caucus's researcher Ness's claim that the American Bar Association (ABA) blatantly discriminated against women and minority men by giving them lower scores when they presented identical credentials, but she did consider a second example of disparate impact: how the ABA's criteria of valuing large firm experience made it nearly impossible for women to pass muster because large firms refused to hire women attorneys. Rather than emphasise women's difference as a claim to their presence on the bench, Martin suggested that if we use objective criteria of merit, women are more deserving than the men Carter appointed. By de-emphasising political connections, Carter's merit commissions let the women candidates' stronger academic credentials emerge. Moreover, Martin suggested that circuit nominating commissions imposed a standard of judicial experience on women but not men candidates because they were skittish about women's abilities. President Reagan placed little priority on diversity but continued to employ a gender double standard. He required women but not men to have had either judicial or prosecutorial experience. Moreover, all of the politically active women appointed by Reagan were active at the national level, in national Republican politics, or presidential or senatorial campaigns (Martin, 1987, p. 140). Martin suggested that women may have had to meet a stronger ideological test than men.[4] She showed the value of using sex as a variable. Comparing men and women provided a basis for rethinking our notions of merit—academic excellence, or knowing a Senator? Is large firm experience perhaps more relevant for the prospective trial judge and judicial experience more relevant for the appellate judge? Interrogating existing standards may expose misogyny by laying bare double standards. Lastly, Martin gave us insight into where a different voice might come from if we find it empirically, and to expect it to be transitory and variable.

According to Martin (2004b), Bush (41)'s[5] record of appointing women improved upon Reagan's and even Carter's, although his interest in appointing women occurred only after the Clarence Thomas hearings, and half of these appointments date from the year he ran unsuccessfully for re-election. Moreover, he mostly elevated women Reagan had appointed, rather than expanded the number of women overall serving on the federal bench. President Bush, therefore, only after the Thomas confirmation, like candidate Reagan before him, perceived an electoral advantage in appointing more women to the federal bench. (Reagan had promised to appoint a woman to the US Supreme Court.) White men were a minority of Clinton's appointments and Clinton's judicial selection team included many women.

Martin's findings were supported and elaborated by other studies. Scherer (2005) showed that Clinton appointed the largest number of women and the largest percentage of women to the bench of any president. Women nominees, however, were more likely to run into trouble with the Republican-controlled Senate. Although diverse, Clinton's appointees were ideologically moderate and indistinguishable in their votes from Bush (41)'s judges. Clinton's women appointees were more likely than men to be sitting judges and less likely to come from private firms. More women, however, now have experience as prosecutors, particularly in the US Attorney's offices, a traditional pipeline to the bench. Presidents seem to hold women to a higher standard of experience either as a judge or a prosecutor than men. Studies by Citizens for Independent Courts showed that the Senate took five months to take action on Clinton's male appointees, while they took eight months to take action on Clinton's female and minority appointees (Biskupic, 2000).

Williams (2007) examined gender and ambition for judicial office among Texas lawyers. Although she found fewer women in her sample declaring ambition for judicial office, she found women more likely than men to express ambition after controlling for other factors. Jensen and Martinek (2007) examined how women candidates fared in judicial elections, finding women, but especially Republican women, to be more successful than men. Githens's 1995 study as a participant observer on the Maryland judicial nominating commission, however, showed the importance of thinking of gender as a social process even as we simply compare the standards imposed on men versus women. Ambition is a social construction, not an inherent sex trait that boys or girls either have or lack at birth; rather it is nourished in some and discouraged in others—nourished, in fact, through the very social processes such as how judicial nominating commissions treat applicants (Lawless & Fox, 2005). Githens demonstrated that the Maryland judicial nominating commission treated men and women with aspirations for the bench differently. Commissioners perceived women as 'uppity' for seeking to rise above their station. Conversely, commissioners regarded men who applied for judgeships as lacking in ambition since judgeships paid far less than practice in a large firm.

3.2. *Sex differences as inputs and the cause of hypothetical outputs*

Once a sufficient number of women were on the bench to study, research on the barriers to women's full equality in securing judicial office receded and the question of how decisions of women judges differed from those of men came to dominate. In 1981, Cook surveyed the 170 women sitting on state courts, and a comparative sample of men. She hypothesised that women as a group would be more feminist than men on women's rights cases. Yet from the very beginning, she eschewed an essentialist approach. Cook dismissed what she called the biological model "that women will exhibit a different style of decision-making and emphasize different substantive goals compatible with certain intrinsic characteristics of the sex" (1981, p. 216), arguing that such a model—the precursor to the different voice—poses no challenge to the existing order of women's separate spheres. Rejecting both models, Cook embraced a socialisation model and added a feminist political philosophy: because women experience sexism and discrimination, "male authorities do not feel for or act for women's interests, and women authorities largely do" (1981, p. 217), a finding Patricia Yancey Martin *et al.* (2002) would later refer to as the feminist standpoint.

Cook identified judges by sex, party, and ideology, asked them whether they considered themselves feminist or supportive of the women's movement, and then asked them a couple of hypothetical questions (1981). Cook found gender gaps on each measure. She then administered two hypothetical questions and asked judges to assume that the law would support a decision for either party. One is about temporary alimony for a woman custodial parent to acquire an education, the other for a married mother to be able to change her name to her maiden name despite her husband's disapproval. Cook found consensus on the hypothetical case on alimony; but she also established that attitude and feminism but not sex and party predicted judges' behaviour on the second hypothetical case about name change.

As soon as enough women were on the federal bench to compare, Elaine Martin (1987) demonstrated the significant differences among them. Presidents Carter and Reagan both imposed extra requirements on their women appointees that they did not impose on men, albeit different ones. Carter wanted evidence of a commitment to equal justice under law; Reagan wanted either judicial or prosecutorial experience as well as evidence of involvement in Republican politics. The two groups were in closest agreement as to whether there should be a woman on the Supreme Court (100% Carter women judges/85% Reagan women judges). The gap between the two widened in their support for women in public office, and grew widest (95% to 37.5%) in their positive support for the women's movement. Martin showed that not all women judges think alike. By having previously exposed the gendered selection mechanisms, Martin showed why we might expect greater differences between Carter and Reagan women appointees than between Carter and Reagan men appointees.

In the same study, Martin also surveyed women judges attending the 1986 annual meeting of the National Association of Women Judges and compared them to a sample of men judges (1989). She modified Cook's protocol, but asked questions that allowed her to plot the gender ideology of judges and then analysed whether that led to differences in answers on increasing the number of women judges, on women judges' behaviour, on perceptions of gender bias in the courts, and on hypothetical cases that raised gender issues from battered women, to divorce, to abortion. On the important question of whether men's view of women is affected positively by the presence of women judges, men feminists were most strongly in agreement. On the next two questions, on whether women have a unique perspective and the bench does not reflect society without women members, gender, led by women feminists, showed the strongest agreement, followed by women non-feminists, then men feminists, then men non-feminists. Women judges, however, virulently disagreed about the difference gender makes. Women judges, feminists and non-feminists, were more likely than men feminists to agree with statements that women judges behaved differently from men, that they have an ability to bring people together, and that they face special problems in the justice system. Feminism, however, was more important than gender in predicting whether judges agreed with the statement that "judges sometimes treat women attorneys, witnesses or litigants in demeaning, condescending or unprofessional ways".

Martin's study had many methodological limitations. Her sample was not representative, we might question whether her scale revealed meaningful differences, she did not control for other potentially important variables, and she dealt with self-reported opinions and hypothetical cases rather than actual behaviour. Nevertheless, Martin made several important contributions. First, like Cook, she did not assume that sex is a proxy for feminism but investigated when gender produces attitudinal differences empirically. She did not treat gender as a simple dichotomy, but recognised the presence of feminist men, who may differ little from feminist women, and non-feminist women, who seem to differ less than we might think from feminist women and more than we might expect from non-feminist men. Yet her work took an essentialist turn when she condensed it for publication in a reader on women and politics under the heading the "unique contribution of women judges" (Martin, 1993, p. 178). Martin showed that feminist ideology may well be more important than gender in predicting different votes in hypothetical cases, yet treated feminism as dichotomous. The presentation of the work illustrates a recurring problem: the way feminist ideology transmorphs into sex differences and a gender continuum becomes dichotomous sex differences.

In a 1991 conference paper, Martin criticised legal academics' importation of Gilligan and Ruddick as a way of talking about hypothesised differences from the outset, instead of examining the question empirically. Martin surveyed women state and local court judges sitting on the bench in 1987 regarding their views of their representational role and the difference women make. They overwhelmingly rejected the view Martin labels token, that is the view that because of their high visibility, women judges should be more cautious than men in breaking with tradition. The highest agreement was with the statement that we need more women judges because the bench without women does not reflect the total fabric of society (85%). Fewer, but an overwhelming majority, agreed with the view that "women have certain unique perspectives and life experiences different from men that ought to be represented on the bench" (80%). Fewer still (62%) responded that women judges are probably more sensitive to claimants raising issues of sexual discrimination than are men. The biggest divisions among women, however, were with what she labels voice: that women judges have an ability in the decision-making process to bring people together in a way that men don't. The largest group (40%) disagreed with this statement, 30% agreed and 30% were neutral.

More recently, sociologist Patricia Yancey Martin examined Florida judges and found that "compared with men judges and attorneys, women judges and attorneys were more conscious of gender inequality, observed more gender bias in legal settings, and showed a stronger connection between experiences with gender bias and feminist consciousness" (Martin *et al.*, 2002, p. 669). Drawing on feminist standpoint theory, however, Martin *et al.* argue that feminist consciousness is a political achievement, not an automatic consequence of being a woman or experiencing life as a woman. Women observed more gender bias dynamics, and were more likely than men to agree with a variety of feminist principles ranging from property division post-divorce, to rejecting rape myths and negative stereotypes about domestic violence. The findings held across race. While not making claims directly for outputs, Martin *et al.* argued that the presence of women judges will make the legal system more objective, more legitimate in the eyes of women claimants, and help all judges raise their consciousness on these issues.

3.3. *Decisions as outputs*

The first study of the effects of women judges found no differences between men and women in their sentencing behaviour, even in rape cases, nor evidence that the gender of the judge interacted with the gender of the defendant (Kritzer & Uhlman, 1977; Palmer, 2001). Later analysis of the same data confirmed that although men and women judges did not differ in their overall sentencing behaviour, women judges were twice as likely as men judges to send women to jail (Gruhl *et al.*, 1981). Women judges, more so than men, treated men and women defendants similarly. Illustrative of the complex and often paradoxical way we think about gender, Kritzer and Uhlman had hypothesised that women would fear crime more than men and therefore would be tougher on criminals, particularly rapists. Gruhl *et al.*, however, hypothesised that women would be more lenient. Perhaps the most important finding, however, was buried in a footnote where Gruhl *et al.* noted that in their miniscule sample of seven, from which they were trying to determine whether sex determines sentencing behaviour, "for all three dependent variables there are more differences among the seven women judges than between the men and women judges" (1981, p. 314). Once sex was introduced into the equation as a variable, however, gender became a dichotomous difference.

In 1983, Gottschall compared the voting of Carter appointees on the Court of Appeals over a two-year period to see if they were liberal activists, as critics charged. He found Carter's appointees to be similar to those of other Democratic administrations and different from Republican appointees. In order to look for gender effects, Gottschall only compared white women to white men, displaying the view of gender as a residual variable, that which is not confounded by other factors, rather than understanding gender intersectionally. He found little difference between men and women on rights of accused and prisoners and some differences for race and sex discrimination cases, with the caveat that he analysed only 19 votes cast by women. Another study of federal district judges found male judges to be more liberal and women more likely to defer to government (Walker & Barrow, 1985). It found no significant differences between male and female US District Court judges on issues of women's rights or criminal policy. Women judges, however, were more likely to uphold government regulation and less likely to support personal liberty claims. Allen and Wall's (1987) study showed that four out of five women on four state Supreme Courts were the court's most liberal members.

Sue Davis's study of judges on the Ninth Circuit Court of Appeals (1992–93) was grounded in feminist theory. She acknowledged the critiques of Gilligan as well as the ways in which scholars often misread or misinterpret her work (Kenney, 1995). Recognising that finding a different, female, or feminine voice in one woman jurist hardly proves anything about the category of women, Davis searched for evidence of the different voice by pairing the women judges on the Ninth Circuit with their most similar men—men appointed by the same president, similar in education and background and at a similar location on the liberal–conservative spectrum. Davis's different voice looks more like a feminist voice than does Gilligan's. For Davis, the different voice is one that asks about gender; it considers the impact of the challenged practice on women. Such a voice recognises a role for the state in protecting members of the community and in valuing connection. Perhaps most controversially, the different voice eschews bright-line legal rules in lieu of pragmatism and contextual reasoning. Davis looked at equal protection and civil rights cases. She found many of the elements of the different voice in the cases she examined, but little evidence of gender differences between paired men and women, let alone a dichotomy. She concluded with agnosticism as to whether Gilligan was wrong altogether, as applied to the judiciary, or whether the sort of women who become federal judges are the sort of women who think like men. Paradoxically, her findings did not lead her to a strong criticism of Gilligan, or to reject the different voice as a way to frame gender and judging. Instead, she leaves us with the possibility that the wrong sort of women serve on the bench (too manly?) or that the male system overpowers the feminist voice.

Davis's study offered the important insight that both men and women used feminist tools of analysis in their reasoning in landmark equal protection cases out of the Ninth Circuit. Moreover, this reasoning looked a lot like other kinds of legal reasoning. What's fair? Who is disadvantaged by this rule? Who is left out of the picture by this abstraction? Whose perspective and labour is valued? Whose is devalued? Which citizens do the police protect, and which do they scorn as provoking and therefore deserving their own beatings? Some of the judges (in one case a man) fail to see the injustice in sex discrimination, but there are men who do see it, and all of the women do. Both men and women judges occasionally struggle to do justice rather than strictly follow rules, and other judges criticise them vigorously in their opinions for results oriented decisions. Davis found that whether one approached sex discrimination law as a feminist matters—it determines outcomes in important cases. Women and some men employed feminist tools of analysis. The feminist mode of reasoning is neither foreign to legal reasoning, nor inherent in women's bodies. Davis took a step forward in empirically showing that while women are likely to apply a feminist analysis of equal protection cases, some, but not all, men do too. In the end, however, she retreated from an anti-essentialist view of gender and questioned whether women judges could give full expression to either their full femininity or feminism, suggesting that only "the right sort of women"—women who accepted the yoke of the law—would be appointed in the first place.

In a subsequent study, Davis *et al.* (1993; see also Songer *et al.*, 1994) expanded the exploration of the different voice from the Ninth Circuit to the entire Court of Appeals and beyond equal treatment cases to cases on criminal procedural and obscenity. Where her matched pairs showed little difference on the Ninth Circuit, Davis *et al.* found women judges on the Court of Appeals as a whole more likely than their male colleagues to support claimants in sex discrimination cases (63–46%), and more likely than their colleagues to support the defendants in search and seizure cases (17.7–10.9%), although they found no significant differences in obscenity cases. The difference narrowed somewhat but persisted when they compared women appointed by Democratic presidents to men in employment discrimination cases, and disappeared between Republican-appointed men and women. Nor did they find differences when they factored the party of the appointing president into her analysis of search and seizure cases.

Davis and colleagues laboured to apply Gilligan whereas one might think her previous study would lead her in the opposite direction. She first interpreted the finding that women seem more likely than their male colleagues to see the harm of sex discrimination as consistent with an ethic of care that gives weight to the harm of community exclusion. Although they cited harsh critics of the Gilligan approach (Epstein, 1988), they were non-committal about what their findings show. The first alternative they considered was that the psychological and legal theories of difference were wrong. Women could support claimants in sex discrimination cases because they have experienced discrimination directly, or have encountered gender-based obstacles in their lives, or have affinity with those who have. Alternatively, perhaps the difference is not evident in a vote? They noted that to the extent they found women speaking in a different voice on the Ninth Circuit, men did too. The third possibility they considered was that law crushes the different voice, and women, as newcomers, cannot withstand law's hostility to an ethic of care. Lastly, women of the generation who are likely to be judges might either have had the ethic of care stamped out of them, or they might have been especially chosen for judicial office because they lacked this supposedly essential gender trait in the first place.

Calling for further study, Davis *et al.* ended by pointing out that until women's different approaches to legal reasoning are welcomed in the study of law, we will not really know whether women have a distinctive impact on the legal system. Implicit in their conclusion was the assumption that women are different, and we just have not been clever enough to uncover that difference empirically; alternatively, that the power of law has suppressed the difference, despite the contradictory evidence that differences were fleeting, a function of partisanship or liberalness, and despite the strong evidence that Davis found in her close textual analysis of the Ninth Circuit that men were asking the woman question and using feminist modes of analysis too. Missed was the opportunity to point out how tricky it is to operationalise Gilligan and marry a gender analysis to an ethic of care.

By 1994, Songer *et al.* equated feminist legal scholarship with the Gilligan position of difference. Gone was the thoughtful asking the woman question of the early Ninth Circuit work. Still they found little evidence of the different voice. Employing a predictive model, they found gender to add nothing to the predictive power in either obscenity cases or in search and seizure cases. As predicted, presidential appointment effects were strong. The gender of judges, however, was strongly related to the probability of a liberal vote in job discrimination cases (38% probability for men, 75% for women). They recognised that women could be more attentive to discrimination generally because of their experiences rather than because they reason in a different voice; but they then returned to the different voice as the dominant frame. They then mused whether law school stamps out the different voice in favour of rights and hierarchies—suggesting that it represses the different voice in everything but discrimination cases.

Rather than seeing law silencing women judges' different voice, perhaps what we see in Davis is political science repressing Davis's more anti-essentialist approach over time. Although she starts with a disfavoured topic—how gender affects judging—she begins with doctrinal analysis, perhaps the discipline's least approved of method.

She moves to a statistical analysis of opinions and at last, to a predictive model. In the process, however, we lose the critical eye and sophistication of feminist theory with which she began; the different voice frame thus becomes more conservative and essentialist. What is striking is that the further she moves down the path of statistical analysis, the farther away we get from any real support of the different voice with the possible exception of sex discrimination cases. Yet Gilligan remains firmly entrenched as the dominant gender frame.

3.4. *Outputs in sex discrimination cases*

"Research on state supreme courts, the US Courts of Appeals, and the US Supreme Court consistently has shown that women judges tend to be the strongest supporters of women's rights claims, regardless of their ideology" (Palmer, 2001, p. 91). Yet even that finding has varied, depending on the time period. In her 2003 essay for the *UC Davis Law Review* reviewing political science studies of whether men and women decide cases differently, legal academic Theresa Beiner is forced to conclude that "the effects of race and gender of judge are inconclusive" (p. 610). In a recent example, Jennifer Segal studied President Clinton's judicial appointees to the district courts and found the traditional (i.e. white male) judges to be more liberal (pro-plaintiff in sex discrimination cases) than non-traditional (women and minority men) appointees. Even if one might concede that as Clinton faced a Republican-dominated Senate, he knew that women nominees faced more intense scrutiny than men, one can hardly conclude, based upon Segal's findings, that Clinton's women appointees spoke in a distinctive feminine or feminist voice.

In addition to casting votes which may or may not diverge from those of colleagues, women judges may influence their male colleagues. When political scientist Nancy Crowe looked for this evidence in sex discrimination cases on the US Court of Appeals between 1981 and 1996, she found no evidence of such an effect (1999). Jennifer Peresie, however, examined how, over a three-year period where the doctrine was relatively stable, the presence of female judges on three-judge federal appellate panels affected collegial outcomes in Title VII cases on sexual harassment and sex discrimination (2005). She found that plaintiffs were twice as likely to prevail when a woman judge was on the bench. The presence of a woman judge increased the probability that a man judge would support the plaintiff. Peresie criticised previous studies for failing to control for individual characteristics other than gender, thereby magnifying the gender effect, and for not controlling for significant doctrinal changes. Peresie found that judges appointed by Democratic presidents were the most pro-plaintiff and that Democratic men and Republican women were similarly pro-plaintiff. Interestingly, Peresie found men and women judges more different from each other on an individual level in sexual harassment cases but the influence of women judges greater in sex discrimination cases. Peresie lacked an adequate theoretical account of these differences. Boyd *et al.* also found that the presence of a woman on a panel hearing a sex discrimination case made it more likely that the panel would result in a pro-plaintiff decision (2007). They believe the effect to be deliberative and to result in men changing their behaviour.

3.5. *Outputs in divorce cases*

Elaine Martin's more recent work examines state supreme courts and rulings in divorce cases (2004a). Martin zeroed in on divorce cases as the place where we might most expect gender rather than feminism to lead to differences in behaviour on the part of men and women judges, and examined the non-unanimous case decisions of the Michigan State Supreme Court over 13 years. She found Democrats to be more liberal than Republicans, African-Americans different from whites on one issue only, discrimination, and men and women to differ from each other but in the opposite direction.

> Men cast 52.3% of their votes as liberals in discrimination cases while women cast only 38.3%. The reason for this result may simply be that during most of the time period under study there was only one Democratic woman justice, who, as a former prosecutor and criminal trial court judges, was somewhat less liberal than her fellow male Democrats in two of the three issue areas (Martin, 2000, p. 1225).

This comment reveals what I find problematic about this line of research. The researcher is drawing on the tools of social science to look for patterned behaviour rather than telling idiosyncratic stories of individual judges and courts and why they decided as they did—either by reading opinions, or by drawing on history, biography, and journalism. But although we are looking at the Michigan Supreme Court over time, we are still explaining variance of a small number of people and a small number of women and minority men. So we assume gender (not feminism) leads to a difference in votes in discrimination cases, and when we do not find it, we explain it away by referring to the particular details of the case itself. The gender assumption remains even though the evidence forcefully not only fails to support it, but contradicts it.

Martin first added Minnesota and Wisconsin to her study, then all state high courts, to examine her hunch that although other studies found few gender differences, divorce cases would provide "the most fertile ground for discovering the impact of judicial gender" (2004a, p. 2). This telling phrasing reveals her belief that, finally, women's true difference from men in the form of their gendered life experiences will be evident in their decision making. Martin labelled what she hopes to find: the representative voice. She found that women judges are more likely than men to support a woman litigant in divorce cases. This difference is more pronounced if there are three women on the court but LESS if there are two—a non-linear relationship Martin cannot explain. Men are more supportive of women litigants when they serve with only one other woman and less likely if they are chosen by merit systems. Women who have more trial court experience are more supportive of women litigants.

As Martin tried to make theoretical sense of these results, the fundamental flaw in these studies emerged: the researcher looked for and either found or failed to find sex differences. A story is produced to suggest why essential differences are masked, or inconsistently found, but the research does not deploy the evidence to help us decide which story is more persuasive. A common story draws on one reading of Kanter—that women tokens, isolated on the bench, or in their profession, behave just like men. But once women reach critical mass, their true differences can emerge. The evidence that Martin and Cook have gathered on women judges in the United States suggests that the earliest women judges (particularly Republican appointees) may have been the most openly feminist, with the exception of Justice O'Connor. Davis tested for the different voice, failed to find it, and left us with the view that it is masked rather than does not exist. Peresie's theories could not explain why a woman member of a panel influenced sex discrimination cases more than sexual harassment cases. Rather than continuing to repeat the running of sex as a variable to test for the different voice, I think it is time for rethinking our theories of gender and judging where Cook began and Martin *et al.* developed.

4. Seeing gender one judge at a time

4.1. *Men judges' women's rights orientation*

As a judicial behaviouralist who adopted the attitudinal model long before it was identified as such, Cook did not see judges at the highest appellate levels as enmeshed in a discursive structure that constrained their decision making and shaped their arguments (i.e. as bound by law) but rather as able to pick and choose from precedent and interpretive canons to support their policy preferences. Rather than engaging in a textual exegesis of rules, precedents, and legal arguments, Cook mined legal texts for evidence of judicial attitudes and policy orientations. What mattered to her was who judges were and what they thought and believed about everything, not just law and the judicial role:

> In these cases, what is important is how the Justice feels about women—women on welfare, pregnant teachers, women officers, women jurors—and their demands, in relation to how the Justice feels about the other party—industry, grade school, the military establishment, the courts—and its expectations for the female role (Cook, 1978a, pp. 54–5).

Cook plotted each of the justices based upon their votes on women's rights cases and the views they express in their opinions, other writings, and speeches. Her searing critique ended with an aside: "The paternalism of the male Supreme Court justices which shines through these cases may only be ended with their closer association with female justices" (1978, p. 78). Yet Cook's assumption that women judges will necessarily support women's rights claims more strongly than feminist men is complicated by her own later analysis of the jurisprudence of Justice O'Connor. Cook also compared two women judges' views on women's rights: Florence Allen's and Sandra Day O'Connor's. Allen, a suffragist, was part of a vast network of women's groups and saw herself as a representative of women; in contrast, men politicians picked O'Connor once Ronald Reagan had promised a seat for a woman and O'Connor looked ahead to the time when sex identity would lose its significance (Cook, 1982, p. 326).

4.2. *Doctrinal and biographical analyses of Justice O'Connor*

One of the most troubling strands of argument in the field of gender and judging has been the assertion that Justice O'Connor used communitarian, holistic, teleological and contextual reasoning, dubbed the feminine voice, rather than liberal, individualistic, atomistic, non-teleological, abstract and rule-based reasoning (Davis, 1993, p. 136). No one could credibly argue that Justice O'Connor had a distinctly feminist voice, although she did take a feminist position on some issues, particularly relative to her more conservative colleagues, but her gender arguably mattered because she deployed a distinctly 'feminine' style of reasoning. This argument was put most fully by legal academic Suzanna Sherry (1986), but several others advanced it as well (Behuniak-Long, 1992; Sullivan & Goldzwig, 1996). When political scientist Sue Davis put these claims to a rigorous empirical test, however, she found little evidence to support them, finding merely that Justice O'Connor was less conservative than Justice Rehnquist on some issues and showed greater support for equality claims than other conservatives (1993). It was hard to argue that O'Connor's reasoning is distinctly feminine, when her positions were shared by Justices Souter and Kennedy and not Ginsburg. Political scientist Jilda Aliotta (1995) reached the same conclusion.

An ongoing puzzle is why Davis, as well as Martin, and others who recognised the theoretical criticisms of Gilligan and found little empirical support in her research, continued to use Sherry's theories to frame questions about Justice O'Connor and gender and judging and further, why they gave Sherry's arguments pride of place when so many feminist legal academics dismissed her argument as nonsensical. Davis's empirical analysis demolished Sherry's argument; yet she concluded, "O'Connor does not appear to speak 'in a difference voice', but the possibility remains that other women judges do" (1993, p. 139). Justice O'Connor (echoing many of the NAWJ members that Martin surveyed) herself dismissed as absurd the idea that she employed a uniquely or distinctly feminine approach to legal reasoning (O'Connor, 1991, p. 1546). To be sure, O'Connor's jurisprudence eschewed bright-line legal rules and she seemed to revel in her power as the swing justice, questioning advocates about facts of particular cases at oral argument. With only one case, it is impossible to demonstrate a connection between her gender and her style of reasoning. What is astonishing, however, is the determination of observers to find that distinct female essence of judging, rather than ask how her experiences, including gender, have shaped her perspectives, as gender and other life experiences have shaped those of each of the men justices.

Although brief, Cook's analysis of Justice O'Connor contrasted favourably with the analysis of many of her successors. Unlike the overwhelming majority of women judges Cook had surveyed, Justice O'Connor neither self-identified as a feminist nor supported widespread access to abortion. Cook documented O'Connor's experience of sex discrimination and her work as a legislator in passing some sex equality legislation while recognising that her commitment to women's equality was weak. She reminded us that upon President Reagan's assumption of the presidency, right-wing Republicans effectively vetoed women judicial candidates as "too feminist" (Cook, 1988, p. 12) and noted that Reagan's choice of O'Connor "offered more symbol than substance to other women" (1988, p. 15). Cook's scalogram analysis of the 18 sex equality cases O'Connor had then considered (Cook excludes abortion cases from this analysis) showed five male justices more favourable to sex equality than O'Connor.

Cook completed a fuller and more comprehensive analysis of O'Connor's role in the Burger Court in 1991. Beginning with an analysis of O'Connor's background and her confirmation hearings, she moved into an analysis of her jurisprudence and found that Justice Brennan, not Justice O'Connor, consistently took the lead in favour of gender equality. O'Connor ranked sixth (Cook, 1991, p. 248). Cook concludes:

> O'Connor performed as the woman justice on the Court only in her extrajudicial activities as a speaker and writer. After her first term, when she raised her voice vigorously for a strong constitutional guarantee of gender equality but for weak remedies for gender discrimination, she retired as a spokesperson on women's rights. She never challenged a Court opinion that denied gender equality. The one attitude that could be associated with her personal experience as a mother in American culture was her sensitivity to children, which appeared in criminal, free expression, and church–state cases ... O'Connor's contributions to the Burger Court's jurisprudence were characterized by her political sensibility, driven by her structural principles, and *unmarked by her gender* (Cook, 1991, pp. 272–3, emphasis added).

Cook's choice of words is telling. Gender means feminine or feminist essence. Unlike Cook, I would urge us to see everyone as marked by gender, men and women, but in different ways and with different effects. Even Cook, the most anti-essentialist of the three scholars I examined here more closely, returned to the assumption of difference. O'Connor was a disappointment because she did not speak in a feminist voice, the voice Cook was hoping for when she criticised the all-male Supreme Court's rulings on sex discrimination.

4.3. *Becoming Justice Blackmun*

In writing her judicial biography of Justice Blackmun, legal correspondent for the *New York Times* Linda Greenhouse had early access to the justice's newly released papers (2005). We learn that Justice Blackmun, most known as the author of *Roe v. Wade*, had a daughter who became pregnant out of wedlock, married, lost the baby through miscarriage, and subsequently divorced. All we learned from his notation after Ruth Bader Ginsburg's oral arguments on landmark equal protection cases is that she had worn a red ribbon in her hair. Greenhouse's remarkable book showed how Justice Blackmun came to feminism through the issue of reproductive freedom, and thereby came to diverge from the other Republican-appointed justices, most poignantly, his lifelong friend, Warren Burger. We learned more about gender, women, and feminism from Greenhouse's approach than from Sherry's. First, not only do men have gender, but they have experiences that mark them by gender, as well as positions on women's rights issues. Second, as feminist standpoint theory would lead us to recognise, gender consciousness is acquired, not an automatic component of biological identity. Nor, as such, is it dichotomous. It varies among men and women and between them in ways that are perhaps patterned but which may be patterned differently across time. Third, we must trace its existence empirically rather than assume it.

4.4. *Each judge influences others, but in unpredictable ways*

In their 1990 *Women and Politics* article, O'Connor and Segal examined how the addition of one justice, Sandra Day O'Connor, to the Court may have moved Justice Rehnquist more toward the centre on sex discrimination cases. Perhaps, too, Justice Ginsburg's arguments led him to join the majority in the Virginia Military Institute case and perhaps even in *Nevada v. Hibbs* (Kenney, 2004). As intriguing as O'Connor and Segal's findings are for thinking about the difference women make in collegial courts, Barbara Palmer's analysis of Justice Ginsburg's effect on her male colleagues (2002) shows the same confounding results that Martin found as the number of women increased on state supreme courts (2004a). Palmer found that although O'Connor and Ginsburg wrote more than their share of decisions in sex discrimination cases and are the spokespeople for the Court on women, some male colleagues have become more supportive of women's rights claims because of Ginsburg's addition; others have become less so, making it difficult to argue for a clear gender effect.

5. Other effects of women on the bench

If significant gender differences exist, they may manifest themselves in other ways than in producing a dichotomous difference in votes cast in cases (Beiner, 2003; Martin, 1989). Women might conduct their trial courtrooms differently from men by refusing to allow well-documented sexist behaviour; they might act differently as administrators: for example, hiring more women law clerks.[6] Men lawyers and men judges might moderate their behaviour, as might women jurors, lawyers, and litigants. In many but not all cases, a woman justice on a state supreme court called for the creation of a state gender bias taskforce (Martin, 1989, p. 79) and women judges were almost always leaders in establishing race bias taskforces (Resnik, 1988).

Martin surveyed the 1989 National Association of Women Judges conference attendees about the impact of women judges. Ninety-eight percent agreed that women judges were role models for women attorneys. Nearly 90% reported making a special effort to encourage other women to run for judicial office. Nearly three-quarters of women agreed that women judges in general work to heighten the sensitivity of other judges to the problem of gender bias although only one third reported that they personally had made a difference in how men judges thought about the gender impact of their decisions. More than half (52%) reported making a difference through substantive decisions. When pressed for specific examples, women judges mentioned sensitising judges to some of their most flagrant sexist practices (47%), being a role model in the sense of making women jurors or litigants feel more comfortable (35%), changing substantive law on domestic violence or divorce (30%), engaging in equitable hiring behaviour (24%), and participating in their state's gender bias taskforce (15%). Martin's study shows the wide spectrum of women judges' views about the difference gender makes.

A 2003 study of the 15 women chief justices of state supreme courts—an all-time high—examined their state of the judiciary messages for evidence that they placed more emphasis on women's issues than male chief justices (Turner & Breslin, 2003). The authors deserve praise for looking for the significance of gender beyond dichotomous votes on cases and noting that as administrators of their state's judicial systems, chief judges can advance reforms such as those concerning juvenile courts, family courts, gender bias studies, and battered women's programmes. The study uncovered enormous variation among the chief judges, men and women, even on women's issues. While the presence of a woman chief judge positively and significantly impacted the likelihood of mentioning a women's issue, the number of mentions does not increase with an increased number of women on the court. Rather, it had the opposite effect. They found no statistical significance for the claim that women chief justices are more likely to make women's issues a priority.

6. Conclusions

How does gender matter? Does it produce different outcomes in judicial decisions? The scholarly studies I discuss in this paper show that researchers have used sex as a proxy for feminist, that is, more likely to be concerned with children and better at juvenile justice, pro-defendant in sex discrimination cases, pro-choice, pro-woman in divorce, employing communitarian reasoning, inclined to seek mediate solutions, likely to raise women's issues in speeches, and likely to inflict harsh or lenient sentences. Only occasionally has the evidence shown that sex is a proxy for the assumed attribute. We need to examine the strength of the empirical basis for the claim of difference (what was the sample size? How representative of the judiciary as a whole? Did the researchers control for other explanatory variables?). Even when researchers uncovered a difference, it predicted different outcomes only in some cases, while other predictors, such as party or ideology, predicted differences more reliably in others. We need to take great care in how we talk about sex differences. Strangely, findings of no difference never seem to challenge the fundamental assumption of difference, nor deter the search for it.

Women and men do have different life experiences. Some, but not all, women are mothers. Some, but not all, women are in heterosexual marriages where they do the lion's share of caring labour. All experience the world as a woman, subject to the risks of sexual violence, gender devaluation, and exclusion and discrimination. Rather than identify essential sex differences, perhaps we should understand gender as producing tendencies among generational cohorts. When the women who are now senior judges entered the legal profession, they had profound experiences of exclusion. Many, such as Justice Sandra Day O'Connor and Minnesota Supreme Court Justice Rosalie Wahl, did not enter large law firms but instead worked for the government on mental health issues or, as many women did because it was one of the few places where parents could work part-time, worked for public defenders

(Kenney, 2001). We can expect women who serve on the bench in Texas, for example, who have run as Republicans, served as prosecutors, and spent their time with the victims of violent crime, to have very different outlooks and to bring to the bench different experiences than women who have worked for a public defender. The Republican women who President Bush (43) appointed might be as different from earlier Republican women appointed to the bench as they were from Democratic women appointees. Even women of the same age cohort do not necessarily share a feminist consciousness. One need only consider the differences between Justices O'Connor and Ginsburg and between Justices Marshall and Thomas for the point to be clear. We must move from an assumption of essential sex differences to a discussion of gender.

It is time to re-examine the application of Rosabeth Moss Kanter's classic work on gender and organisations, *Men and Women of the Corporation* (1977), to courts. Kanter was profoundly anti-essentialist. Her organisational analysis focused on structural conditions to predict behaviour rather than essential sex differences to explain why tokens may conform to the dominant group. On the other hand, scholars often misapply her findings to claim that once women reach critical mass their 'true' (read dichotomous, uniform, and feminist) differences can emerge. More recent studies have questioned Kanter's assumption that resistance to women's presence in male-dominated institutions would diminish as women moved from minority to parity (MacCorquodale & Jenson, 1993; Yoder, 1991). We should apply these insights to evidence of increasing challenges to women judges. Rosemary Hunter's analysis of women judges in Australia shows that behind the recent numbers of women appointments "lurks an undercurrent of hostility toward women judges, which shows no sign of abating in the near future" (2006, p. 281). According to Hunter, women judges experience what Rosabeth Moss Kanter called heightened attention: their qualifications are disputed, and their colleagues (on and off the bench) show open hostility to them. She notes that women judges' colleagues simply "hold them in contempt for simply being women" (p. 295). The assumption is that men are the natural occupants of such positions, that women obtain them through political manoeuvring, not merit, and that enough women have been appointed. Moreover, evidence from Canada suggests that women judges are far more likely than men to have their objectivity challenged and gender-based conflicts of interest asserted (Backhouse, 2003; Omatsu, 1997). Litigants seem to miss the irony that if the gender of the woman judge poses a conflict in a rape or employment discrimination case, the same goes for the gender of a male judge. We should recognise that a feminist consciousness is a political achievement, not an inevitable result of being female or living life as a woman. So, too, should we understand that the creation of a group of judges, men and women, who bring a gender lens to judging, is an organisational accomplishment and not an automatic result when a certain number of women judges join a court. In fact, the evidence suggests that women may feel less compelled to articulate 'a woman's point of view' the more women serving on a court. The question is not simply in adding more women to the mix, but in creating organisations attentive to gender devaluation.

Gender is a relevant category for social interaction, and the absence or presence of women may change group dynamics; but that does not mean it does so in fixed, predictable, and static ways. Particularly on collegiate courts, I think there is a strong case to be made for injecting people with different experiences of all sorts rather than for using gender as an automatic proxy for feminist, liberal, or compassionate toward the downtrodden. The gender composition of groups matters in often subtle ways, determining what comments might be intolerable and how issues are framed as well as what kinds of evidence and arguments the group considers. It matters, then, that Lady Brenda Hale is a woman, but perhaps more important is that she is an expert in family law and has championed no-fault divorce as a law commissioner. She is the author of the first text on women and the law (Hale & Atkins, 1984) and brings a sophisticated understanding of gender issues to her analysis.[7]

The work of more than 70 scholars in the Collaborative Research Network on Gender and Judging of the Law and Society Association shows the rich possibilities of a gender analysis. When done well, using sex as a variable can expose discrimination or important sex differences. When done badly, it can assume rather than discover essential sex differences in ways that are not helpful for understanding judicial behaviour. Across many methods, from statistical analysis of judicial opinions, to historical case studies of judicial campaigns to doctrinal analysis of equal protection decisions, a gender analysis, where gender is a social process, has much to offer our understanding of judging.

Acknowledgements

I would like to thank Myra Marx Ferree, Kathleen Laughlin, Judith Resnik, and Patricia Yancey Martin for their helpful comments on the paper. I would also like to thank Amber Shipley and Lura Barber for research assistance. Thanks, too, for the helpful comments from the Gender and Judging Collaborative Research Network of the Law and Society Association.

Notes

[1] See the special issue of *Politics & Gender on Intersectionality*, 2(3), (2007).

[2] Within political science, those who identify as judicial behaviourists adopt quantitative methods rather than qualitative methods, share the values of social science, and see judges as using legal rules to justify their policy choices rather than determining them (Mather, 1994, p. 77).

[3] In employment discrimination law, disparate impact (known as indirect discrimination in the United Kingdom and European Union) occurs when employers use a sex neutral characteristic, such as a height or weight-lifting requirement or the requirement that one be a veteran. The requirement is formally neutral since some women are tall, some can lift heavy weights, and some are veterans, but fewer women than men can comply with any of these requirements. The burden then shifts to the employer to show that the requirement is necessary for the job. So in this case, fewer women than men may be known to the president (or senator), but is being known the best predictor of who will make a good judge?

[4] Carroll's data show Reagan-appointed women judges to be far less supportive of the women's movement even than other Republican women politicians, while Carter's appointees were well within the range of Democratic women politicians (1985).

[5] George Herbert Walker Bush was the 41st president of the United States from 1989 to 1993. George W. Bush was the 43rd president of the United States, taking office in 2001. To distinguish them, we tend to refer to them as Bush (41) and Bush (43).

[6] Cook drew attention to this issue early on. The existing evidence raises interesting points about sex and feminism. Justice Brennan refused to hire women clerks on the grounds that his secretary (later his wife after he was widowed) would not permit it. Justice O'Connor made it a priority, as did Justice Marshall. Justice Ginsburg, however, does not have a good record. Blackmun hired more women law clerks than all the sitting justices combined, and during his last ten years on the Court, a majority of his clerks were women (Greenhouse, 2005, p. 208).

[7] Erika Rackley's work on Hale (2006), like Linda Greenhouse's work on Blackmun (2005), shows how gender matters in individual cases.

References

Aliotta, Jilda (1995) Justice O'Connor and the equal protection clause: a feminine voice?, *Judicature*, 78, p. 232.

Allen, David & Wall, Diane (1987) The behavior of women state supreme court justices: are they tokens or outsiders?, *Justice System Journal*, 12, pp. 232–45.

Alozie, Nicholas O. (1996) Selection methods and the recruitment of women to state courts of last resort, *Social Science Quarterly*, 77, pp. 110–26.

Backhouse, Constance (2003) The chilly climate for women judges: reflections on the backlash from the Ewanchuk case, *Canadian Journal of Women and the Law*, 15(1), pp. 167–93.

Behuniak-Long, Susan (1992) Justice Sandra Day O'Connor and the power of maternal legal thinking, *Review of Politics*, 54, pp. 417–44.

Beiner, Theresa M. (2003) The elusive (but worthwhile) quest for a diverse bench in the new millennium, *University of California Davis Law Review*, 36, pp. 597–615.

Biskupic, Joan (2000) Politics snares court, hopes of minorities and women, *USA Today*, 22 August.

Boyd, Christina, Epstein, Lee & Martin, Andrew D. (2007) Untangling the causal effects of sex on judging, available at: http://adm.wustl.edu/media/working/genderjudging.pdf.

Bratton, Kathleen A. & Spill, Rorie L. (2002) Existing diversity and judicial selection: the role of appointment method in establishing gender diversity in state supreme courts, *Social Science Quarterly*, 83, pp. 504–18.

Carroll, Susan (1985) *Women as Candidates in American Politics* (Bloomington, Indiana University Press).

Chamallas, Martha (2003) *Introduction to Feminist Legal Theory*, 2nd edition. (New York, Aspen).

Cook, Beverly Blair (1978a) The Burger court and women's rights 1971–77, in: Winifred L. Hepperle & Laura Crites (Eds) *Women in the Courts* (Williamsburg, National Center for State Courts), pp. 47–83. Reprinting *American Politics Quarterly* article.

Cook, Beverly Blair (1978b) Women judges: the end of tokenism, in: Winifred L. Hepperle & Laura Crites (Eds) *Women in the Courts* (Williamsburg, National Center for State Courts), pp. 84–105.

Cook, Beverly Blair (1980a) Florence Allen, in: Barbara Sicherman & Carol Hurd Green (Eds) *Notable American Women: The Modern Period—A Biographical Dictionary* (Cambridge, Harvard University Press), pp. 11–3.

Cook, Beverly Blair (1980b) Political culture and selection of women judges in trial courts, in: Debra W. Stewart (Ed.) *Women in Local Politics* , pp. 42–60.

Cook, Beverly Blair (1981) Will women judges make a difference in women's legal rights? A prediction from attitudes and simulated behaviour, in: Margherita Rendel (Ed.) *Women, Power and Political Systems* (New York, St. Martin's Press), pp. 216–39.

Cook, Beverly Blair (1982) Women as supreme court candidates: from Florence Allen to Sandra O'Connor, *Judicature*, 65(6), pp. 314–26.

Cook, Beverly Blair (1988) Women as judges, in: Beverly B. Cook, Leslie F. Goldstein, Karen O'Connor & Susette M. Talarico (Eds) *Women in the Judicial Process* (Washington, DC, American Political Science Association), pp. 9–24.

Cook, Beverly Blair (1991) Justice Sandra Day O'Connor: transition to a Republican court agenda, in: Charles M. Lamb & Stephen C. Halpern (Eds) *The Burger Court: Political and Judicial Profiles* (Buffalo, SUNY Press), pp. 238–75.

Crowe, Nancy E. (1999). Diversity on the US Courts of Appeals: how the sexual and racial composition of panels affects decision making. Paper prepared for the American Political Science Association Annual Meeting, Atlanta.

Davis, Sue (1992–93) Do women judges speak 'in a different voice?' Carol Gilligan, feminist legal theory, and the Ninth Circuit, *Wisconsin Women's Law Journal*, 8, pp. 143–73.

Davis, Sue (1993) The voice of Sandra Day O'Connor, *Judicature*, 77(3), pp. 134–9.

Davis, Sue, Haire, Susan & Songer, Donald R. (1993) Voting behavior and gender on the US Courts of Appeals, *Judicature*, 77(3), pp. 129–33.

Epstein, Cynthia Fuchs (1988) *Deceptive Distinctions: Sex, Gender, and the Social Order* (New Haven, Yale University Press).

Faderman, Lillian (2000) *To Believe in Women: What Lesbians Have Done for America—A History* (Boston, Mariner Books).

Githens, Marianne (1995) Getting appointed to the state court: the gender dimension, *Women and Politics*, 15(4), pp. 1–24.

Gottschall, Jon (1983) Carter's judicial appointments: the influence of affirmative action and merit selection on voting on the US Court of Appeals, *Judicature*, 67(4), pp. 165–73.

Greenhouse, Linda (2005) *Becoming Justice Blackmun: Harry Blackmun's Supreme Court Journey* (New York, Times Books).

Gruhl, John, Spohn, Cassia & Welch, Susan (1981) Women as policymakers: the case of trial judges, *American Journal of Political Science*, 25, pp. 308–22.

Hale, Brenda & Atkins, Susan (1984) *Women and the Law* (Oxford, Blackwell).

Hunter, Rosemary (2006) The high price of success: the backlash against women judges, in: Elizabeth Sheehy & Sheila McIntrye (Eds) *Calling for Change: Women, Law, and the Legal Profession Ten Years After Touchstones for Change* (University of Ottowa Press), pp. 281–301.

Jensen, Jennifer M. & Martinek, Wendy L. (2007). Gender, race, and ambition in the New York State Supreme Court. Paper prepared for presentation at the Seventh Annual Conference on State Politics and Policy, University of Texas at Austin, 23–24 February, 2007, Available at: http://www.unc.edu/depts/polisci/statepol/conferences/2007/papers/Jensen%20and%20Martinek.pdf.

Kanter, Rossabeth Moss (1977) *Men and Women of the Corporation* (New York, Basic Books).

Kenney, Sally J. (1995) Women, gender, feminism, and law: ruminations of a feminist academic, *Women and Politics*, 15(3), pp. 43–69.

Kenney, Sally J. (1996) New research on gendered political institutions, *Political Research Quarterly*, 49(2), pp. 445–66.

Kenney, Sally J. (2001) Thank you for being ready: Minnesota's First Supreme Court Justice, Rosalie Waht. Public policy teaching case, http://www.hhh.umn.edu/centers/wpp/case-studies.html#kenney2.

Kenney, Sally J. (2004). The constitutional status of the *Family and Medical Leave Act*, paper presented at the *Afterbirth Conference*, Minneapolis, Minnesota, 1 October, 2004, Humphrey Institute of Public Affairs, Available at: http://www.hhh.umn.edu/centers/wpp/afterbirth/pdf/kenney.pdf (accessed 22 August 2008).

Kritzer, Herbert M. & Uhlman, Thomas M. (1977) Sisterhood in the courtroom: sex of judge and defendant in criminal case disposition, *The Social Science Journal*, 14(2), pp. 77–88.

Lawless, Jennifer Law & Fox, Richard L. (2005) *It Takes a Candidate: Why Women Don't Run for Office* (Cambridge, Cambridge University Press).

MacCorquodale, Patricia & Jenson, Gary (1993) Women in the law: partners or tokens?, *Gender and Society*, 17(4), pp. 582–93.

Martin, Elaine (1982) Women on the federal bench: a comparative profile, *Judicature*, 65(6), pp. 307–13.

Martin, Elaine (1987) Gender and judicial selection: a comparison of the Reagan and Carter administrations, *Judicature*, 71(3), pp. 136–42.

Martin, Elaine (1989) Differences in men and women judges: perspective on gender, *Journal of Political Science*, 17, pp. 74–85.

Martin, Elaine (1991). Judicial role models: a women judges' network, unpublished paper presented at the *Midwest Political Science Association*, 18–20 April.

Martin, Elaine (1993) Views from the state bench: gender roles and judicial roles, in: Lois Lovelace Duke (Ed.) *Women in Politics: Outsiders or Insiders?* (Englewood Cliffs, NJ, Prentice Hall).

Martin, Elaine (2000) Gender, race, and partisanship on the Michigan Supreme Court, *Albany Law Review*, 63, pp. 1205–36.

Martin, Elaine (2004a). Taking sides: the impact of judicial gender on decisions in divorce law, unpublished paper presented at the *Midwest Political Science Association*.

Martin, Elaine (2004b) Gender and presidential judicial selection, *Women and Politics*, 26(3/4), pp. 109–29.

Martin, Patricia Yancey, Reynolds, John R. & Keith, Shelley (2002) Gender bias and feminist consciousness among judges and attorneys: a standpoint theory analysis, *Signs*, 27(3), pp. 665–702.

Mather, Lynn (1994) Introducing a feminist pioneer in judicial politics: Beverly Blair Cook, *PS: Political Science & Politics*, 27(1), pp. 76–8.

O'Connor, Karen & Segal, Jeffrey (1990) Justice Sandra Day O'Connor and the Supreme Court's reaction to its first female member, *Women and Politics*, 10(2), pp. 95–103.

O'Connor, Sandra Day (1991) Portia's progress, *New York University Law Review*, 66, pp. 1553–4.

Omatsu, Maryka (1997) The fiction of judicial impartiality, *Canadian Journal of Women and the Law*, 9(1), pp. 1–16.

Organ, Joan Ellen (1998) *Sexuality as a Category of Historical Analysis: A Study of Judge Florence E. Allen, 1884–1966*, PhD Dissertation, (Department of History, Case Western University).

Palmer, Barbara (2001) Women in the American judiciary: their influence and impact, *Women and Politics*, 23(3), pp. 89–99.

Palmer, Barbara (2002) Justice Ruth Bader Ginsburg and the Supreme Court's reaction to its second female member, *Women and Politics*, 24(1), pp. 1–23.

Peresie, Jennifer (2005) Female judges matter: gender and collegial decisionmaking in the federal appellate courts, *Yale Law Journal*, 114, pp. 1759–90.

Rackley, Erika (2006) Difference in the House of Lords, *Social & Legal Studies*, 15(2), pp. 163–86.

Resnik, Judith (1988) On the bias: feminist reconsiderations of the aspirations for our judges, *Southern California Law Review*, 61, pp. 1877–944.

Scherer, Nancy (2005) *Scoring Points: Politicians, Activists, and the Lower Federal Court Appointment Process* (Palo Alto, Stanford University Press).

Schultz, Ulrike & Shaw, Gisela (Eds) (2003) *Women in the World's Legal Professions* (Oxford, Hart).

Segal, Jennifer (2000) Representative decision making on the federal bench: Clinton's district court appointees, *Political Research Quarterly*, 53, p. 137.

Sherry, Suzanna (1986) Civic virtue and the feminine voice in constitutional adjudication, *Virginia Law Review*, 72, pp. 543–615.

Songer, Donald R., Davis, Sue & Haire, Susan (1994) A reappraisal of diversification in the federal courts: gender effects in the Courts of Appeals, *Journal of Politics*, 56(2), pp. 425–9.

Sullivan, Patricia A. & Goldzwig, Steven R. (1996) Abortion and undue burdens: Justice Sandra Day O'Connor and judicial decision-making, *Women and Politics*, 16(3), pp. 27–54.

Turner, Robert C. & Breslin, Beau (2003). The impact of female state chief judges on the administration of state judiciaries, paper presented at the *America Political Science Association Annual Meeting*, Philadelphia, 28–31 August.

Walker, Thomas & Barrow, Deborah (1985) The diversification of the federal bench: policy and process ramifications, *Journal of Politics*, 47, pp. 596–617.

Williams, Margaret (2007) Ambition, gender, and the judiciary, *Political Research Quarterly*, 61(1), pp. 68–78.

Yoder, Janice D. (1991) Rethinking tokenism: looking beyond numbers, *Gender & Society*, 5, pp. 178–92.

Family judges in the city of Buenos Aires: a view from within

BEATRIZ KOHEN
Asociación por los Derechos Civiles, Buenos Aires, Argentina

ABSTRACT *This paper summarises the main findings of a study of gender differences in the values and attitudes of family judges carried out in Buenos Aires, Argentina. The study explored how men and women judges understood their profession and its requirements, their representation of the ideal family judge, their motivation to become family judges, the way they experienced the power they wield, and their opinion on the supposed contributions women judges might bring to the family judiciary. The study's findings were analysed in terms of Gilligan's ethic of justice/ethic of care approach. Two key results emerged. Firstly, there were no clear-cut differences between men and women in terms of their adherence to an ethic of justice or of care respectively. Secondly, distinct gender differences were apparent in the way women judges approached decision-making.*

I. Some preliminary remarks

As a relatively new section of the judiciary, the Family Courts of the city of Buenos Aires, a previously male dominated area in which women judges had recently outnumbered men, seemed an ideal milieu to study the impact of the large number of women in the judiciary in the context of an emerging democracy.

At the time when I started this project (2000), existing research on women in the judiciary was scarce, and the little there was touched only tangentially on the issue of gender difference. This study was the first comprehensive attempt to depict the situation of women in the legal professions in Buenos Aires. It was also the first research project to study the Family Courts as well as the first to consider women judges and the difference they might make to the administration of justice. The unavailability of relevant knowledge and data meant that I had to start from a very low base, putting together a considerable body of existing and new information to supply my research into family judges with the necessary theoretical, socio-historical and institutional context.

I began by analysing the theoretical framework provided by feminist legal theory, paying particular attention to the ways legal feminism had explained the situation of women in the legal professions. I found myself before a very rich, prolific, complex and controversial theoretical tradition working across disciplinary boundaries and paralleling the development of feminism, a theoretical body that has progressed in different strands, the main tenets of which are not necessarily mutually exclusive.

The analysis of 'cultural feminism' (Gilligan, 1982; Gilligan *et al.*, 1985; Menkel-Meadow, 1989, 1995, 1996; Bender, 1997)—the strand within legal feminism that oriented my research—against the backdrop of the main debates within feminist legal theory provoked much reflection about the research questions, its aims and the risks involved in the proposed enquiry. The current debate within feminist legal theory acknowledges the theoretical problems involved in the subject matter and takes the anti-essentialist critique seriously. The discussion of the dangers of essentialism entailed in the cultural feminist approach pointed to the need to design a research strategy aiming at counteracting such risks (Heyes, 1997; Conaghan, 2000; Drakopolou, 2000; Schultz, 2003a, 2003b). In line with the work of other researchers working internationally on women in the legal professions, I considered the issue in a new light, bringing complexity and caution into it. Accordingly, my research project was set in a specific environment—the Family Courts of the city of Buenos Aires—searching for results only applicable to its particular context. This enquiry was thus sceptical and cautious with respect to the attribution of the care orientation to women in law and considered other aspects besides gender and different social forces that could be related to the values and attitudes that women could bring to judging (Schultz, 2003a, 2003b).

The acquaintance with the various strands within feminist legal theory facilitated the appreciation of the different theoretical and methodological tools these currents could supply for the advance of this research. Therefore, the enquiry resorted to research tools devised by the different strands of legal feminism. The methods of liberal feminism, intending to examine the quantitative participation of women in society, were very helpful to investigate the situation of women within the legal profession in Buenos Aires, while the approach of difference feminism proved most valuable for the exploration of the impact of gender on the values and attitudes of men and women judges.

Likewise, the review of the main socio-historical trends giving rise to women's increasing participation within the professions in Argentina demonstrated the multifarious relationships between the strengthening of democratic institutions and the advance of women within society. The analysis of Argentinean women's incorporation into education and their fight to obtain civil and political rights in the context of the systemic fluctuations of the country's emerging democracy and its fragile economy proved to be extremely useful. It revealed that while a democratic context is crucial for women's social progress, even within democratic rule, women's demands for equality are relatively marginal. Thus, while democratic rule appears as a necessary requisite for women's advancement in society, it is, nevertheless, not a sufficient condition. This explains part of the difficulties in promoting significant transformations in gender related issues.

II. An overview of the main research findings

Women's participation within the legal professions

The description of women's participation in the different branches of the legal profession constitutes a necessary base line that was previously unavailable. As such, it will be extremely helpful for further research. It basically showed that, like in other parts of the world, law is an inhospitable institution when it comes to incorporating women (Menkel-Meadow, 1995, 1997; Jack & Jack, 1988; Mossman, 1986, 1988, 1989; Harrington, 1994; Freyer, 1995; Thornton, 1996; McGlynn, 1996, 1998a, 1998b, 1998c, 1999, 2003; Sommerlad, 1998a, 1998b, 2003; Schultz & Shaw, 2003; Botelho Junqueira, 1997a, 1997b, 1997c, 1997d, 1999, 2003; Boigeol, 2003; Hunter, 2003a, 2003b).

The analysis of the situation of women in the legal professions in Argentina demonstrated that the large increase in the number of women receiving legal education was not making itself felt in terms of women's participation in the legal labour market.

Despite women's advances, all areas of legal practice exhibited a high degree of vertical and horizontal segregation, the large legal firm being the main locus of discrimination. Women were mostly situated at the lower end of the hierarchy of the firms and only very rarely became partners. While large law firms proved to be inimical to the incorporation of women, legal education and the judiciary appeared as branches of the profession where women could develop careers more easily in conjunction with family responsibilities. In the view of the judges that participated in this study, this explains women's preference for the judiciary over large law firms.

One remarkable finding was that women as law teachers—generally a part-time and low-paid branch of the profession—worked on a full-time basis more often than men Although even when they held important roles as members of the UBA Law School faculty hierarchy, they frequently occupied the less prestigious and more time-consuming posts, performing pastoral and housekeeping tasks.

Similarly, women judges were concentrated in the lower instances of the judiciary, within the sections more related to their traditional family roles. Although the participation of women in second instance courts and in the Supreme Courts of the provinces was increasing, there were no women at the National Supreme Court until 2005; since that time there have been two of them (Mackinson, 1985, 1987, 1988, 1991; Mackinson & Goldstein, 1988; Gastrón, 1988, 1991; Kohen, 2005a, 2005b).

Women judges in Family Courts

The examination of recent trends in family life and family law provided a valuable context for the study of family judges. Women's increased participation in paid employment as a result of their enlarged educational opportunities and growing male unemployment appears as one of the more striking phenomena over the last 25 years in Argentine society. Even if its effects need still to be fully studied, this appeared as a very important issue framing the work of family law judges (Torrado, 2003; Wainerman, 2003).

The creation of Family Courts coincided with a period of profound changes initiated by the restoration of democracy. Embedded in a general societal trend to update family law and eliminate gender inequalities within the law, it should be seen as an aspect of the modernisation of family law centred around the passing of the law of divorce, and as a response to the demands posed by changes in family life. Thus, if this study of Family Law Courts presents a partial view of the situation of women within the judiciary, it certainly relates to a key period in Argentinean history. This period, characterised by important transformations, coincided with a time of relatively intense activity of the women's movement, which became more involved in matters strongly related to gender.

The high number of women in the family law judiciary, as compared to other sections of the judiciary, parallels the transition from private to public undergone by Argentine women in recent times. The family law judiciary represents a bridge between the private sphere of the home and the public realm of the law and legal institutions. In that sense, it is analogous to women's public participation in other branches of the state, such as the legislature and the executive, in which women are frequently in charge of areas related to the roles they have traditionally performed within the family.

The proportion of women among family judges has been growing steadily since the creation of the Family Courts in 1989. More than half of family judges were women at the time when the research was carried out. The findings show a considerable uniformity in the composition of Family Courts: the judges were all white, able bodied and had received a Catholic upbringing; most came from middle class backgrounds, were or had been married and had children. In such a homogeneous context, the sex of the judges seemed a strong criterion for differentiation and so did their age, since women were, on average, nine years younger than men judges. Men and women family judges also differed with respect to their practice of the Catholic religion, men seeming to practise the Catholic religion more often than women, although all of them had had a Catholic upbringing. Civil status also varied with gender: while men were all married, half of the women were widows, separated or divorced. Men and women judges in the family law section also differed in terms of their educational attainment and career trajectories. Women had a higher level of educational attainment and men a longer seniority in the judicial post. While men judges had had continuous careers, the women judges' careers had often been discontinuous.

As members of the first generation of women judges, the judges participating in this study were pioneers who occupied positions of prestige stemming from their professional roles. Thus they broke certain patterns in relation to their family and social role models. However, the responses of both men and women judges revealed that these women belonged to a transitional generation. Since parental responsibilities within their families had not been redefined in accordance with their increased participation in the public sphere, their domestic responsibilities had affected their career choices and chances for advancement. Thus, I found that younger women judges who were mothers of young children were significantly overburdened as a consequence of the traditional parental role allocation along gender lines. The discontinuities in the women's careers, due to interruptions related to motherhood and child caring, had certainly had negative effects on their chances of professional advancement.

Bearing in mind the situation of women within the judiciary and the effects of the double shift, I borrow the expression coined by the Spanish sociologist M.A. García de León (1994, p. 76) to characterise the women judges in this study as members of "a discriminated elite". Whereas men's roles as economic providers inspired their career choices, women judges showed a stronger vocational orientation and understood their work in a 'missionary' fashion more often than the men.

Reason for the large proportion of women in family law and the family judiciary

My analysis of women's participation in the judiciary showed that the large entry of women is concentrated mainly at the first instance level in the Civil, Family and Labour Courts. Women are located more often at the bottom of the judicial pyramid; the sections of the judiciary that host more women are the less prestigious ones, because the cases dealt with by these courts involve small amounts of money and have little political impact. This situation mirrors the reality observed by international research studies on women jurists in many jurisdictions (Schultz, 2003a, p. xlvii).

As I shared those findings with the family judges that participated in the research, the important proportion of women in family law and the family law judiciary was seen partly as a matter of social pressure and partly as a matter of preference or choice. As Schultz (2003b, p. 282) has put it "Self selection and allocation go in tandem".

The judges explained the large numbers of women lawyers in family law mostly as a consequence of men leaving the family law area to look for more profitable or prestigious sectors as women entered the legal profession. Both men and women magistrates explained the large proportion of women among the family judges in terms of family gender roles. In fact, the central roles of men and women within the family, i.e. men's role as economic providers and women's role as in charge of home and children, were the reasons given by the judges throughout the research to justify important choices and decisions.

The traditional sexual division of labour within the family emerged as a factor determining the choices men and women members of the legal profession make when they opt for the sections in which to develop a career. Although there is less economic incentive in the judiciary than in large law firms, women seem to prefer the judiciary because of its stability and fixed hours and because it seems easier to combine with motherhood. The shorter working day of Family Courts as compared to Criminal Courts, the fact that Family Courts work only in the mornings, rather than women's preference for the family specialty, was highlighted by the respondents as the main reason for the large numbers of women in Family Courts.

In addition, women's preference for the family subject matter was considered as a given by both men and women judges and related to their different personal experiences and their greater involvement with the family. In the view of the judges, through such an involvement, women developed both the preference and the capacities that made them more suitable to deal with family matters. This coincides with Thornton's findings in the Australian context who argued that: "Family law like raising children is based on experiences and practices with which everyone (particularly women) are thought to be familiar rather than on acquired, technocratic knowledge" (Thornton, 1996, p. 279).

However, particularly women judges believed that the family law judiciary requires specialised knowledge and training. Accordingly, they related the large numbers of women in the family judiciary to women's higher propensity to add further specialised training to their legal studies.

The judges' opinions on the difference women can make to the administration of justice

With respect to the contribution that women judges could make to the judiciary, the responses obtained from men and women were very different. While women judges initially tended to deny any capacity that could be derived from gender, men judges very much sustained the traditional stereotype. Men judges thought that women had a potential to make a big difference in the administration of justice, particularly in the family law judiciary where, as they claimed, the humanity that women brought was necessary and welcome. Women's initial denial of any gender differences that might affect their activity as judges was frequently reversed with the progress of the interview, when they identified some tendencies which, to some extent, contradicted their first response (Hunter, 2002). Bearing in mind the masculine character of law, this first denial could be explained as a strategy on the part of women judges to anticipate and avoid discrimination by asserting that gender does not make any difference in adjudication and that women can administer justice as well as men.

A point of convergence among men and women judges was women's greater tendency to resort to interdisciplinarity as an aid and essential tool for their work as family law judges. It was not surprising that women who, for a long time had not participated in the creation of the law, attempt to expand its boundaries to make it more reflective of their conceptions on social health, and more responsive to the needs of the litigants.

Women judges' greater tendency towards interdisciplinarity can be interpreted in terms of various factors: in the first place, as a consequence of a greater exposure in their education to disciplines such as sociology, psychology, anthropology and social work. In the second place, it can be concluded that referring to a consistent body of knowledge in the psycho-social field on which to base their decisions can provide the women judges with a sense of self confidence which, as newcomers to the profession, they might otherwise be lacking. In the third place, I associate women's tendency to interdisciplinarity with their propensity to look at family problems in their full complexity with a greater sensitivity to the context and a different conception of psycho-social health and to understand the problems at a more complex level (Fox Keller, 1985). Thus, according to their testimonies, they not only tended to attempt to find a legal solution to the cases but also to work out a solution to the underlying conflicts in order to prevent new ones. Actually, the most significant contribution that women seemed to be making to the family law judiciary consists in the introduction of an interdisciplinary approach to the resolution of family problems. It was also noted that, while the women judges appear as the 'champions of interdisciplinarity', the Supreme Court does not allow judges to have members of the 'psy' professions as full members of their staff. The so-called interdisciplinary team is composed of two social workers. Various judges in the sample referred to their having made a special request to the Supreme Court to add a psychologist or a psychoanalyst to their staff. Their request was repeatedly rejected. This means that here their voices are not heard. That fits in with Thornton's observation that women remain marginal within the legal field (Thornton, 1996, p. 3). Nevertheless, apart from resorting to the cooperation of professionals from the social and state provided health services and of independent experts nominated and authorised by the judiciary whom the judges are entitled to consult a limited number of times a year, both men and women judges (probably more often women than men) deploy strategies that enable them to rely frequently on the collaboration of psychiatrists or psychologists that aid the court free of charge.

Overall, both men and women judges eventually mentioned the existence of certain gender-specific attributes that women judges contribute to the activity of judging with a potential to introduce changes to the family law judiciary. In their opinion, women aim at making the family judiciary more sensitive to the reality of the litigants undergoing a family conflict. More particularly, women brought an improved understanding of the underlying non-legal problems. Mostly men judges appeared somewhat critical of what they thought was an excessive reliance on the 'psy' disciplines.

Awareness of discrimination and of the effects of gender in the family

I also examined the judges' perceptions of discrimination within the judiciary and the family amidst a general discussion on their awareness of difference in general. Although some of the judges were faintly aware of some degree of discrimination within the judiciary, be it relating to gender or to other differences, in general they thought of it as a relatively egalitarian institution and referred to discrimination as something that mainly occurred in the past and was destined to disappear with the introduction of a new and more transparent system for the selection and appointment of judges. In fact, the previous system for the selection of judges was clearly obscure and anachronistic and allowed for the reproduction of the status quo in terms of the composition of the judiciary, namely that judges were all white, Catholic, male, blue eyed, belonging to the middle to upper classes. It will be very interesting to examine how gender impinges on the process of selection of new judges by the 'Consejo de la Magistratura', the new organ created to select and designate judges. We need to be looking at whether the new system promotes gender equity or whether instead it reproduces the previous state of affairs. This requires an examination of both the process of selections and its results from a gender perspective.

The lack of awareness of gender discrimination within the judiciary extended to their perceptions with respect to women's situation within society and within the family. In spite of the fact that the discourse of the judges shows some recognition of the effects of gender on the lives of the people involved in legal conflicts, the lack of a comprehensive critical gender perspective is worthy of notice. It suggests a remarkable degree of tolerance regarding injustice on the part of those whose task is to administer justice. As those who make important decisions affecting the future of the families that come to court, family judges would benefit from a more complete vision of the effects of gender on family life and on the lives of its individual members.

While both men and women judges were resistant to acknowledge discrimination within the judiciary and the family they were very aware of the potential for discriminatory practices involved in their own work. They were conscious of the danger of symbolic violence they might exert through the imposition of a family model that might not coincide with reality. This revealed a tendency to contextual thinking that was also evident when they described the way they reached their decisions in the resolution of the cases that came before them.

Characteristics of the ideal judge according to men and women judges

I asked the judges to name and describe the characteristics of the ideal family judge (Toharia, 1995). Although I observed a considerable overlap in terms of the qualities attributed by men and women judges to the 'ideal' family judge, there were differences of emphasis as well as of attributes selected. Qualities such as empathy, immediacy, sensitivity to the context, humility, lack of prejudice, honesty, and knowledge of the law often appeared in the discourse of both men and women judges. The abilities that clearly differentiated the men judges' ideal were objectivity, equanimity, equidistance, composure, thoughtfulness, moderation. The need for the judge to be well acquainted with interdisciplinary knowledge and to view his/her work as a public service were the required characteristics of an 'ideal' family law judge emphasised by women judges. I associated these different abilities highlighted by men and women judges with a tendency towards a more individual work style on the part of the men judges and a tendency to a more collective work style on the part of the women judges.

As the ideal of women appeared to be more demanding than that of men, I proposed that the difficulty to live up to such a demanding ideal could partly explain their more acute sense of discomfort with the power and responsibility associated with their role and their professed difficulties in exerting authority.

Although the aim of my research was not to test the cultural feminist approach in the context of the family law judiciary, I used its conceptual framework to orient my enquiry on gender differences among the family judges. Following Gilligan's model of two different moral orientations associated with gender, Menkel-Meadow speculated on the possibility that, once the number of women in the legal profession became significant, differences might emerge between men's and women's professional attitudes. While men would approach their work with an 'ethic of justice', women would deploy an 'ethic of care' (Gilligan, 1982; Menkel-Meadow, 1989, 1995; Sherry, 1986a, 1986b; Tronto, 1996; West, 1988, 1997; Sevenhuijsen, 1996).

However, my own findings, in keeping with those of scholars from other countries, were not conclusive. While some of the results of my work with family judges seem to substantiate the cultural feminist thesis, others do not.

On the one hand, there was no essential difference in the way the judges reached their decisions. Both women and men judges stated that they first decided on a fair solution and only then looked for the law that would give legal support to that solution. Apart from challenging one of the main tenets of the civil law system according to which civil law judges are just "the mouth of the law" (Merryman, 1989), this suggests a tendency present in both sexes towards contextual thinking more typical of the 'ethic of care', underlining the relevance of the real persons underneath the judges' robes, their moral values and personal conceptions of justice and the high level of discretion actually involved in adjudication.

On the other hand, my study did suggest that, while men judges stress the importance of objectivity, neutrality and equidistance, women emphasise vocation, care and personal involvement. In addition to this, the cultural feminist thesis about different moral orientations associated with gender would be supported by the way women view their professional activity as a service to the community and experience the power they wield as a strong responsibility (Jones, 1993). However, although women lay a stronger emphasis on empathy, immediacy and a contextual approach, the fact that men as well as women deem those aspects important would suggest that men judges, too, embrace certain qualities more characteristic of the 'women's voice' and the 'ethic of care'. This casts doubt on the appropriateness of Gilligan's assertion with respect to the prevalence of either the 'ethic of care' or the 'ethic of justice' in the majority of the cases.

Of course, the very nature of the family subject matter could help to explain my findings. After all, the presence of children who are frequently abused and of women suffering from domestic violence and epitomising those in need of care in family conflicts, would justify the deployment of the 'ethic of care' among family judges, irrespective of their gender (Flanagan & Jackson, 1994). For this reason, corresponding research in other branches of the judiciary would help to clarify the issue.

Religion could provide another possible explanation for both male and female family judges' adoption of a care approach, given that care and compassion constitute central imperatives of the Catholic ethic. All of the judges in the sample had a Catholic upbringing, most of the men practised the Catholic religion, and the men judges who appeared as the most caring were those who explicitly expressed the strongest adherence to Catholic principles. It is worth remembering that Gilligan's work was set up in the North-American scene with an overall preponderance of the Protestant religion, thus not reflecting the particularities of the Argentine case. Presumably, the contents of a 'Catholic ethic of care' would be somewhat different from those of a 'feminist ethic of care'. While these ethical approaches are not mutually exclusive, one could expect the former to be rather conservative, while the latter would be more progressive. What my research clearly shows is that the deployment of an ethic of care does not lead to an adherence to feminism on the part of either men or women judges.

III. Concluding remarks

Despite the fact that women judges in my study laid a stronger emphasis on care than men judges, both tended to deploy their caring capacities when exercising their work as family judges. Both argued that a caring approach makes a difference to those coming to court searching for a legal resolution to their family problems must be valued positively as an important constituent of an adequate judicial service, along with the more traditional requirements, such as knowledge of the law, fairness and honesty. This evidence will help to undermine the conventional stereotype that family law is an area for which women are better suited than men.

This paper summarises the main findings of a study of gender differences in the values and attitudes of family judges carried out in Buenos Aires, Argentina. The study explored how men and women judges understood their profession and its requirements, their representation of the ideal family judge, their motivation to become family judges, the way they experienced the power they wield, and their opinion on the supposed contributions women judges might bring to the family judiciary.

The study's findings were analysed in terms of Gilligan's ethic of justice/ethic of care approach.

Two key results emerged. Firstly, there were no clear-cut differences between men and women in terms of their adherence to an ethic of justice or of care, respectively. Secondly, distinct gender differences were apparent in the way women judges approached decision-making. The most significant contribution that women seemed to be making to the family judiciary consists of the introduction of an interdisciplinary approach to the resolution of family problems.

Research on women in the judiciary is still embryonic in Argentina, my own study having been the first empirical project to address gender within the judiciary. As women's participation in the legal realm increases noticeably and we encounter women in authoritative positions within the judiciary more often, new and exciting possibilities for research materialise. I hope this first attempt will pave the way for a new body of scholarship to emerge.

References

Bender, L. (1997) From gender difference to feminist solidarity: using Carol Gilligan and an ethic of care in law, in: Hilaire Barnett (Ed.) *Sourcebook on Feminist Jurisprudence* (Great Britain, Cavendish Publishing Limited), pp. 203–11.

Boigeol, A. (2003) Male strategies in the face of the feminisation of a profession: the case of the French judiciary, in: U. Schultz & G. Shaw (Eds) *Women in the World's Legal Professions*, Oñati International Series in Law and Society (Oxford & Portland, OR, Hart Publishing), pp. 401–18.

Botelho Junqueira, E. (1997a) A juiza-mulher: conflictos e impasses no espaco da casa, *Serie Pesquisa* N°2, Junho (Rio de Janeiro, Instituto Direito e Sociedade (IDES)).

Botelho Junqueira, E. (1997b) A feminizacao da magistratura, *Serie Pesquisa* N°3, Agosto (Rio de Janeiro, Instituto Direito e Sociedade (IDES)).

Botelho Junqueira, E. (1997c) A experiencia das mulheres na magistratura: a conquista de um espaco, *Serie Pesquisa* N°4, Agosto (Rio de Janeiro, Instituto Direito e Sociedade (IDES)).

Botelho Junqueira, E. (1997d) A contribuicao da mulher a administracao de justice, *Serie Pesquisa* N°5 (Rio de Janeiro, Instituto Direito e Sociedade (IDES)).

Botelho Junqueira, E. (1999) *A professionalizacao da mulher na advogacia. Relatorio Final* (Rio de Janeiro, Fundacao Carlos Chagas).

Botelho Junqueira, E. (2003) Women in the judiciary: a perspective from Brazil, in: U. Schultz & G. Shaw (Eds) *Women in the World's Legal Professions*, Oñati International Series in Law and Society (Oxford & Portland, OR, Hart Publishing), pp. 437–50.

Conaghan, J. (2000) Reassessing the feminist legal project in law, *Journal of Law and Society*, 27(3), pp. 351–85.

Drakopolou, M. (2000) The ethic of care, female subjectivity and feminist legal scholarship, *Feminist Legal Studies*, 8, pp. 199–226.

Flanagan, O. & Jackson, C. (1994) Situating feminism, from thought to action, in: M.J. Larrabee (Ed.) *The Ethic of Care* (Sage International), p. 74.

Fox Keller, E. (1985) *Reflections on Gender and Science* (New Haven, CT & London, Yale University Press).

Freyer, J.A. (1995) Women litigators in search of a care-oriented judicial system, *Journal of Gender and the Law*, 4(199), pp. 199–218.

Garcia de León, M.A. (1994) *Elites Discriminadas Sobre el Poder de las Mujeres* (Colombia, Anthropos).

Gastrón, A. (1988). Situación de la mujer en la Facultad de Derecho y Ciencias Sociales de la UBA, paper presented at the Conference *La juventud en la Argentina, ¿y la mujer joven?* organised by Subsecretaría de Juventud, Buenos Aires, organised by Subsecretaría de Juventud.

Gastrón, A. (1991) *Situación actual de la mujer en el poder judicial argentino* (Buenos Aires, Premio Coca Cola en las Artes y las Ciencias).

Gilligan, C. (1982) *In a Different Voice: Psychological Theory and Women's Development* (Cambridge, MA, Harvard University Press).

Gilligan, C., Mackinnon, Menkel-Meadow, C. *et al.* (1985) The James MacKormic Mitchell lecture: feminist discourse moral values and the law, a conversation, *Buffalo Law Review*, 34, p. 1.

Harrington, M. (1994) *Women Lawyers. Rewriting the Rules* (USA, Plume, Penguin Books).

Heyes, C.J. (1997) Anti-essentialism in practice: Carol Gilligan and feminist philosophy, *Hypatia, Bloomington*, 1(3), pp. 149–63.

Hunter, R. (2002) Talking up equality: women barristers and the denial of discrimination, *Feminist Legal Studies*, 10, pp. 113–20.

Hunter, R. (2003a) Women in the legal profession: the Australian profile, in: U. Schultz & G. Shaw (Eds) *Women in the World's Legal Professions*, Oñati International Series in Law and Society (Oxford & Portland, OR, Hart Publishing), pp. 87–102.

Hunter, R. (2003b) Women barristers and gender difference in Australia, in: U. Schultz & G. Shaw (Eds) *Women in the World's Legal Professions*, Oñati International Series in Law and Society (Oxford & Portland, OR, Hart Publishing), pp. 103–22.

Jack, D. & Jack, R. (1988) Women lawyers, archetypes and alternatives, in: C. Gilligan, J.V. Ward & J.M. Taylor (Eds) *Mapping the Moral Domain* (Cambridge, MA, Harvard University Press).

Jones, K. (1993) *Compassionate Authority, Democracy and the Representation of Women* (New York, Routledge).

Kohen, B. (2005a) Dónde están las mujeres del derecho en la ciudad de Buenos Aires, *Revista Academia* n°6 (Facultad de Derecho de UBA).

Kohen, B. (2005b) Más mujeres en la justicia: los argumentos más frecuentes, *Revista Academia* n°6 (Facultad de Derecho de UBA).

Mackinson, G. (1985) *El juez Ideal* (Buenos Aires, Facultad de Derecho UBA).

Mackinson, G. (1987) *Sociología del Poder Judicial* (Buenos Aires, Ediciones Sociología del Derecho).

Mackinson, G. (1988) La mujer y el derecho. Estudio sobre las variaciones de la matrícula femenina en la Facultad de Derecho y Ciencias Sociales de la UBA, *Revista de Sociología del Derecho*, (No. 2 and 4).

Mackinson, G. (1991) *La escuela de la Magistratura: Modernización y Eficiencia* (Universidad de Buenos Aires, Facultad de Derecho y Ciencias Sociales, Secretaría de Ciencia y Técnica).

Mackinson, G. & Goldstein, M. (1988) *La Magistratura de Buenos Aires. Un estudio sociológico* (Buenos Aires, Literaria Jurídica).

Merryman, J. (1993) *The Civil Law Tradition* (Stanford, Stanford University Press).

McGlynn, C. (1996) A different voice?, *New Law Journal*, 31 May, p. 816.

McGlynn, C. (1998a) *The Woman Lawyer, Making the Difference* (London, Butterworths).

McGlynn, C. (Ed.) (1998b) *Legal Feminisms: Theory and Practice* (London, Ashgate Publishing Limited).

McGlynn, C. (1998c) Will women judges make a difference?, *New Law Journal*, 29 May, p. 813.

McGlynn, C. (1999) Judging women differently: gender, the judiciary and reform, in: S. Millns & N. Witty (Eds) *Feminist Perspectives on Public Law* (London, Cavendish), pp. 87–106.

McGlynn, C. (2003) The status of women lawyers in the United Kingdom, in: U. Schultz & G. Shaw (Eds) *Women in the World's Legal Professions*, Oñati International Series in Law and Society (Oxford & Portland, OR, Hart Publishing), pp. 138–58.

Menkel-Meadow, C. (1989) Feminisation of the legal profession, the comparative sociology of women lawyers, in: R. Abel & P. Lewis (Eds) *Lawyers in Society, Comparative Theories* (University of California Press), pp. 196–255.

Menkel-Meadow, C. (1995) Portia's redux: another look at gender, feminism and legal ethics, in: C. Sampford (Ed.) *Legal Ethics and Legal Practice: Contemporary Issues* (Oxford, Clarendon Press).

Menkel-Meadow, C. (1996) Women's ways of 'knowing' law: feminist legal epistemology, pedagogy and jurisprudence, in: N. Goldberger, J. Tarule, B. Clinchy & M. Belenky (Eds) *Knowledge; Difference and Power, Essays Inspired in Women's Ways of Knowing* (New York, Basic Books), pp. 57–84.

Menkel-Meadow, C. (1997) Portia in a different voice: speculations on a woman's lawyering process, in: B. Hilaire (Ed.) *Sourcebook on Feminist Jurisprudence* (Great Britain, Cavendish Publishing Limited), pp. 196–203.

Merryman, J. (1993) *The Civil Law Tradition* (Stanford, Stanford University Press).

Mossman, M.J. (1986) Feminism and legal method: the difference it makes, *Australian Journal of Law and Society*, 3, pp. 30–52.

Mossman, M.J. (1988) Invisible constraints on lawyering and leadership: the case of women lawyers, *Ottawa Law Review*, 20, p. 567.

Mossman, M.J. (1989) *Gender Bias and the Legal Profession: Challenges and Choices. Research Consultation on How to Study Gender Bias and the Law, The Courts and the Legal Profession* (Vancouver, BC, Osgoode Hall—School of York University).

Schultz, U. (2003a) Introduction: women in the world's legal professions: overview and synthesis, in: U. Schultz & G. Shaw (Eds) *Women in the World's Legal Professions*, Oñati International Series in Law and Society (Oxford & Portland, OR, Hart Publishing), pp. xxv–liv, Oñati International Series in Law and Society.

Schultz, U. (2003b) The status of women lawyers in Germany, in: U. Schultz & G. Shaw (Eds) *Women in the World's Legal Professions*, Oñati International Series in Law and Society (Oxford & Portland, OR, Hart Publishing), pp. 271–94.

Schultz, U. & Shaw, G. (Eds) (2003) *Women in the World's Legal Professions*, Oñati International Series in Law and Society (Oxford & Portland, OR, Hart Publishing).

Sevenhuijsen, S. (1996) *Citizenship and the Ethics of Care, Feminist Considerations on Justice, Morality and Politics* (London, Routledge).

Sherry, S. (1986a) The gender of judges, *Law and Inequality*, 159(198), p. 160.

Sherry, S. (1986b) Civic virtue and the feminine voice of constitutional adjudication, *Virginia Law Review*, 72(3), pp. 543–616.

Sommerlad, H. (1998a) The gendering of the professional subject: commitment, choice and social closure in the legal profession, in: C. McGlynn (Ed.) *Legal Feminisms: Theory and Practice* (London, Ashgate Publishing Limited).

Sommerlad, H. (1998b) *Gender, Choice and Commitment, Women Solicitors in England and Wales and the Struggle for Equal Status* (Dartmouth, Ashgate).

Sommerlad, H. (2003) Can women lawyer differently?, in: U. Schultz & G. Shaw (Eds) *Women in the World's Legal Professions*, Oñati International Series in Law and Society (Oxford & Portland, OR, Hart Publishing), pp. 191–224.

Thornton, M. (1996) *Dissonnance and Distrust: Women in the Legal Profession* (Melbourne, Oxford University Press).

Toharia, A. (1975) *El juez español* (Madrid, Tecnos).

Torrado, S. (2003) *Historia de la Familia, en la Argentina Moderna (1870–2000)* (Buenos Aires, Ediciones de la Flor).

Tronto, J. (1996) *Moral Boundaries, a Political Argument for an Ethic of Care* (London, Routledge).

Wainerman, C. (2002) *Familia Trabajo y Género.un Mundo de Nuevas Relaciones* (Buenos Aires, UNICEF/ Fondo de Cultura Económica).

West, R. (1988) Jurisprudence and gender, *The University of Chicago Law Review*, 55(1), pp. 1–72.

West, R. (1997) *Caring for Justice* (New York & London, New York University Press).

Women and the judiciary in Syria: appointments process, training and career paths

MONIQUE C. CARDINAL
Faculté de théologie et de sciences religieuses, Université Laval, Québec, Canada

ABSTRACT *This article describes the recruitment, training and career paths of women judges and public prosecutors in Syria over a period of 30 years (1975–2005). It analyses both quantitative and qualitative data drawn from official statistics and interviews conducted with 67 women judges and public prosecutors in Syria's largest cities, Damascus and Aleppo. The paper focuses on how training of the judiciary has changed since the founding of the new Institute of Judicial Studies and the effect this change has had on women's career paths. The entry of women to the judiciary in 1975 and the restructuring of the training system in 2002 are the two most important events in the recent history of the judiciary in Syria.*

1. Introduction

Nisrīn Āghā, a young woman jurist from Syria, was one of the top nine candidates to get a perfect score on the National Judicial Examination held on 27 April 2007. This examination is taken after legal studies at the university and allows candidates to join the Institute of Judicial Studies (*al-Ma'had al-qada'ī*) for a two-year programme in order to train as judges and public prosecutors. The examination of 2007 was new: the first multiple-choice test to be used to recruit young jurists. Because scores were computer-generated, a larger number of candidates than in the past sat for the exam: 1,374 signed up, 165 did not show, 850 passed (i.e. had a score of at least 70%) and 219 or 26% of them were women.[1] In order to create a greater pool of candidates to choose from, the Ministry of Justice had adopted the new exam format, increased the age limit from 30 to 32 and lowered standards: law graduates needed only a grade point average of 58% (while the previous year 61% had been required).[2] Obviously, Syria is in need of more judges and public prosecutors.

Another noteworthy accomplishment is that of Hanān al-Bayrūtī who, along with a man colleague, graduated from the Institute of Judicial Studies (IJS) in July 2007 at the top of her class with the score of 96.17 out of 100. It was the first time since the new Institute had opened in 2002 that a woman had finished the two-year training programme in the highest ranks. These recent successes resemble past ones, for example, when women jurists qualified in the first National Judicial Examination open to them in 1977. They completed the one-year training programme with the best scores on the final exams.[3] Throughout the years, women judges and public prosecutors have had to maintain the highest standards in order to prove to the Ministry of Justice and Syrian society at large that they are indeed capable of holding judicial office.

This article aims to describe the recruitment, training and career paths of women judges and public prosecutors in Syria over a period of 30 years (1975–2005). It examines how the training of the judiciary has changed since the founding of the new IJS and the effect this change has had on women's career paths. The entry of women to the judiciary in 1975 and the restructuring of the training system in 2002 are the two most important events in the recent history of the judiciary in Syria. Both events have transformed the administration of justice in Syria. This article does not aim to examine the impact of women and the IJS on the working of the judiciary—that will be the subject of an upcoming contribution—however, it lays the groundwork for future thought.

2. The judiciary of Syria, a civil law country

The civil law judicial system of Syria is based on the French system and is divided into two court structures: ordinary courts and administrative courts. This article focuses on the appointments process of judges and public prosecutors of the ordinary courts. The Syrian judiciary is a career judiciary. The selection process is founded on academic merit and competitive examinations. A candidate must have a degree in law but is not required to practise as a lawyer in order to participate in the exams. After having passed the National Judicial Examination, the newly-recruited appointees undergo a two-year training programme at the IJS situated in the capital of Syria, Damascus. If they successfully complete the programme and pass the final examinations, they are appointed as judges to the lower courts, as deputy public prosecutors or investigating judges. They move up the judicial ranks based on seniority and positive evaluations. The mandatory retirement age of judges and public prosecutors was recently increased (December 2006) to 70 years of age.[4]

3. The current National Judicial Examination

The National Judicial Examination consists of two parts: a written and an oral one. Those candidates who pass the written examination qualify to take the oral examination. If they pass this second examination they are appointed as judicial trainees and receive a salary for two years during their training at the IJS.

The subjects covered in the written examination are civil and criminal law, civil and criminal procedural law and law of evidence. Each section is worth 20 marks and, in order to pass, the candidate must obtain a total grade of 70, providing that for any given section he or she does not score less than eight.[5] The oral examination is conducted by the High Judiciary Council (*majlis al-quadā̀ al-aʿlā*). This council is responsible for the nomination, promotion, transfer, discipline, removal, approval of retirement, leave of absence and resignation of judges and public prosecutors (all decisions to be signed by the minister of justice as stated in article 65 of the Judicial Authority Law no. 98 of 1961 with amendments). The most senior (and powerful) judges of the Syrian judiciary sit on the council: the minister of justice, the president and the two vice-presidents of the Court of Cassation, the attorney-general of the Syrian Arab Republic and the director of the Judicial Inspection Department.[6] Officially the President of the Syrian Arab Republic is the head of the High Judiciary Council, but it is the minister of justice who acts in his place. All new appointments to the judiciary are issued in a decree signed by the President. Table 1 gives the results of candidates granted permission to sit for the National Judicial Examination of the first four cohorts of the IJS.[7]

Recently, the oral examination has been decisive in determining which candidates are nominated as trainee judges and public prosecutors (Figure 2). It will have a crunching effect for the new trainees of 2007–08: the 850 candidates who passed the written examination must be reduced to about 100 since the IJS cannot accommodate a greater number of entrants.[8]

Figure 1 shows that men candidates have consistently performed better in the written exam, but over time women's performance has improved globally. In addition, women and men have a similar success rate in the oral exam (Figure 2), an indication that this exam[9] has not been used, unlike in other countries,[10] as a means to limit the number of women entering the judiciary. Oral examinations have the reputation of being more subjective and can generate results that differ significantly from the evaluation process of written examinations. The results of Figure 2 confirm that the women candidates of the IJS were not subject to any overt discrimination in the selection process for the period 2002–05. In fact, the average percentage of women appointed to the judiciary since 2002, 34% (Table 1), is extremely high when compared to results of the past.

Table 1. *Cohorts of the Institute of Judicial Studies*

				Written exam			Oral exam			
	Candidates admitted			Successful candidates			Successful candidates			
Cohorts	Men	Women	Total	Men	Women	Total	Men	Women	Total	% of women
2002–1st	17	10	27	13	6	19	13	6	19	32
2003–2nd	32	22	54	24	14	38	23	13	36	36
2003–3rd	29	19	48	20	11	31	15	8	23	35
2005–4th	129	80	209	86	50	136	39	20	59	34

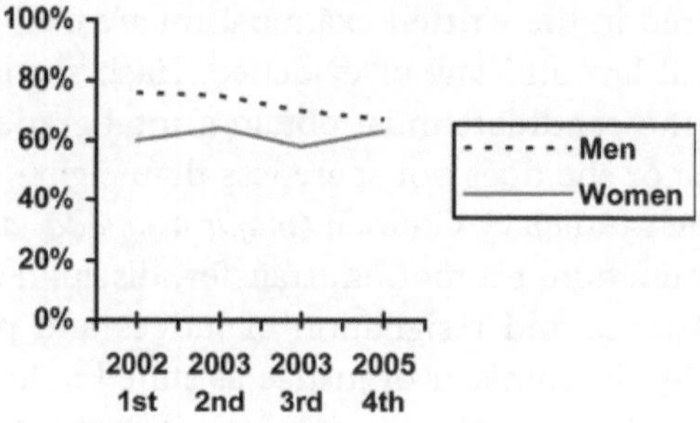

Figure 1. *Success rates in written exam*

4. Past National Judicial Examinations

The National Judicial Examination of 1977, the first open to women, consisted only of an oral examination. The applicants were drawn from a pool of public sector employees who had law degrees. At the time, the government was unable to recruit women lawyers because their number was insufficient to supply enough candidates. For example, in 1975, when the first woman member of the judiciary was appointed, there were only four reputable, actively practising women lawyers at the Damascus courthouse,[11] one of whom, Ghāda Murād, fit the profile: a successful lawyer of nine years' experience with a promising career before her (at the time, she was only 34).[12]

The 21 women applicants who passed the judicial oral examination of 1977 worked in a variety of jobs in the public sector: state bank employees, teachers, an executive member of the Women's General Union, director of the contract department of the state-owned electricity company, court official at the Aleppo courthouse, civil servants in different ministries, school director, assistant director at an all-girls' school, employees in a state-owned foreign trade company, administrator in the Faculty of Fine Arts of Damascus University, employee in a state-owned milling company, manager of a state department store, etc.[13] Nine of the 21 women candidates completed the one-year training programme in 1978 and, in 1979, were appointed public prosecutors in Damascus (three), Latakia (one), Idlib (two), Aleppo (one), Homs (one) and Deir ez-Zor (one).[14] That was a success rate of 43%, while the success rate of men proved to be 28%: 45 of the 162 men candidates were appointed. Nonetheless, only 17% of the total number of appointees were women.

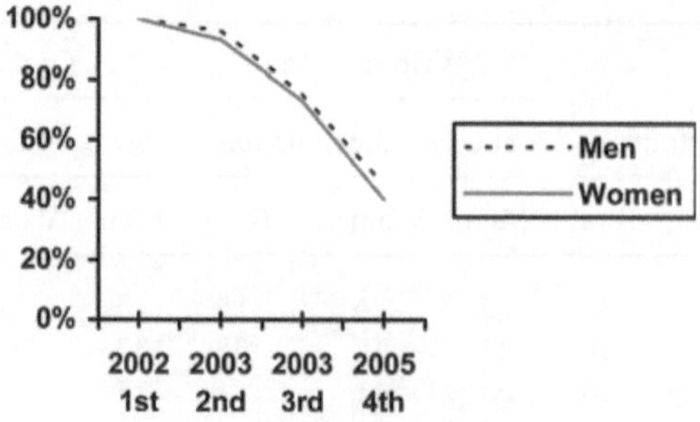

Figure 2. *Success rates in oral exam*

Table 2. *Recruits of National Judicial Examinations*

Year of appointment	Men	Women	Total	% of Women
1979	45	9	54	17
1981	120	7	127	6
1986	119	10	129	8
1993	207	43	250	17
1995	320	53	373	14
1998	215	27	242	11

A woman judge of this first generation relates how she entered the judiciary not of her own doing. Some young men employees under her supervision at the state-owned electricity company wanted to take the judicial oral examination which they had seen advertised at the Damascus courthouse[15] and decided to sign her up as well. Her mother encouraged her to participate in the exam, and she recalls that she was very calm and easily answered the questions about civil and criminal law put to her. She passed the exam, but her men colleagues did not.[16] Her story is typical of women of her generation. Not a single one imagined that she would pursue a career in the judiciary. Before then, it had not been a career option open to women.

In subsequent National Judicial Examinations, the number of women recruits was relatively low (except in 1993) as indicated in Table 2.[17]

How does one explain the higher percentage of women appointees, 34%, in recent years? A possible explanation is the increase in the number of women law graduates. Table 3 shows the number of law graduates over a 30-year period for the two largest universities, Damascus and Aleppo, which, until recently, were the only institutions of legal education in Syria.[18] The years selected correspond to the dates of the National Judicial Examinations.

Table 3. *Law graduates, 1975–2005*

	Damascus University				Aleppo University			
Year	Men	Women	Total	% of women	Men	Women	Total	% of women
1975–76	163	15	178	8	–	–	–	–
1978–79	248	23	271	8	–	–	–	–
1981–82	452	49	501	10	–	–	–	–
1985–86	545	54	599	9	176	15	191	8
1992–93	893	210	1,103	19	578	99	677	15
1995–96	1,022	343	1,365	25	697	122	819	15
1997–98	1,306	461	1,767	26	1,054	210	1,264	17
2001–02	755	287	1,042	28	497	119	616	19
2002–03	822	386	1,208	32	485	114	599	19
2003–04	890	387	1,277	30	534	127	661	19
2004–05	1,104	454	1,588	29	419	95	514	18

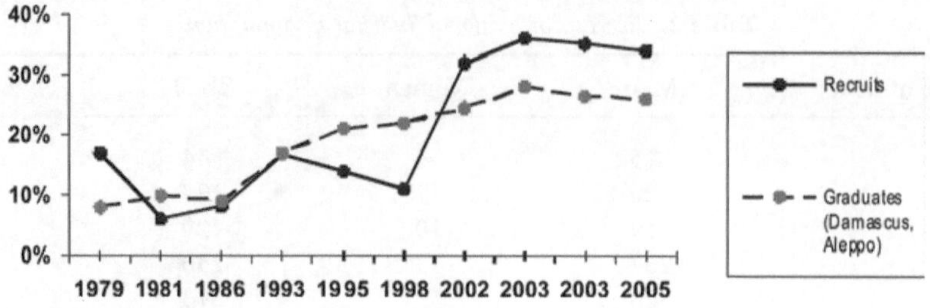

Figure 3. *Women judicial recruits and law graduates*

The percentages of Tables 2 and 3 represented in Figure 3 show that the appointment of women judges and public prosecutors in comparison to women law graduates was disproportionate for the first generation of women appointees: 17% of judges and public prosecutors appointed in 1979 were women while the average percentage of women law graduates from the mid-1970s to the early 1980s was around 9%. Appointment policy of the Ministry of Justice can account for the significant number of women who entered the judiciary in 1979. At the time, the Ministry's aim was to introduce as many women as possible to the judiciary and, in order to do so, as mentioned earlier, recruited among public sector employees with law degrees because this was the largest available pool of well-educated women workers in Syria. From the mid-1980s to the early 1990s, the percentage of women judicial appointees corresponded to that of women law graduates in Syria (Damascus + Aleppo graduates). However, the percentage of women judicial recruits decreased significantly in comparison to the percentage of women law graduates in the mid- and late 1990s. It is only with the founding of the IJS in 2002 that the percentage of women judicial recruits exceeded that of women law graduates in Syria. The higher percentage of women judicial recruits in recent years is perhaps indicative of a proactive policy on the part of the Ministry of Justice to increase the overall number of women members of the judiciary. However, further research is required in order to determine if, indeed, the Ministry has adopted such a policy.

5. Damascus, capital of women judges and public prosecutors

The greater number of women law graduates at Damascus University in comparison to Aleppo University (Table 3) translates into a higher number of women judges and public prosecutors in the capital. In December 2004, there were 66 women judges and public prosecutors (and 210 men) in Damascus, while for the same year, there were only 16 women judges and public prosecutors (and 208 men) in Aleppo.[19] In all, 24% of judges and public prosecutors in Damascus were women, double the national average of 12% in 2004; the percentage of women judges and public prosecutors in Aleppo was 7%. Though Aleppo is the second largest city after Damascus, there exist important differences between the two in regards to women's higher education and participation in the workforce. In 2004, only 8% of women in Aleppo had access to a secondary or university education in comparison to 23% of women in

Damascus (Courbage, 2007, p. 203). Likewise, while women made up approximately 12.4% of the Syrian workforce (other than agricultural work) in 2003, their participation in paid labour was less in Aleppo: 6% (Courbage, 2007, pp. 187, 204).[20] The much lower percentage of educated women in Aleppo explains why fewer women work in the legal profession. To the contrary, women judges and public prosecutors (in addition to women court clerks and judicial staff) have been more visible at the Damascus courthouse since women were first appointed to the judiciary in the 1970s. It is possible that this visibility has had the effect of attracting larger numbers of women jurists to judicial office in the capital in comparison to other cities in Syria where women judges and public prosecutors are few in number. One cannot deny the importance of role modelling when it comes to career choice. If it is true to say that the more women law graduates there are, the greater the number of potential women candidates for judicial office, it is even truer to say that the greater the number of women judges and public prosecutors who work in the courthouses, the more the public, the men—lawyers, judges and public prosecutors—get used to working with them. In people's minds, it has become more socially acceptable for women to hold judicial office than in the past. As a result, more and more women jurists choose the judiciary as a career. But, as earlier demonstrated, government policy of raising and lowering the standards for admission also greatly determines the outcome of the judicial selection process.

6. Social profiles of women judges and public prosecutors

Higher education at public universities is state-financed in Syria. Top scores on the baccalauréat exam (the grade 12 national examination) enable a student to enter the best faculties at university: medicine, dentistry, pharmacology, information technology, engineering . . . and law. Thus, career choice depends more on academic merit than on the socioeconomic status of a person—i.e. the ability to pay for an education—as in the case of a private university system. A change in mentalities and free access to higher education are factors that have contributed to more women obtaining degrees and entering the workforce. During a series of 67 interviews[21] the author conducted with women judges and public prosecutors in Syria (Damascus, its countryside and Aleppo)[22] over a period of three years (2004–07), it became apparent that these women come from a wide variety of social backgrounds.

A significant proportion of women, 18%, have fathers who work in the legal profession (judge, lawyer and court clerk), while military officers and low-ranking civil servants each account for 16% of the women's fathers' professions. Merchants (14%), teachers (6%) and police officers (5%) follow in number (Figure 4). Women's access to higher education has resulted in a greater social mobility as demonstrated by the fact that some of the women's fathers are farmers, a tailor, carpenter, mechanic and driver.[23] The most important difference in social status is between the mothers and their daughters: 89% of the women judges' and public prosecutors' mothers are homemakers. As for those mothers who work, the majority of them are teachers (6%, Figure 5).[24] It is today's women professionals who constitute on a wider scale the first generation of working mothers in Syria.

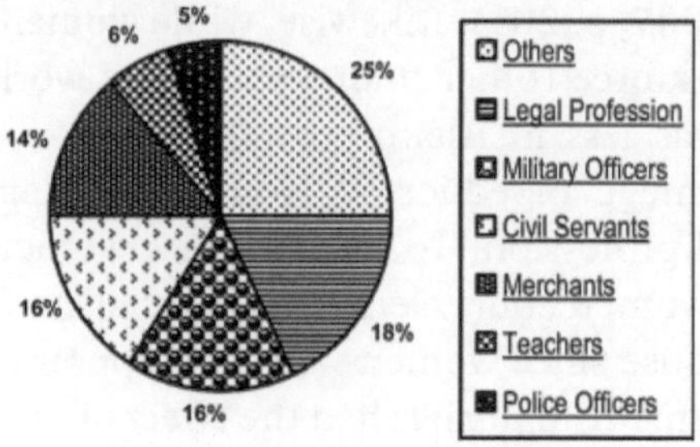

Figure 4. *Fathers' professions*

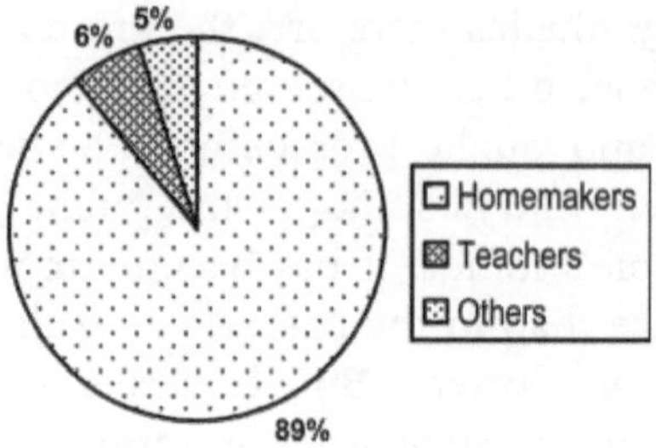

Figure 5. *Mothers' professions*

These findings differ from those of Mahmoud M. Hamad in the first part of his contribution, 'The politics of judicial selection in Egypt' (Hamad, 2006, pp. 262–3). Hamad hypothesises, without sufficient data, that members of the Egyptian judiciary are from 'the upper-middle or upper stratum of society' (Hamad, 2006, p. 263) with 'over one-half of the new appointees [being] relatives of sitting or former judges [...] [s]iblings of government ministers, MPs, governors, university professors, and top officials of the military–bureaucratic establishment' (Hamad, 2006, p. 276, footnote 14). This was not the case with Syrian judges and public prosecutors surveyed in this article—but, then again, only women and not men members of the judiciary were interviewed. In Syria, it is a well-established fact that state-financed higher education has played a major role in enabling gifted high-school graduates of lower socio-economic status (of the two sexes) to acquire a university education and work in a profession that often differs from the professions of their parents, particularly mothers as was observed. In regards to women's appointment to the judiciary, government policy was the determining factor as previously mentioned. It is common knowledge that without government support, Syrian women simply would not have entered the judiciary when they did, given the widespread public resistance and lukewarm enthusiasm of the (male) legal profession to women holding judicial office in the 1970s.

7. Education and career paths

The interviews conducted also provided information on the women's age at appointment, the number of years they trained and practised as lawyers, those who obtained an LLM, their marital status and number of children.

The selection process adopted by the IJS in 2002 requires that candidates be between 26 and 30 years of age—(32 as of spring 2007). Before 2002, 18 women appointees were under the age of 26 (30%) while 11 were over the age of 30 (18%). Among the young appointees, only two had completed an LLM and three had practised as lawyers. Among the older candidates, it can be observed that from 1993 onwards, more and more women were lawyers before their appointment to the judiciary. In addition, it is striking that since 1998, a greater proportion of women, 35%, have obtained an advanced law degree (LLM) while before, only 2% had. It became apparent that the older the candidate upon appointment, the more legal experience and education she had. For example, two judges, who were respectively appointed at the ages of 51 and 49, were at their third career change: they had previously worked as an English teacher and a lawyer, a court clerk and a notary.[25] By increasing the age of appointment to 26 as a condition to participate in the 2002 National Judicial Examination, the Ministry of Justice aimed to attract a greater proportion of candidates who had more legal experience and education.

Among the six graduates of the IJS interviewed,[26] two had an LLM, one had practised as a lawyer for six years, another one had both an LLM and practised as a lawyer for three years and, finally, a fifth graduate had completed $1\frac{1}{2}$ years of training as a lawyer. The new selection process of the IJS seems to encourage potential candidates to increase their legal knowledge and experience before applying. The fact that men are required to do compulsory military service for two years after graduating from university could also explain why the minimum age requirement was increased to 26.[27] Since women do not do military service, one might conclude that they acquire more training in law, either as lawyers or by obtaining a higher degree than their men counterparts who participate in the National Judicial Examination. However, data on men judicial candidates must be compiled in order to determine if the women do have higher degrees or more experience as lawyers than the men.

Despite the age limits imposed by the new selection process of 2002, the Ministry of Justice continues to periodically recruit mature candidates who have practised as lawyers for either 10 or 16 years. These candidates neither sit the National Judicial Examination nor are they required to complete the two-year training programme at the IJS. Rather, they undergo an evaluation process conducted by the High Judiciary Council. This form of recruitment is practised by the Ministry when there is a shortage of judges in the higher courts. For example, one woman, recruited as a lawyer of 16 years' experience, was appointed to a civil appeal court in 2003 at the age of 42.[28] However, the percentage of women recruited as mature candidates in comparison to those recruited to train at the IJS is lower. For example in 2003, 15% of lawyers of 16 years' experience (or more) recruited as mature candidates were women,[29] while, for the same year, approximately 36% of the new trainees at the IJS were women (Table 1). The Syrian example confirms the results of comparative studies of the appointments process and training of judges in common and civil law countries. These studies show that the proportion of women entering the judiciary in common law countries, whose recruitment pool is constituted almost exclusively of mature candidates, is systematically lower than in civil law countries, where the majority of candidates are selected according to their scores on competitive examinations and academic merit (see Schultz & Shaw, 2003, p. xxxvii). Interrupted career paths and part-time working schedules due to family commitments disadvantage women in a selection process based on years of continuous practice in the different branches of the legal profession.

8. Career choices and family commitments

Of the 67 women judges and public prosecutors interviewed, 25 (37%) had finished their two-year apprenticeship as a lawyer in order to earn the title of *maître* (*ustādh*), 18 of whom had practised law (27%) for an extended period. This information, when cross-referenced with marital status, shows that before appointment to the judiciary, a greater proportion of single women (47%, nine out of 19) practised as lawyers in comparison to married/divorced women (19%, nine out of 48). A majority of the interviewees claimed they preferred the judiciary as a career over the advocacy because of job security and the regular work schedule.[30] Many women did not like the competitive nature of the advocacy, the long hours, the running around at the courthouse in the mornings and the constant contact with clients in the afternoons. They felt that being a judge was a more dignified career for a woman and allowed them to better cope with family commitments and work. The bringing up of children and household duties explain, in part, why women prefer the regular schedule and salary of a judge and public prosecutor over the more risky business of exercising a liberal profession. Of the 67 women interviewed, 48 were married or divorced (72%), and only three of them had not had children. The average number of children per woman was 2.27, a figure considerably lower than the fertility rate of Syria which was 3.58 in 2004.[31] As other women civil servants, women members of the judiciary benefit from the usual paid maternity leave: 120 days for the first child, 90 for the second, 75 for the third ... but they receive no paid maternity leave for the fourth.[32] This policy of reducing maternity leave in proportion to a greater number of children is the government's way of discouraging women from having too many children in order to lower the extremely high birth-rate of Syria.[33] Of the 48 mothers interviewed, three have four children and therefore did not receive any paid maternity leave for their last child, while 14 of the women who have three children did not receive adequate paid maternity leave for their youngest child. In addition, there are no government day care centres made available for women judges and public prosecutors. Women are often criticised by men colleagues and court staff for taking too much leave of absence and too many sick days, which cause case loads to build up. There is a general sentiment among men colleagues and court staff that many women judges and public prosecutors do not fully assume their professional responsibilities. During interviews, it also became clear that the married women with family commitments preferred to preside over a criminal court, since less research and time are required to decide a case. In addition, before and after pregnancy, women judges often request that they be transferred to the public prosecutor's office because being a prosecutor is basically an office job and does not require that case files be taken home. Civil law is seen more as the single woman's, widowed or divorced woman's (with few or no children) domain. Many interviewees stated that civil law is 'as vast as an ocean', and to decide a civil law case can be extremely time-consuming. Since the majority of women judges are mothers and spouses, it is not surprising that many of them do not work in civil law for an extended period of time. Of the seven women judges of the 1979 and 1981 cohorts who, as the highest-ranking judges, are now assigned full-time to the different divisions of the Court of Cassation according to their area of specialisation,[34] only one works in civil law.[35]

9. Training

The IJS offers a programme that provides both theoretical and practical training in the courts and public prosecutor's office. Seminars are given in the following areas of law: 30 hours (each) in civil law and civil procedural law; 25 hours in criminal procedural law and law of evidence; 20 hours in the areas of criminal, personal status, property, modern technology and commercial law; 15 hours in rent law, foreign language (French and English), Arabic and judicial ethics. The trainees also learn computer and Internet skills and are presented short lectures on administrative law, labour law, the Judicial Authority Law and the Bar Association Law, the judicial police and forensic medicine. In addition, they periodically visit different facilities: property records offices, police stations, forensic medicine divisions, union offices, centres for young offenders, etc. As for training at the courthouse, the trainees spend three months in the public prosecutor's office and the investigating judges' division, and three months in the lower courts, focusing on civil and criminal cases, the procedure for implementing civil court decisions and personal status and property cases. Non-attendance is strictly monitored and any trainee that has not been to a minimum of 80% of lectures and practical training cannot take the final exams (written and oral). In order to pass any given subject, the trainee must obtain at least 60%. Upon successfully completing the two-year programme, the trainee is then officially sworn in as a member of the judiciary[36] and appointed by the High Judiciary Council to a lower court (civil or criminal peace court, personal status court), to the public prosecutor's office or as an investigating judge.[37]

9.1. *Women trainers and trainees*

Since the IJS opened in 2002, two senior women judges have participated in training the recruits. Ghāda Murād, the first woman to join the Syrian judiciary in 1975, teaches evidence law, and Lutfiyya 'Ubayd, a judge of the first generation of women appointed in 1979, taught criminal law at the IJS while acting as the programme director. These two women first participated in the training of judges as early as 1993.[38] For a one-month period, all appointees attended lectures at the Damascus courthouse—and thus were taught by Judges Murād and 'Ubayd—and then returned to their respective city centres to do training for a total of five months equally divided between six sections at the courthouses of Damascus, Aleppo and Homs:[39] (1) public prosecutor's office; (2) civil peace court; (3) criminal peace court; (4) investigating judges' division; (5) personal status court or juvenile court;[40] and (6) the civil court executive judges' division.[41] Before the new programme of the IJS, most training sessions were for a six-month period, except for the first training session women were admitted to in 1978 which lasted, as already mentioned, a full year. It, therefore, took an average of 16 years after women first entered the judiciary for them to acquire the expertise (and confidence of their men colleagues) to train incoming judges and public prosecutors. In addition, they played a direct role in the selection process when Justice Ghāda Murād was appointed attorney-general of Syria in 1998, the first woman to hold such a position in the Arab world. As a member of the High Judiciary Council, she had a word in deciding which candidate would become a member of the judiciary. However, her voice was one among many. Since her retirement in August 2006, there is no longer a woman who is member of the High Judiciary Council and officially has a say in the selection process.

During the interviews, some women judges and public prosecutors appointed before 2002 stated that they trained for a shorter period than six months. For example, practising lawyers with six years experience once recruited for the judiciary only had to train for one month before holding office.[42] Likewise, the women court clerks with a degree in law, commonly known at the courthouse as 'the maidens of the court' (*banāt al-qasr*), who passed the National Judicial Examination, also only trained for a short period or were exempted from training because of their many years of experience laboriously writing out the court minutes as dictated by the presiding judge[43] and keeping court files.[44]

10. Trends over the past 30 years: the budding career woman

The new IJS was created with the intention of improving the quality of judicial training. First, training was extended to two years providing for more lecture hours on law and longer periods of courthouse experience. Second, the minimum age requirement was increased to 26, allowing men to do their military service after law school while encouraging all candidates to obtain an advanced law degree or experience as a lawyer. It was noted previously that the majority of women graduates of the IJS have more legal knowledge and experience than previous generations of women judges and public prosecutors. On the whole, the IJS has been successful in redefining standards of the profession and providing quality training.

What is striking about the past generations of women judges and public prosecutors is the variety of their career paths. The first generation started off as public sector employees and ended up as public prosecutors, a radical career change. Some women of the generations to follow gradually entered the profession, first as court clerks while completing their law degrees, then as examination candidates and judicial trainees. A handful of women, because of no age restrictions, were able to change their careers: the homemakers and mothers went back to school to fulfil a childhood dream of studying law while the working woman tired of her career choice, for example teaching, redid her high school final examinations in order to be admitted to university, studied law, practised as a lawyer, and then passed the National Judicial Examination with flying colours. Also, the experienced lawyers were (and still are) periodically given the opportunity to join the judicial ranks. Many talented women, because of state-financed higher education and the flexibility of the judicial training system, were able to find their way to the judiciary if they so desired. In light of the past, the new entrance requirements and training programme of the IJS may appear restrictive and discriminating towards those candidates who do not fit the mould. However, young women today are more career-minded than in the past. A university degree is no longer a pretext to finding a husband, killing time before one comes along, or settling for a low-ranking job in the public service. The judiciary has become a viable career for women in Syria, and the most talented law school students see it as an option, especially the women, since this type of legal employment has a regular work schedule, pays well (given the substantial increase in salaries and allowances in October 2005)[45] and provides security in old age.

11. Conclusion

Though Syria's judicial system, appointments process and training institute are based on the French model, the composition of its judiciary is very different with regards to women membership. Unlike the French, the Syrian judiciary has not experienced the feminisation of its ranks.[46] Women in Syria make up only 12% of the judiciary with their number now close to the 200 mark.[47] In a recent contribution, Anne Boigeol attributes the feminisation of the judiciary in France to three factors: (1) an increased number of women law graduates; (2) an appointments process based on academic merit and competitive examination; and (3) a lack of interest of men in the judicial professions (Boigeol, 2003, pp. 404–7). The introduction to this article paid tribute to the academic success of women judicial candidates over the years and it was observed that the selection process in Syria, because it is based on merit and competitive examinations, works to the advantage of women.[48] However, statistics show that the percentage of women law graduates in Syria is still relatively low, 23.5%,[49] and, therefore, has not significantly contributed to an increase in the number of potential women candidates for judicial office. Rather, it is recent government policy which seems to be the deciding factor in the higher proportion of women judicial trainees since 2002. It remains to be seen if the fifth cohort of the IJS will include as many women trainees as the previous ones.

The judiciary in Syria has remained male-dominated and men's interest in the profession is still strong, given the recent rise in salaries and the power associated with judicial office. In order to overcome this male hegemony, the Ministry of Justice has had to adopt special measures to appoint women judges and public prosecutors to regions in Syria where women in the judicial ranks are under-represented or non-existent. In December 2005, there was only one woman public prosecutor in the southern governorate of al-Suweida (as compared to 23 men, judges and public prosecutors), and no women in neighbouring Dar'ā (with 41 men).[50] To remedy this absence of women public prosecutors and judges in the South, all new trainees of the IJS appointed to the courthouses of al-Suweida and Dar'ā in 2005 were women: four women judges in al-Suweida, and two women judges and two women public prosecutors in Dar'a.[51] These young women trainees recently graduated in July 2007, among them Hanān al-Bayrūtī with the top score as previously mentioned, and are now eligible for judicial office. The South is the last frontier of the Syrian landscape that women jurists have to conquer, and the best of them are doing so with the support of the Ministry. As in the past, the Ministry of Justice of Syria continues to apply a proactive policy of appointing women to the judiciary, but in a gradual manner in order not to stir up the more conservative factions of Syrian society who still believe that women should not hold judicial office.

Acknowledgements

The author is indebted to the judges and public prosecutors (mostly women but some men) of Syria who, without exception, were generous with their time and agreed to answer questions. In addition, employees of the Ministry of Justice are to be thanked for the information they provided from the Personnel Records, Statistics Bureau and Archives. Finally, this research would not have been possible without the permission granted by the Ministers of Culture and Justice, and the chief public prosecutors of the courthouses visited in Syria. Last but not least, the author expresses her profound gratitude to the directors, staff and researchers of the Institut du Proche-Orient (formerly IFEAD) in Damascus for providing a rich and stimulating research environment.

Part of this research was funded by a Cardinal-Maurice-Roy Grant of Université Laval, Québec, Canada.

Notes

[1] Decrees no. 3181 L, 11 November 2006/28 Shawāl 1427 H (Muslim Hijrī dates are also indicated when available. H stands for the Hijrī calendar); no. 794 L, 29 April 2007/12 Rabī' al-thānī 1427 H, and visit to the Institute of Judicial Studies (*al-Ma'had al-qadā'ī*), 14 May 2007. Full diacritics of the Arabic transliterations are not given in the article.

[2] Ministry of Justice, Decrees no. 1462 L, 18 April 2002; no. 2824 L, 21 August 2002/13 Jumādā al-thāniyya 1423 H; no. 471 L, 30 January 2003/27 Dhū al-Qa'da 1423 H. The GPA of 2003 and 2002 had been even higher: respectively 63% and 65%. Though these grade averages may seem low, top ranking law students in Syrian universities rarely score over 65%.

[3] As stated by Ghāda Murād, first woman appointed to the Syrian judiciary in 1975, in an interview granted to the magazine of the Women's General Union (a popular organisation of the ruling Ba'th Socialist Party), *al-Mar'a al-'arabiyya* [*The Arab Woman*], 1978, 140, p. 11.

[4] Law no. 64, 27 December 2006.

[5] Article 9, Decrees no. 3181L, 19 November 2006/28 Shawāl 1428 H; no. 2065L, 17 July 2004/2 Jumādā al-thāniyya 1425 H; no. 431L, 30 January 2003/28 Dhū al-Qa'da 1423 H; no. 2824L, 21 August 2002/13 Jumādā al-thāniyya 1423H, and Article 8, Decree no. 1462L, 18 April 2002.

[6] Article 66 of the Judicial Authority Law no. 98 of 1961 (with amendments). In addition, a deputy minister of the Ministry of Justice is also member of the Council. Ministers and deputy ministers of justice in Syria are senior members of the judiciary who have acted as judges and public prosecutors in the ordinary courts and, in certain cases, in the administrative courts.

[7] Decrees no. 1910L, 20 May 2002/8 Rabī'al-awwal 1423 H; no. 2117L, 9 June 2002/29 Rabī' al-awwal 1423 H; no. 2934L, 4 September 2002/27 Jumādā al-thāniyya 1423 H; 2984L, 14 September 2002/8 Rajab 1423 H; Presidential Decree no. 347, 5 October 2002/29 Rajab 1423 H; Decrees no. 3229L, 2 October 2002/26 Rajab 1423 H; no. 3467L, 21 October 2002/15 Sha'bān 1423 H; no. 19L, 4 January 2003/2 Dhū al-Qa'da 1423 H; Presidential Decree no. 52,

4 February 2003/3 Dhū al-Hijja 1423 H; Decrees no. 863L, 6 March 2003/3 Muharram 1423 H; no. 1295L, 24 March 2003/21 Muharram 1424 H; no. 2718L, 18 June 2003/18 Rabī' al-thānī 1424 H; Presidential Decree no. 301, 24 August 2003/26 Jumādā al-thāniyya 1424 H; Decrees no. 266L, 19 January 2005/9 Dhū al-Hijja 1425 H; no. 844L, 2 March 2005/21 Muharram 1426 H; no. 2284L, 3 July 2005/27 Jumādā al-awwal 1426 H; Presidential Decree no. 410, 3 October 2005/30 Sha'bān 1426 H.

[8] Interview at the Ministry of Justice, 14 May 2007.

[9] Data are lacking for the National Judicial Examinations that predate 2002.

[10] For example, France in the 1990s. Though the evidence was not conclusive, many judges and public prosecutors, both men and women, interviewed by the French sociologist, Anne Boigeol, were convinced that the oral exam was used to limit the number of women entering the judiciary in France in an attempt to curb the feminisation of the judicial corps (Boigeol, 1993, pp. 497–8).

[11] Interview 26 June 2006.

[12] Ghāda Murād was recruited as a mature candidate and, therefore, did not sit the National Judicial Examination. See Section 7, Education and career paths, for more information on the recruitment of mature candidates.

[13] *al-Mar'a al-'arabiyya* [*The Arab Woman*], 1978, 121, pp. 47–9 and interview of 3 June 2004.

[14] Legislative Decree no. 540, 10 March 1979 published in The Official Gazette of the Syrian Arabic Republic, vol. 2 (*al-Jarīda al-rasmiyya li-l-jumhūriyya al-'arabiyya al-sūriyya, al-juz' al-thānī*), 1981, 28, pp. 4910–2.

[15] The dates for the National Judicial Examinations are systematically advertised in the daily newspapers, on television, at the courthouses and the main and regional offices of the Bar.

[16] Interview 3 June 2004.

[17] Figures are taken from the following Presidential Decrees: no. 540, 5 March 1979/6 Rabī' al-thānī 1399 H; no. 759, 29 December 1981/3 Rabī' al-awwal 1402 H; nos. 192, 200 and 209, 23 August 1986/18 Dhū al-Hijja 1406 H; no. 113, 26 May 1993/5 Dhū al-Hijja 1413 H; no. 310, 16 November 1995/23 Jumādā al-thāniyya 1416 H; no. 19, 14 June 1998/19 Safar 1419 H.

[18] *Statistical Abstract*, 1975–2006 (Damascus, Central Bureau of Statistics). Since 1919, all students to graduate in law attended Damascus University—formally known as the Syrian University—the first modern university in Syria. It was only in June 1985 that students graduated in law at Aleppo University. Three other state universities in Syria, al-Ba'th (Homs), Tishrīn (Latakia) and al-Furāt (al-Hasaka and Deir ez-Zor), now offer a degree in law. However, statistics for these universities are not available.

[19] Ministry of Justice, Statistics Bureau. I do not quote figures for 2005 and 2006 because they are not accurate for Damascus.

[20] A report on women's status in Syria prepared by the Central Statistics Bureau and Women's General Union of Syria in collaboration with UNIFEM (*Taqrīr awdā' al-mar'a fī sūriyya*) states that women's participation in the workforce was 21.4% in 2002. *Tishreen* (Syrian daily newspaper), 17 December 2005, p. 3. This source does not specify if agricultural work is included in this percentage.

[21] The Ministry of Justice in Syria does not publish an annual report that gives information on the social background, legal education and experience, marital status, rank and career patterns of the judiciary. Therefore, interviews are the key source for providing information on the lives and careers of Syrian judges and public prosecutors.

[22] These three governorates comprise 68% (2004) of women judges and public prosecutors in Syria. Further interviews are to be done in the central and south cities of Homs, Hama, Latakia, Tartus, al-Suweida and Dar'a in 2008.

[23] Other professions are military judge, mayor, technician, employee in an oil company, engineer, hotel owner, military, writer, politician and factory owner. Information is not available for four of the interviewees' fathers.

[24] The other working mothers are a school director, seamstress and accountant. Information for the mother of one of the interviewees is not available.

[25] Interviews 18 and 24 October 2004.

[26] Interviews 22, 28 and 29 June 2006; 5 June 2007.

[27] The Judicial Authority Law no. 98 of 1961 (with amendments), article 70/5, states that a trainee judge or public prosecutor must be at least 22 years of age.

[28] Interview 25 June 2006.

[29] Decree no. 185, 22 May 2003/21 Rabīʿ al-awwal 1424 H. Four out of the 26 candidates recruited were women. In a more recent recruitment of senior lawyers of 10 or 16 years' experience, only three out of the 68 successful applicants were women (4%). Decree no. 84, 10 March 2008/3 Rabīʿ al-awwal 1429.

[30] Women's preference for the judiciary over the advocacy has been observed by other researchers, notably Boigeol (2003), pp. 408–9.

[31] 2004 Census of Population, *Statistical Abstract 2006* (Damascus, Central Bureau of Statistics), Table 8/2, p. 68.

[32] Article 53 of the State Employment Law (*al-Nizām al-asāsī l-il-ʿāmilīn fī-l-dawla*) no. 50 of 6 December 2004/23 Shawwal 1425 H.

[33] Over a 10-year period (1994–2004), the population of Syria increased from 13,756,000 to 17,980,000 with an annual growth rate of 2.68% (Courbage, 2007, p. 185).

[34] Some 16% of full-time judges (seven out of 43) in the Court of Cassation are women. Interview at the Ministry of Justice, 21 July 2007.

[35] As previously stated in Section 4, the first cohort of women to enter the judiciary in 1979 all started out as public prosecutors and most of them, when appointed to the bench, pursued a career in criminal law. This explains why almost all of these senior women judges are now assigned to the criminal divisions of the Court of Cassation.

[36] The trainee takes the oath of judicial office as stated in article 77 of the Judicial Authority Law: 'I swear by God to judge among people fairly and to respect the law'.

[37] Programme information as explained in the Internal Regulations of the IJS, Decree no. 467 N, 27 March 2002/13 Muharram 1423 H.

[38] Their names figure in the list of trainer judges of Decree no. 70, article 1, 28 June 1993/9 Muharram 1414 H.

[39] These three cities were the training centres for villages and cities in the south (Damascus), in the mid-region (Homs) and in the north (Aleppo) of Syria.

[40] Women judges are not appointed to personal status courts. Therefore, they do this part of their training in the juvenile courts. Since the entry of women to the judiciary, judges and public prosecutors appointed to juvenile courts are almost exclusively women, at least in the courthouses of Damascus and Aleppo.

[41] Decree no. 66, article 4, 21 June 1993/2 Muharram 1414 H.

[42] Interviews 27 October 2004 and 17 July 2007.

[43] In Syria, court sessions are not transcribed verbatim. It is the presiding judge who dictates what is written into the case file, be it a testimony or other verbal exchanges. Case files are not computerised and court proceedings are not taped.

[44] Interviews 20, 23 June and 17, 18 October 2004.

[45] Presidential Decrees no. 92, 93 and 94, 3 October 2005.

[46] In 1975, the first woman in Syria was appointed to the judiciary, while in France more than half of the new entrants to the *École nationale de la magistrature* (training institute for the judiciary) were women (Boigeol, 1999, p. 160). Other civil law jurisdictions also have a majority of women judges (see Schultz & Shaw, 2003, pp. xxxvii–xxxviii, xlvi).

[47] These figures, though not precise, are a reasonable estimate. They are based on statistics dating from 2004 and the last four cohorts of women graduates of the IJS.

[48] In contrast, case studies of common law jurisdictions demonstrate that a judicial selection system structured on the consultation process (a form of networking), the self-replication of the judiciary (basically male) and the requirement of many uninterrupted years of advocacy does not correspond to women's career patterns and judicial culture and, therefore, is a barrier to their advancement and appointment to the judiciary (Malleson, 2003, 2006).

[49] This is the national average of 2004 based on the number of women law school graduates of Damascus and Aleppo Universities.

[50] Ministry of Justice, Statistics Bureau, 25 June 2006. In a visit to Dar'ā on 13 September 2005, the minister of justice, Muhammad al-Ghafarī, spoke of the necessity to appoint women to the region's courts: *Tishreen*, 14 September 2005, p. 3.

[51] Presidential Decree no. 410, 3 October 2005/30 Sha'bān 1426 H. Recent statistics of the Ministry show that the number of women appointed to al-Suweida and Dar'a as of 31 December 2007 were four in each governorate.

References

Boigeol, A. (1993) La magistrature française au féminin: entre spécificité et banalisation, *Droit et Société*, 25, pp. 489–523.

Boigeol, A. (1999) Les magistrates en France: des stratégies particulières?, in: A. Delvillé & O. Paye (Eds) *Les femmes et le droit: constructions idéologiques et pratiques sociales* (Bruxelles, Facultés universitaires Saint-Louis), pp. 149–73.

Boigeol, A. (2003) Male strategies in the face of the feminisation of a profession: the case of the French judiciary, in: U. Schultz & G. Shaw (Eds) *Women in the World's Legal Professions* (Oxford & Portland, OR, Hart), pp. 410–8.

Courbage, Y. (2007) La population de la Syrie: des réticences à la transition (démographique), in: B. Dupret, Z. Ghazzal, Y. Courbage & M. Al-Dbiyat (Eds) *La Syrie au présent: reflets d'une société* (Arles, Actes sud & Paris, Sindbad), pp. 179–213.

Hamad, M.H. (2006) The politics of judicial selection in Egypt, in: K. Malleson & P.H. Russell (Eds) *Appointing Judges in an Age of Judicial Power* (Toronto, University of Toronto Press), pp. 260–79.

Malleson, K. (2003) Prospects for parity: the position of women in the judiciary in England and Wales, in: U. Schultz & G. Shaw (Eds) *Women in the World's Legal Professions* (Oxford & Portland, OR, Hart), pp. 176–89.

Malleson, K. (2006) Rethinking the merit principle in judicial selection, *Journal of Law and Society*, 33(1), pp. 126–40.

Schultz, U. & Shaw, G. (Eds) (2003) *Women in the World's Legal Professions* (Oxford & Portland, OR, Hart).

Index

Page numbers in *Italics* represent tables.
Page numbers in **Bold** represent figures.
Page numbers followed by n represent endnotes.